The Iranian Green Movement of 2009

The Iranian Green Movement of 2009

Reverberating Echoes of Resistance

Maral Karimi

LEXINGTON BOOKS
Lanham • Boulder • New York • London

Published by Lexington Books
An imprint of The Rowman & Littlefield Publishing Group, Inc.
4501 Forbes Boulevard, Suite 200, Lanham, Maryland 20706
www.rowman.com

Unit A, Whitacre Mews, 26-34 Stannary Street, London SE11 4AB

British Library Cataloguing in Publication Information Available

Library of Congress Cataloging-in-Publication Data

Names: Karimi, Maral, 1979- author.
Title: The Iranian green movement of 2009 : reverberating echoes of resistance / Maral Karimi.
Description: Lanham, Maryland : Lexington Books, 2018. | Includes bibliographical references and index.
Identifiers: LCCN 2018013925 (print) | LCCN 2018026398 (ebook) | ISBN 9781498558679 (electronic) | ISBN 9781498558662 (cloth : alk. paper)
Subjects: LCSH: Protest movements—Iran—History—21st century. | Iran—History—Election protests, 2009. | Iran—Politics and government—1997- | Iran—Politics and government—1979-1997. | Communication in politics—Iran—History. | Social media—Iran—History. | YouTube (Electronic resource) | Discourse analysis.
Classification: LCC DS318.9 (ebook) | LCC DS318.9 .K37 2018 (print) | DDC 322.4/409550905—dc23
LC record available at https://lccn.loc.gov/2018013925

♾™ The paper used in this publication meets the minimum requirements of American National Standard for Information Sciences—Permanence of Paper for Printed Library Materials, ANSI/NISO Z39.48-1992.

Printed in the United States of America

To the women of Iran
in their brave struggle for equality

Contents

Acknowledgments

Intellectual endeavors are often exercised not in isolation but in collaboration and conversations with other thinkers. This book is no exception as it is the outcome of years of intense intellectual labor and collaboration with insightful, generous, and bright individuals from across educational institutions and countries. First, I want to thank everyone at York University for welcoming me and for providing my research with a home. I would like to specially acknowledge Dr. Minoo Derayeh, Dr. Cheryl van Daalen-Smith, and Fiona Fernandez for their guidance and support during my time at the university.

My sincere gratitude goes to my mentor, Professor Ojelanki Ngwenyama, for introducing me to the art of scholarship. For the privilege of the countless hours he patiently spent training me in philosophy, critical discourse analysis, and hermeneutics, so I could fulfill my passion and do what I love, I am forever thankful. Dr. Ngwenyama is director of the Institute for Innovation and Technology Management at Ryerson University, where I've had the privilege of serving as a research associate for almost a decade. The institute has provided an outstanding context within which to learn the various theories and methodologies this book draws on.

It was through the institute that I came to know and collaborate with two of my most esteemed colleagues: Dr. Mohamed Elmi and Hanna Woldeyohannes, from whom I received much encouragement for this book. Over the years I have been fortunate to engage with them in critical debate and explore the arguments discussed in this book, and I have benefited from their intellectual input, feedback, and expertise on various subjects including scientific argumentation and methodology.

The arguments in the epilogue to this book were devised with tremendous theoretical as well as editorial assistance from Dr. Charles Simon. In this regard, Dr. Simon's intimate understanding of Iran's political economy and history has been an incredible source of intellectual nourishment for me. For hours of debates and conversations exploring the different themes of this work, and for his unwavering enthusiasm for my research, I am forever indebted to him. I am also grateful to my editor Joseph Parry at Lexington Books for his patience and goodwill in overseeing the publication of this book.

I must thank my family, my parents, and my sister for their continued support and emotional boost. I specially owe a great debt of gratitude to my two beautiful children Delaram and Roozbeh for sharing their infancy and toddler years with the demands of this project. To my husband, Hooman Javdan, without whose encouragement this journey would not have begun, I am forever grateful. His love, his continued support and cheer, his selfless sacrifices, and his help with our children made it possible for me to continue writing over the years.

List of Tables

Abbreviations

CDA   Critical Discourse Analysis

CST   Critical Social Theory

IRGC   Islamic Revolutionary Guards Corps

IRI   Islamic Republic of Iran

MKO   Mojahedin Khalgh Organization

SDC   Systematically Distorted Communication

TCA   Theory of Communicative Action

1

The Green Movement

Following the presidential elections held on June 12, 2009, in Iran, massive protests took place contesting those results declaring the incumbent president Mahmoud Ahmadi Nejad the winner by a large margin for a second term. The two Reformist candidates, Mir Hossein Mousavi and Hojatol Islam Mehdi Karoubi, contested the results and called on their supporters to hold a street rally. People responded in large numbers (millions by some estimates) by holding a peaceful march of silence on June 15, 2009, down the streets of Tehran, the capital city, and other major urban centers. While many wore or carried green artifacts, others held signs that simply read, "Where is my vote?" referring to the alleged election fraud. Originally during the campaigns, Mousavi's campaign team introduced green-colored artifacts and signage to differentiate their supporters and signal devotion to Islam since that particular shade of green symbolizes allegiance to Shi'ite Islam.

The government, however, broke up the peaceful protests violently, and Iran witnessed yet another popular uprising that was reminiscent of the Islamic Revolution in 1979. Women and youth had a significant presence in the movement, many of whom were arrested, harassed, tortured, shot at, or killed by government forces loyal to the Supreme Leader Ayatollah Ali Khameneyi. While the protesters were not victorious in pressuring the government to meet their demands and President Ahmadi Nejad stayed to complete his second term, they continued their efforts, led by Mousavi and Karoubi until their house arrest in February 2011. Social media was at its peak, and Twitter, Facebook, and YouTube were some of the key tools used by the protesters, and their leaders, to communicate their stories to the rest of the world, filling the void that was created by the expulsion of foreign journalists, international observers, and independent news outlets.

This book looks at the aspirations of those involved in the movement by analyzing their political communications. I critically examine the public discourse of the primary actors of the Green Movement through social media, which was the medium of communication of choice for many, in order to develop an understanding of the movement and the conditions that contributed to its demise, which can then be applied to the greater Iranian political scene.

There is very little disagreement among politicians and scholars alike of the discontent felt by the Iranian public, although there is a wide spectrum of ideas about the degree to which it was felt. People of Iran, especially the youth, students, women, and the middle classes, have manifested their desire for more political freedom and equal rights through two major events: first, in the 1997 presidential election by bypassing the government-approved candidate to elect a little known cleric Mohammad Khatami and his platform of reform and dialogue, which became known as the 2nd of Khordad Movement; and second, in the Green Movement of 2009. While there is much speculation about the driving motivations of those events, it is clear that the dominant narrative of the regime was being challenged by a considerable cross-section of the society.

To further study the state of Iranian dissent, I have organized this book to focus on the utilization of social media, YouTube particularly, by the leaders of the Green Movement for political communications. Those communications are further analyzed in order to understand the impact of their discourse on the movement, to discern the aspiration of the protesters, and finally to understand the factors contributing to the movement's failure. Additionally, in order to historicize the movement, I have provided a similar analysis of the communications of Ayatollah Ruhollah Khomeini—leader of the 1979 Islamic Revolution and founder of the current regime—during the revolutionary period. In this chapter, I will outline the objectives and motivations of this study as well as its theoretical and methodological framework.

THE OVERARCHING QUESTION AND OBJECTIVE

In this book, I explore and seek answers to the following question: What was the impact of the discourse of the leaders of the 2009 Iranian Green Movement? A key objective of the research is to develop an understanding of the complex nature of the political unrest that resulted in the birth of both the 2nd of Khordad Movement and the Green Movement and the reasons for its subsequent failure. The 2009 Green Movement against the Islamic Republic of Iran was the last in a series of uprisings for freedom and democracy by the Iranian people, starting with the Constitutional Revolution of 1905, the

1949–1953 movement for the nationalization of the oil industry, the 1963 protests against the White Revolution, as well as the 1979 movement that removed the Pahlavi monarchy.

Studying Iran's sociopolitical state is important because several factors place this ancient country in a unique position to influence world affairs significantly. According to the Organization of Petroleum Exporting Countries (OPEC), by the end of 2013 Iran had the third-largest proven crude oil and second-largest proven natural gas reserves in the world (OPEC, 2015) and thus is critically important to the world economy. Additionally, Iran is of geopolitical importance for it is located in the oil-producing hot bed of the Persian Gulf and has strategic control over the Strait of Hormuz, through which 40 percent of the world's traded oil flows (Cordesman, 2007). Moreover, Iran's sheer size and its population of over 80 million (The World Factbook: IRAN, 2018), in addition to the regime's tendency to "export the revolutionary ideas,"[1] make it a significant power in the region.

Through examination of the Green Movement, this book aims to facilitate a greater understanding of the complex nature of the political power struggles and opaque decision-making process in Iran. Studying the increasing dissent in the Islamic Republic that is manifested through political uprisings allows us to better understand the social and political complexities that rule this country and their inevitable impact in the region.

THEORIES AND CONCEPTS

The news media dubbed the Iranian political uprising of 2009 the "Twitter Revolution" (Iran's Twitter Revolution, 2009) and went on to portray the protesters as web-savvy internet users who relied heavily on social media, including YouTube and Facebook, to organize and communicate during the protests. Tusa (2013) and Cross (2010) both question this assertion, and I will further discuss this in chapter 2. Notwithstanding that, for the first time in the history of political uprisings, modern, internet-based social media played a significant role in the political communications of a movement. This emphasis on social media in general and Twitter in particular has prompted several studies that investigate this phenomenon in the context of the Green Movement from various angles (Tusa, 2013; Cross, 2010; Harris, 2012).

However, YouTube as a social media platform has been largely overlooked by researchers of Iranian politics. By virtue of its audiovisual capabilities and its potential for viral reach, YouTube provides a much richer medium of communication and thus presents us with a unique lens through which social interactions can be studied. Research reveals gaps in examining how YouTube was utilized by various social actors involved in the protests as a tool to communicate, organize, and exchange information. Thus, I have organized this research to focus on investigating how the leaders of the movement, i.e., the Reformers, used social media to facilitate communicating to the public their intention to change social and political structures. Further, I will examine the social structures that were the target of change, addressing political repression generally, and the structures of patriarchy, women's rights, and the economy in particular. Through studying the communications of the Green leaders, this project attempts to unravel communication distortions and their impact on the demise of the movement. Ayatollah Khomeini's communications are also examined in order to historically trace the establishment of the above mentioned oppressive structures.

I will investigate how YouTube was utilized as *steering media* to further the political agenda of the protesters. Steering media, such as money and power, enable a state and corporations to control the process of everyday life, thus undermining democratic values, the public sphere, and moral and communicative interactions. Through studying the social media practices and the content generated by those actors, this book aims to facilitate a greater understanding of the current political unrest in Iran, focusing on the root causes of dissent, and analyzing the viability of the Reform Movement as a political alternative.

The study also contributes to the existing scholarship on political communication, social movements, and political activism, which is predominantly conducted in Western and democratic settings. By applying Western concepts of social movements and political communications to a non-democratic setting, this book tests the applicability of such concepts to non-Western nations and contexts. In addition, this inquiry further illuminates the role of social media as an alternative channel of communication in authoritarian regimes such as Iran where traditional media predominantly serve the interests of the ruling elite. Moreover, this project helps to illustrate how increasingly popular social media, such as YouTube, are contributing to demands for civil liberties and democratic social movements by challenging authoritarian regimes. As a preliminary to this discussion, it will be necessary to answer the following five research questions.

RQ1: Who were the key stakeholders and participants in the discourse of the Iranian Green Movement of 2009? In other words, who were the principal "social actors" of the movement, and what were their political orientations and socioeconomic positions?

RQ2: What were the primary aspirations of the key stakeholders of the movement? In other words, what social structures were the principal categories of social actors attempting to alter or preserve by their involvement in the movement?

RQ3: Did the above groups of actors involved in the movement have equal access to political power?

RQ4: Were the aspirations of the key social actors involved in the Green Movement aligned with one another or in contradiction?

RQ5: If contradictory, was there any attempt in the discourse of the movement to bridge the gap? In other words, was the discourse of the leaders of the Green Movement oriented toward building mutual understanding or was it systematically distorted communication oriented toward success?

This research is grounded in critical social theory—more specifically, the theoretical framework for this study is informed by the *theory of structuration* of Anthony Giddens (1984) and the *theory of communicative action* (TCA) of Jürgen Habermas (1984). Broadly speaking, "structuration" is a tool for studying the interactions of social structures and the agency that was at the core of the Green Movement.

To create a wider lens for this research, I have altered the structuration framework to study "social action" based on Habermas's theory of communicative action. Habermas has devoted considerable time and effort to developing the theory of communicative action, which is a rigorous tool for the study of social action and public discourse.

RESEARCH METHODOLOGY AND DATA COLLECTION

My research conducted for this book relies on the principles of *Critical Discourse Analysis* (CDA), grounded in critical hermeneutics and based on the Habermasian theory of communicative action and ideal speech situation, operationalized by Cukier, Ngwenyama, Bauer, and Middleton (2009). Specifically, I rely on Habermas's four-part validity test, which focuses upon *comprehensibility, truth, legitimacy,* and *sincerity* of each claim. These elements are the foundations for our framework for a "heuristic" (Stahl, 2007) approach to identify the Green leaders' claims through empirical observations of communication in the form of YouTube videos.

The CDA application was used to investigate both Ayatollah Khomeini's revolutionary discourse and the Green leaders' validity claims regarding altering structures of *signification, domination, and legitimation* for the period of January 2009 to February 2011 when the leaders were put under house arrest and their communications with supporters were cut.

My research points to evidence of systematic communication distortions on the part of the leaders of the Green Movement and links that to similar distortions in the rhetoric of Ayatollah Khomeini. The evidence illustrates the contradictory and irreconcilable nature of the aspirations of the key stakeholders of the movement and links it to the failure of the uprising. This study also questions the viability of the Reform strategy in the current situation in order to achieve democracy and discusses the role of civil society in that context. The rest of this book is organized as follows.

Chapter 2 places the research in a historical context by providing a comprehensive account and analysis of events leading to the Green Movement. A detailed chronology of the Constitutional Revolution, the Oil Nationalization Movement followed by the 1953 Anglo-American Coup, the White Revolution of 1963, and the 1979 Islamic Revolution all serve as the background to the Green Movement as the most recent upheaval on this contentious political continuum.

Chapter 3 situates the research in a sociological framework and identifies the paradigmatic assumptions to which this research belongs. This chapter will detail the key concepts of the Giddens-Habermas framework of structure-agency and provides an in-depth discussion of public sphere and social action as it pertains to this book.

In chapter 4, I describe and provide justification for the use of CDA as a research methodology in general and the operationalized version developed by Cukier et al. (2009) in particular. Chapter 4 will also offer a detailed description of the means and methods of data collection (i.e., YouTube) and analysis, the software that was utilized, and strategies for data coding and interpretation. Limitations and scope of study will also be reviewed in this chapter.

Chapter 5 provides an overview of the actors participating in the Green Movement and the social structures they attempted to alter. I will provide a brief overview of both the ideological orientation and the intellectual underpinnings of the different actors who participated in that political uprising as well as their goals, their roles, and their aspirations. This exploratory approach allows for a better understanding of the composition of the "Green Wave" and those in opposition to the movement, thus drawing a more comprehensive picture of the movement and the actors involved.

The key actors of the Green Movement can be categorized into three groups: *civil society groups*, the *Islamic Reform Front*, and the *Hardliner Conservatives*. While civil society groups are by definition non-governmental organizations, the Reformers and the Conservatives are the outward manifestation of the two ideological factions among Iran's political leadership elite. Reformers represent the Islamic-Left and the Conservatives the Islamic-Right, among each of which there are smaller factions. Within this chapter, some of the complexities of the political establishment of the Islamic Republic of Iran (IRI) are also explained, which will give us a better understanding of the movement.

In chapter 6, I will examine the political communications of two Reformist campaigns in the movement through YouTube videos then detail the structures that were targeted for change and the type of social actions that were taken to achieve that. This chapter will rely on CDA and ideal speech situation claims as detailed in chapter 5 to investigate the content generated by the above actors through social media.

Similar to chapter 6, chapter 7 analyzes the discourse of Ayatollah Khomeini during the Islamic Revolution, regarding the structures that were targeted for change at that time. A CDA of the leader of the revolution's rhetoric further helps in contextualizing the Green Movement and the institutional, social, and political structures it targeted, many of which were established post revolution.

Finally, chapter 8 draws on the analysis of chapters 6 and 7 to outline the impact and implications of the political discourse of the Green leaders for the movement and its failure. The findings are tested against a theoretical framework for broader implications, including examining the effectiveness of the Reform Movement and the broken condition of the public sphere in Iran, among other findings.

NOTES

1. A common phrase coined by Ayatollah Khomeini.

2

Historicizing the Green Movement

AN OVERVIEW OF THE CHAPTER

This chapter is designed to provide a brief overview of key social movements and cycles of political protest since the onset of the twentieth century, events that significantly shaped modern Iran. The movements chronicled in this chapter are periods of heightened sociopolitical uprising and are key to our understanding of Iran. We focus on those events with the intention of historicizing the Green Movement as well as to reveal the common threads that run through these cycles, such as demands for rule of law, freedom, justice, national independence, and, more recently, democracy and women's rights. This chapter opens with the Constitutional Revolution at the onset of the previous century, the Oil Nationalization Movement and the subsequent Anglo-American Coup in 1953, and the 1979 Islamic Revolution. But first we begin with the encounters of Iran with the Western world in the early 1800s.

IRAN AND WESTERN MODERNITY

In 1812 and again in 1828, following two consecutive military defeats against czarist Russia, the ruling Qajar dynasty (1789–1925) was forced to surrender vast territories under humiliating terms to its northern neighbor. This point in history is considered the inception of Iran's contentious and tumultuous encounter with the modern West. The Russian victories were seen as more than the military superiority of a formidable opponent but as highlighting the social and scientific advances of the modern world in comparison to the dark conditions of traditional Iran. The stark contrast was not lost on the ruling elite of the Qajar, prompting them to adopt a more critical view of the affairs of a country plagued with poverty, backwardness, and loss, impressing upon them the need to search for a solution. The government first responded to Western pressure by taking a number of ambitious initiatives to reform the military, bureaucratic, economic, and education systems, these changes were met with strong resistance from both the Qajar traditionalists of the royal court and the Shiite *ulama* (jurists or clerics) who dominated the ruling classes.

The reforms initiated by the Qajars to strengthen their political position and restore the country's sovereignty, however, ultimately proved to undermine their rule. Although limited, the modernization programs and modernized institutions gave rise to a new generation of intelligentsia, known as *monawarolfekran* (the enlightened minded), whose aspirations—constitutionalism, secularism, and nationalism—went beyond institutional reform and aimed to fundamentally alter the monarchy. Essentially, the Constitutionalists aimed to curb the Shah's absolute and arbitrary rule and give the people a voice in running their affairs as well as to curb foreign interference. In what follows I will briefly discuss those objectives.

The contentious relationship between the intelligentsia and the ruling class ultimately lead to the Constitutional Revolution, in which the progressive forces succeeded in drafting the country's first constitution aimed at curbing the Shah's absolute and arbitrary rule, establishing an independent judiciary, and promoting personal liberties. The decades that followed those historic events witnessed the erosion of those institutions, once again giving rise to tyranny and oppression.

Constitutionalism

Mashrootiat, or Constitutionalism, refers to the revolutionaries' principal demand of limiting the powers of the monarch (the Shah) through a drafted constitution and establishing a parliament (*Majlis*) to foresee its execution. The Constitutionalists' demands were quite progressive for their time and included the establishment of a house of justice (*Adalatkhaneh)* and a written legal code that would serve as the country's first constitution. But perhaps the most revolutionary of these was the introduction of a fundamentally new concept of government: that of an elected, national assembly, or *Majlis-e-Shoraye-Melli* (Majlis for short), to limit the absolute authority of the Shah, essentially establishing a constitutional monarchy. Witnessing the destruction and devastation that had crippled the country for decades prior and the failed attempts at implementing reforms even by such capable prime ministers as Mirza Taghi Khan Amir Kabir and Mirza Taghi Khan Gha'em Magham Farahani, the intellectual and political elite concluded that the answer lay in the person of the Shah, his absolute authority, and arbitrary rule. In other words, once it was clear that, among others, the educational, military, and bureaucratic reforms had failed because they were stifled by the constricting limits of royal despotism, the intelligentsia organized to overhaul the political establishment of late-nineteenth-century Iran from an absolute monarchy to a limited form of parliamentary monarchy. Separation of powers and establishment of a judiciary independent of the Shah were other significant outcomes of constitutionalism.

NATIONAL INDEPENDENCE AND CURBING FOREIGN INTERFERENCE

Iran's strategic geopolitical position in the Persian Gulf had for decades made it a battleground for the colonial interests of primarily czarist Russia and Great Britain. The power play between the British in the southern provinces and Russians in the north is crucial in understanding the context in which the Constitutionalists formulated their demands and forged strategic alliances. One of the major goals of the Constitutionalists was to limit foreign influence in the country because the Qajar Shahs, especially Naseredin Shah, were making all kinds of concession that would almost always unilaterally benefit the colonial powers while briefly filling the royal coffers. Some of the major concessions to the British included selling the rights to build railroads and search for minerals, granting shipping rights to Iran's only navigable river in the south, and allowing the establishment of banks and a monopoly to print banknotes. The Russians on the other hand were successful in securing contracts to pave highways in the north, exploiting the lush Mazandaran forests, establishing a monopoly over the fishing industry in the Caspian, and obtaining the right to exploit coal mines and oil fields in and around Azerbaijan in the north.[1]

During the heat of the Constitutional Revolution, however, while the British sided with the Constitutionalists, Russia supported the Royalists. Russian Cossack brigades even shelled the parliament building at the request of Mohammad Ali Shah, who later fled to Russia when forced by Constitutionalist forces to abdicate the throne.

Secularism

While the Shah and the Royalists, reinforced by foreign interests, posed the most eminent threat, the Constitutionalists were fighting a battle on a third front against the traditional yet powerful Shi'ite ulama, or the clergy. The ulama, holding significant mass mobilizing power, were split on constitutionalism, some, including Ayatollah Abdollah Behbahani and Ayatollah Mohammad Tabatabayi, sided with the intelligentsia in demanding a constitutional monarchy and establishment of a parliament, while others supported the absolute rule of the Shah and *Shari'a*. Sheikh Fazlolah Noori was the most prominent figure opposing constitutionalism, specifically the separation of religion and state and the separation of power into three branches, particularly since the latter stipulated an independent judiciary as well as an elected parliament. Instead he called for *Mashrooteh Mashroo'eh*: constitutionalism contingent on Islamic Shari'a.

As a senior Shi'ite cleric, he naturally opposed separation of religion and state, including an elected assembly (i.e., Majlis) as the law-making organ of the government because, in his view, under Islam all laws are set by Shari'a and interpreted by the Shi'ite jurists (*foqaha*). Instead, his interpretation of Mashrooteh was a consultative assembly of religious experts (*mojtahedin*) to oversee the laws of the land for compatibility with Shari'a. He proposed an appointed assembly that would serve as a consultative forum for the Shah without the executive privileges of the elected Majlis, which was the goal of the Constitutionalists. Moreover, he opposed the separation of power into the three branches of executive, judiciary, and legislative, considered a modern concept at the time, on similar grounds, describing it as a pure straying from the righteous path of god. He argued separation of powers would diminish the monarchy, and thus he aligned himself with the Royalists or, as they are otherwise known, the Absolutists. As well, since the courts and legal matters had historically been the purview of Shari'a and Shi'ite clerics, an independent judiciary would significantly limit their authority.

THE CONSTITUTIONAL REVOLUTION (1905–1909)

Following a series of riots, protests, and strikes at various levels of society, Mozaffareddin Shah consented to the establishment of a parliament in August of 1906, five days prior to his death. According to the constitution, mainly modeled after that of Belgium at the time, the person of the Shah was from then on "under the rule of law, and the crown became a divine gift given to the Shah by the people" (Hirschl, 2011, 24). However, Mozaffareddin Shah's son and successor, Mohammad Ali Shah (r. 1907–1909), a forceful absolutist, decided to abandon the constitution despite having previously pledged to uphold it. On June 24, 1908, Mohammad Ali Shah's hostility toward the movement led him to place the Majlis under siege and with the help of the Russian Cossack Brigade he had the parliament building shelled. A year later however, the Constitutionalists and their allies, collectively known as the

"Freedom Fighters," from across the country marched on Tehran and successfully captured the capital. On the eve of Tehran's capture by the Freedom Fighters, the Majlis held an emergency session in which Mohammad Ali Shah was deposed and his thirteen-year-old son Ahmad Shah (r. 1905–1925) was named his successor.

Following Tehran's capture by the Freedom Fighters, Sheikh Fazlolah Noori was arrested, tried, found guilty of treason, and executed by hanging. Interestingly, Noori's views continued to resurface in subsequent Islamic movements in Iran, including those of Fadayian Islam (in the 1940s and 1950s), but more significantly in Ayatollah Khomeini's formulation of Islamic governance. The idea of a democratic republic in Iran compatible with Islamic guidelines, as you can see, can trace its roots at least as far back as the Constitutional Revolution. One of Ayatollah Khomeini's very first disputes with both radical and moderate forces, including Mehdi Bazargan, the moderate prime minister of Iran's interim government following the 1979 revolution, was over the wording of the referendum on the new regime. While Khomeini and his allies insisted on "Islamic Republic of Iran," secular forces pushed for "Democratic Republic of Iran" (Long and Reich, 1995)—a dispute that was clearly far beyond word play and went to the heart of the competing ideas of the revolutionary factions.

Women and the Constitutional Revolution

While the Constitutional Revolution was admittedly a progressive movement that created enfranchised men, it fell short of enfranchising women. Women, who had participated extensively in the movement, were expressly barred from the political process by the new constitution due to the strong influence of the clergy—an influence that continues to resonate with women's rights activists to date.

REZA KHAN AND THE PAHLAVI DYNASTY

In the decades that followed the Constitutional Revolution, Iran saw the erosion of the Constitutionalists' ideals and was once again the scene of tremendous political transformation, tyranny, and tension. In 1925 Reza Shah Pahlavi, the then prime minister, deposed the last Qajar dynasty monarch, Ahmad Shah Qajar, in a coup and founded the Pahlavi dynasty, which lasted until the 1979 revolution. In August 1941 however, Anglo-Soviet allied powers occupied Iran and imposed a new political landscape on the country once more. The invasion, in which Iran was assaulted by air, land, and naval strikes delivering heavy losses to the Iranian military, was instigated in retaliation to Reza Shah's declaration of neutrality in World War II and refusal to allow Iranian territory to be used as a transport corridor by the Allies for shipment of arms and supplies to Russia in their war efforts against Germany.

Iran is geographically located so that it adjoined Russian territories to the north and the Persian Gulf and the Strait of Hormuz linking it to the Indian Ocean to the south. Russian politicians had always regarded Iran as strategically important since the country was Russia's only link to open waters via the Strait of Hormuz. Reza Shah Pahlavi was forced by the occupying forces to abdicate in favor of his son the crown prince Mohammad Reza Shah Pahlavi in September of that year. Soon after that, Reza Shah was exiled to South Africa, where he spent his final years.

Reza Shah, determined on bringing Iran into the twentieth century, adapted an ambitious modernization process, one that would not be slowed to abide by the new constitution. Establishing large construction projects to extend roads and highways and the first trans-Iranian railway, building industrial plants, introducing a modern and mandatory education system, sponsoring students to study in European universities, and improving public health and building hospitals were some of his initiatives. While Reza Shah's reign saw many infrastructural and technological improvements that the country was in a dire need of, it was also one of tyranny, oppression, corruption, and terror. Although some Constitutionalist intellectuals originally backed his coup against the Qajars, whose rule had become synonymous with Iran's sharp domestic and international decline, they soon realized his efforts were one of modernization and not of modernity.

While ardently championing a Western modernization process, Reza Shah did not tolerate the slightest hint of dissent, criticism, or insubordination. During this time many writers, artists, intellectuals, and even some of his closest political allies were imprisoned, tortured, and murdered at the Shah's behest. The Majlis, thus, became an instrument of his power, stripped of its original spirit of curbing the Shah's arbitrary rule and protecting freedom of expression.

MOHAMAD REZA SHAH (R. 1941–1979) AND THE OIL NATIONALIZATION MOVEMENT

Aside from the 1979 Islamic Revolution that abolished a constitutional monarchy and established a republic, the Oil Nationalization Movement and the subsequent Anglo-American Coup of 1953 represent the most significant moments of Mohammad Reza Shah's thirty-eight-year reign. The Oil Nationalization Movement in Iran, championed by Iran's Prime Minister Dr.

Mohammad Mosaddegh, dissolved the Anglo-Persian Oil Company (AIOC) in 1951 via the Majlis and nationalized the oil industry in order to restrict the increasing interference of the British, Russians, and Americans in Iranian affairs post–World War II. The AIOC, though indirectly, was the legacy of multiple Qajar concessions, including the widely protested Reuter's concession to foreign powers that used force and exploited the weakness of the Shahs to coerce the Iranian state into allowing foreign businesses to control Iran's extraction of natural resources, including that of the oil that was discovered later.

Mosaddegh, along with other like-minded progressive politicians such as Karim Sanjabi[2] and Hossein Fatemi,[3] had founded Iran's National Front, or *Jebheh Melli*, an umbrella organization for a diverse set of forces with liberal-democratic, nationalist, socialist, secular, as well as Islamic tendencies aimed at ending foreign interference and establishing Iran's sovereignty largely through nationalizing Iran's oil industry. In a speech to the Majlis in 1952, Mosaddegh detailed the significant implications of this policy for the overall well-being of the country and the Iranian people.

> Our long years of negotiations with foreign countries . . . have yielded no results thus far. With the oil revenues we could meet our entire budget and combat poverty, disease, and backwardness among our people. Another important consideration is that by the elimination of the power of the British company, we would also eliminate corruption and intrigue, by means of which the internal affairs of our country have been influenced. Once this tutelage has ceased, Iran will have achieved its economic and political independence (Fateh, 1956, 525).

Once both Majlis and the international court ruled in favor of Iran, Mosaddegh and his cabinet refused to allow any further British involvement in the industry, and in retaliation, the British government made sure Iran could not sell its oil in an effort to suffocate Mosaddegh's popular government and incite internal rebellion against him. Without oil revenues, the country soon began to suffer economically, putting a severe strain on Mosaddegh's promised reforms and thus leaving the electorate unhappy with his government. Mosaddegh's increasing popularity and international success in facing off a great colonial power had also intimidated the Shah who feared he too would suffer his father's fate and be dethroned. Mosaddegh though had always maintained he was devoted to a constitutional monarchy and uninterested in overthrowing the government in favor of a republic, and there is no evidence to suggest otherwise. However, despite Mosaddegh's repeated assurances to the contrary, the Shah was determined to undermine and later remove his powerful Prime Minister. Eventually, the British MI6 along with the American Central Intelligence Agency (CIA), allied with the Shah (who had fled to Rome with the queen prior to the coup) the armed forces, and the clergy, overthrew Mosaddegh's government. The CIA and MI6 appointed General

Fazlolah Zahedi, a high-ranking member of the royal military loyal to the Shah, as Mosaddegh's successor. While in the West, and according to newly released CIA documents, the coup was referred to as "Operation Ajax," in Iran it is known as the "Black Coup" in reference to the dark decades that followed Mosaddegh's overthrow.

Mosaddegh was subsequently arrested, sentenced to three years in prison, and later exiled and put under house arrest until his death in 1967. Upon his death he was denied a funeral and was buried in his own living room. Dr. Hossein Fatemi (1917–1954), Mosaddegh's closest associate and political ally and the Minister of Foreign Affairs, was executed by the order of Mohammad Reza Shah's military court for "treason against the Shah." Many others were imprisoned, tortured, or exiled, including Ali Shayegan and Ahmad Zirakzadeh.

Mosaddegh's short-lived government was the closest Iran has come to experiencing democracy in modern times. Throughout his political life, Mosaddegh strove to increase the collective power of the people and Constitutionalist principals versus the power of the crown. He was in favor of a constitutional monarchy in which the balance of power tipped toward the Majlis and not the Shah and the armed forces. Essentially, Mosaddegh's government was fighting the might of two foreign powers (Britain and the United States) as well as the Shah, the clergy, and the increasingly powerful armed forces domestically, while the base of his support was with the intellectuals and in the urban centers.

It is important to reiterate here the impact of the 1953 coup on the Iranian psyche and political uprisings that followed, including the 1979 Islamic Revolution. A large majority of the Iranian people hold the British and especially the Americans responsible for collectively destroying Iran's only semblance of a democratic government to date. This partly explains the animosity felt and exhibited toward the United States. Nationalizing the oil industry was in pursuit of restoring national sovereignty and pride, and it was an attempt to break the cycle of colonial exploitation. However, the coup staged by these foreign powers dealt a heavy blow to those aspirations and unleashed a wave of anger and suffocating frustration that resurfaced in the form of the 1979 revolution—an attempt to restore the country's sovereignty and to establish democracy and freedom.

THE 1979 ISLAMIC REVOLUTION: THE BACKGROUND

The 1979 Islamic Revolution in Iran was an uprising distinguishable in many respects from other armed struggles or civil unrests that occurred around the world in the mid-1970s and early 1980s. It was not only the first Islamic revolution in the world but also the century's last ideological revolution. Ervand Abrahamian (1982) points out that "Khomeini is to the Islamic revolution what Lenin was to the Bolshevik, Mao to the Chinese, and Castro to the Cuban revolutions" (531). The significance of the Iranian revolution was the victory of the political and ideological agendas of a handful of Islamic revolutionary clerics (the ulama) led by Ayatollah Khomeini who wished to establish an Islamic Shia state in Iran. While Mohammad Reza Shah promised a better future by transforming Iran into the world's fifth-major industrial power by the turn of the century, Khomeini and his supporters pointed to the Shah's Western ways, describing them as corrupt and thereby targeting the widening urban-rural divide and a growing yet disenfranchised middle class. Khomeini was essentially promising a Shi'ite utopia where oil revenues would be distributed equally among all Muslim Iranians, particularly the "hut residents,"[4] and public transit, hydropower, gas, and water would be free for everyone. The Shah largely relied on modern means of mass communication, such as television and the print media, while Khomeini developed a media mix that consisted of both traditional (e.g., gatherings in mosques) and modern communication systems (e.g., audio cassettes, flyers, and interviews with foreign journalists).

The radicalized Shi'ite clerics, the unlikely members of the Iranian civil society, integrated with the traditional merchants, or the "Bazaari" class, acted as vehicles for the Islamic revolution in Iran. The small but well-organized revolutionary clerics allied with the Bazaari were able to use their financial resources as well as the mosques to coordinate religious gatherings (e.g., on religious holy days and days of religious mourning) for mobilizing the masses against the Shah's secular programs, programs that undermined the clergy's authority.

I need to point out here that while the Constitutional Revolution was largely a secular movement that sought to curb the authority of the clergy, and while Reza Shah's secular policies had put the clerical class on the defensive, for the most part Mohammad Reza Shah had managed a cordial relationship with the clergy. In a mutually beneficial relationship, a large majority of senior Ayatollahs and leading Shi'ite figures, including Grand Ayatollahs Ha'eri and Boroujerdi, adopted a *quietist* policy or *Taghieh* and stayed out of political affairs, essentially lending their tacit support to the Shah, and Mohamad Reza Shah in return did not follow his father's harsh anti-clergy policies—for example, reversing Reza Shah's policy and exempting the clergy from military service in a gesture of respect.

Khomeini though, was an exception to this general pattern. Grand Ayatollah Boroujerdi, who was one of the leading *Marja*'s at the time and Khomeini's mentor, had specifically forbidden him to become involved in political matters. However, following the senior Ayatollah's death in 1961, Khomeini was free to pursue his political aspirations, especially since he was now considered a leading *Marja'* himself.

However, even at the height of the revolution, only a fraction of Shi'ite clerics joined the pro-Khomeini movement, while a majority of high-ranking Grand Ayatollah and sources of emulation (*Marja' Taghlid*) including Grand Ayatollah Shari'atmadari maintained their conservative stance, remaining suspicious of the radicalized youth and of Khomeini's ways and avoiding direct involvement in the revolutionary movement—a fact that changed once Khomeini rose to power after 1979.

THE WHITE REVOLUTION AND KHOMEINI'S RISE TO FAME

Let's look back at the 1960s when the monarchy was experiencing a deep crisis after the failure of its economic modernization project that began with the land reforms, or the White Revolution in 1962. The program, which in theory sought to dismantle large concentrations of landholdings by aristocrats and the clergy in favor of farmers, had sparked fury among the former classes and proved unsuccessful for the recipients. The clergy were especially unhappy because they believed expropriation of large parcels of land would weaken the dominance of religious institutions.[5] Ayatollah Khomeini was particularly appalled by the program's more secular policies such as granting suffrage to women and allowing secular local elections that would extend election and appointment to local offices to Iran's non-Muslim minorities such as Christians, Jews, Baha'is, and Zoroastrians. Despite the quietist tradition of the clergy at the time, Khomeini took an outspoken stance against the program.

> I have repeatedly pointed out that the government has evil intentions and is opposed to the ordinances of Islam . . . The Ministry of Justice has made clear its opposition to the ordinances of Islam by various measures like the abolition of the requirement that judges be Muslim and male; henceforth, Jews, Christians, and the enemies of Islam and the Muslims are to decide on affairs concerning the honor and person of the Muslims (Khomeini, 2015, 175).

He also took a strong stance against women's suffrage, calling gender equality a Western plot that would corrupt and demoralize Iranians' Islamic values.

In June 1963 Khomeini gave a famous speech in Feyzieh Seminary in Qom criticizing, for the first time, the person of the Shah and his brutality toward seminary students protesting the White Revolution earlier that month, comparing him to Sunni Muslim Caliph Yazid, a corrupt tyrant by Shi'ite accounts. Khomeni was detained two days later, and following that news street protests erupted in major cities in which around four hundred people lost their lives. Khomeini was released from detention but placed under house arrest until August 1963. A year later, however, in October 1964, Khomeini took to the pulpit again to publicly denounce the Shah and the United States in light of a newly passed "Capitulation" law in which the Shah granted diplomatic immunity to American military personnel in Iran. The law essentially granted U.S. military staff and their families protection from prosecution by the Iranian judiciary, instead allowing them to be tried in the United States and under U.S. law. The Capitulation was widely viewed with indignation as a privilege granted to the Americans, which further undermined Iranian sovereignty and re-opened the wounds of the 1953 coup.

Khomeini's denunciation of "Capitulation" in yet another sharp-tongued speech ultimately got him exiled to Turkey and shortly after to the holy Shi'ite city of Najaf in Iraq, where he spent most of the next more than fourteen years.

MAPPING THE ISLAMIST GROUPS
IN THE 1979 ISLAMIC REVOLUTION

Like most political uprisings, the Iranian revolution began with a host of diverse and at times opposing forces, from radical Islamists to secular liberals and democrats, and, of course, a thriving rainbow of leftists and communist forces. In the end, however, the Khomeinists managed to triumph over other perhaps more progressive forces and stir the nation into an ideological, totalitarian regime. This is why I have dedicated this book to studying the dynamics, perils, and promises of the Islamic political agenda in key historical moments over the past four decades. It is by no means my intention to diminish the bravery, political prowess, and sacrifices made over the decades, both during the Pahlavi era and the Islamic reign, by the Iranian Left (in all its forms and shapes, from the Group of 53 to the Tudeh Party, the Fadayian, and others), the National Front, secular and liberal democrats, and especially women's groups. This chapter is not a survey of the many social actors or an analysis of the causes of the Iranian revolution, it is simply meant to historicize both the 1979 revolution and the 2009 Green Movement and to study the political communications of their leaders, thus focusing on the Islamic forces to which all those figures belong.

Four general groups can be distinguished within the spectrum of Islamic political orientation. The first is radical Islam, as represented by supporters of Ali Shariati. The second is militant Islam, as expounded by Ayatollah Khomeini. The third category, liberal Islam, whose adherents seek political power through non-violent means, is mainly represented by the Iran Freedom Movement, an offshoot of the National Front, whose leader Mehdi Bazargan was later appointed by Khomeini the interim government's prime minister. The fourth group can be categorized as traditionalist Islam, which appealed to the overwhelming majority of the clergy who were against any radical and/

or militant changes in Iran and generally adopted quietism on state matters. Despite their differences in political agendas, the first three groups were united under the leadership of Khomeini, whose campaign hinged on such slogans as "Islamic authenticity," "freedom" for the oppressed, and "justice" for the economically downtrodden. Additionally, the Bazaaris in particular were directly attacked by the Shah through such policies as an anti-profiteering campaign of the mid-1970s. The historical marriage of the Shi'ite clerics and the Iranian Bazaar is revealed in the fact that the clergy's financial resources originate through the vast sums contributed by believers (mostly members of the Bazaar) as religious taxes, or the "Imam's share."

Under pressure from the Shah's regime, Khomeini was deported from Iraq in 1978 for instigating anti-regime protests. After multiple unsuccessful attempts to stay in neighboring states such as Kuwait and Turkey, he was finally granted asylum in France. While in Paris, the Ayatollah held daily sermons in the tradition of Shiite seminaries that were attended by Iranian dissidents, students, politicians, and residents abroad. Toward the end of 1978 it became apparent to the world that a revolution was in fact happening in Iran and that Khomeini was its ultimate leader, spiritually at least. A series of press conferences, interviews, articles, and daily reports in the international media illustrated the attention the world afforded this event and its leaders. Ayatollah Khomeini accepted the reporters with open arms, answering their questions and making promises to the revolutionaries of Iran and to the world about the future of the country should the movement be successful. He recognized the power of the modern media, embraced it to communicate his message, and continued this trend throughout the first years of the revolution.

Furthermore, Khomeini's claims about his political aspirations, and his stance on such issues as women, the direction of the new government, and individual freedoms during the pre-revolution era substantially differed from his post-revolutionary course of action. Khomeini changed from a soft-spoken, spiritual leader in Paris to an authoritative father-figure guiding and supervising the transition of power in early days after the revolution and finally to a vengeful and inflexible dictator asserting his vision of an ideological political Islam. His public stance changed as he gained influence. In Paris, he claimed he would play the role of a "guide" (Khomeini, 2008, 4:389) to the new government and that "the religious authorities will not rule by themselves; they will rather supervise and direct those executive affairs" (Khomeini, 2008, 4:148). After returning to Iran, Khomeini claimed that the ulama were essential to the operation of the government (Khomeini, 2008, 13:15), and ultimately in later years he established himself as the Supreme Leader.

CHAPTER SUMMARY

My intention in this chapter has been to historicize the Green Movement of 2009 and provide more context for this latest social movement in contemporary Iran. However, as you can see by now, certain themes run through all those uprisings, which have come at great cost to the country, both in human lives and otherwise. From the Constitutional Revolution in 1905 to the Green Movement of 2009, one can't help but recognize that the Iranian people's demands for justice, freedom, and democracy continue to surface, reminding us that despite the heavy costs paid so far by this nation, those demands remain unfulfilled as of yet. The desire for a free and just society, and for emancipation continues to return in generation after generation of Iranian people, which explains the cycles of protests, large-scale demonstrations, and revolutions every few decades. Critical to our understanding of the Green Movement is the context in which it takes place, a context that includes the oppressive legacy of the 1979 revolution put in place by Khomeini and his allies. We will delve deeper into this discussion over the next few chapters.

NOTES

1. For more on this topic see Abrahamian (1982).
2. Dr. Karim Sanjabi (1904–1995) was an Iranian politician and a founding member of the National Front who also served as Mosaddegh's minister of culture and education.
3. Dr. Hossein Fatemi (1917) was another one of Mosaddegh's close allies and served as his minister of foreign affairs. Dr. Fatemi is known to have brought forward the proposal for nationalization of Iran's oil and gas assets.
4. "Hut dwellers," or *Kookh neshinan*, refers to Khomeini's frequent reference to the poor and the underprivileged in comparison to *Kakh Neshinan*, or "palace dwellers."
5. Like the Catholic Church, the Muslim clergy control religious endowments, or *Oghaf,* which generally include large parcels of land.

3

The Green Movement through a Conceptual Lens: Structuration, Social Action, and the Public Sphere

AN OVERVIEW OF THE THEORETICAL FRAMEWORK

The conceptual framework for this book is grounded in critical social theory and is based on the theory of structuration of Anthony Giddens and the theory of communicative action (TCA) of Jürgen Habermas. Structuration theory is a widely tested social theory based on the interactions of social structures and agency (Giddens, 1984), which are at the core of my work. Structuration is an ontological framework for the study of human social activities, that is, recurrent social activities and their transformations (Giddens, 1984). Both the 1979 Islamic Revolution and the Green Movement of 2009 witnessed the activities of a set of social actors attempting to transform the sociopolitical structures of the ruling regimes. Structuration theory focuses on understanding conflict, contradiction, and modes of domination and forces of emancipation, all of which are at play in political movements.

However, since the study of production and consumption of media content that take place through the interactions of structure and agency is ultimately the goal of this study, I have decided to alter the framework to examine social action, an integral part of the theory of structuration, through TCA. Media usage in the context of the *public sphere*, as demonstrated by both theorists, falls within the realm of social action and must be studied as such. TCA in my view provides greater flexibility and offers deeper understanding of social action, especially as it pertains to media usage, since Habermas has done extensive work on the subject. Both frameworks are essentially similar in that they both examine the interactions of human agents with social structures within the context of the public sphere. However, by combining the two frameworks, I have created a stronger, more appropriate lens with which to conduct my study.

The social interactions of structure and agency occur in the context of the public sphere, as noted, a discursive arena of social life where private individuals gather to discuss matters of public concern. Thus, I will examine both theories against the backdrop of the public sphere. Jürgen Habermas has done extensive work on developing this concept, and thus this inquiry will be based on his concept of the notion of the public sphere.

The remainder of this chapter is organized as follows: situating the research in a sociological framework, briefly describing the various concepts of the theory of structuration, discussing various types of social action based on the theory of communicative action, detailing the concept of the public sphere and its guiding principles and then discussing those conditions in the context of Iran, and particularizing for this study the various concepts above and coding them for later analysis of the data.

SITUATING THE RESEARCH

This research broadly and primarily falls into the humanist paradigm and is anchored in critical social theory (CST). Traditional social theorists view themselves as observers of social conditions and focus on describing and understanding social phenomenon. On the other hand, critical social theorists, including Habermas and Giddens, believe that researchers are not mere observers but their very presence influences and is influenced by sociopolitical systems. In other words, critical social scientists go beyond developing a sound explanation of a social situation and extend their responsibilities to include the critique of unjust and oppressive conditions from which the actors seek emancipation. I am interested in critically interrogating what I believe are deep-seated, structural contradictions within the present sociopolitical and economic systems in Iran that are instigating widespread dissent.

Additionally, CST researchers are sensitive to the *lifeworlds* of the social actors they study. Lifeworlds are a taken-for-granted stock of knowledge, the shared normative social and cultural backdrop against which individuals interact, which reflect meaning extracted from within the social context of the actors. In other words, CST is concerned with interpreting and mapping the meanings of the actions of social actors from their own perspective, and therefore it recognizes that social context is imperative not only to meaning construction but also to the activities the social actors participate in. Thus, CST considers social actors as intelligent beings who can create and enact their own meaning and thus can be critical of it.

CST is concerned with a critique of oppressive sociopolitical situations, hegemony, and emancipatory forces from domination, and it thus provides suitable theoretical grounds for this research. Additionally, Habermas, one of the main contributors to CST, has already developed a communication theory: TCA.

THE THEORY OF STRUCTURATION: CONCEPTS AND COMPONENTS

Structuration theory considers agency and structure as a duality through which human agents draw upon certain understandings of norms and power relations during social action and thus produce and reproduce social structure. Therefore, Giddens does not give primacy to either agency or structure and treats them as an interdependent phenomenon in this theory. Structuration theory asserts that structures do not exist in any concrete sense, but they are instantiations of social actions over time intervals. In this way, structuration suggests a duality between structure and agency in which social structures enable and constrain the actions of human agency. Human agents draw upon the rules and resources presented by structures to enable them in their social activities while at the same time they are constrained by those structures. Let's use traffic laws as an example: while this structure provides rules and resources for drivers to draw upon while operating a vehicle, they also constrain the actions of those drivers, i.e., one is prohibited from going through a red light.

In another view, social structures constitute both the medium and the outcome of social interactions. They constitute the medium because they provide the rules and resources necessary to facilitate interactions. Social structures also constitute the outcome since they only exist through instantiation, and the rules and resources only exist as long as they are acknowledged and applied by the agency. They have no existence independent of the social practices they constitute. For example, in a university setting, rules and regulations, whether explicitly stated, such as an academic code of conduct, or taken for granted, such as the customs governing student-teacher relations, form the medium. At the same time, the concept of a university is only meaningful through its instantiation, i.e., as long as students attend the institute and follow its rules for the purpose of higher learning. If one day all students, teachers, and staff decided to abandon the institute, all that would be left would be buildings and objects. Below, I will briefly discuss the various concepts of the theory of structuration.

Agency

Agency is the capability of human agents to consciously act in social settings. Giddens (1984) draws a distinction between the capability and the intention to act, stating that agency is not the intention of performing an act but implies the power to do so. For instance, a student protester on the streets of Tehran may be capable of joining the ranks of his fellow protesters in setting a police car on fire but have no intention to do so for fear of retaliation or just out of principle. Giddens asserts that the concept of agency refers to what an agent "does," regardless of intentionality. Along the same lines, actions that agency performs may have known and intentional consequences as well as unknown and unintentional ones. Nevertheless, even unintended consequences may systematically feed back into the system and contribute to the unacknowledged conditions of future acts. By way of an example, I may pour salt into my coffee thinking it is sugar and after finding out it was salt decide not to drink the coffee. Although I actually intended to sweeten my coffee and drink it, salty coffee is an unintended consequence of my action, which has contributed to my further action of not drinking the coffee.

Agency and Power

On another note, it is important to point out that agency occurs in a continuous flow of action rather than in individual yet combined acts. Therefore, agency can be viewed as the power that enables an individual actor to intervene in this flow and alter the events should he choose to (Giddens, 1984). As such, agents are not merely routinely following the rules presented by the social structure within which their actions fall. But they have the power, i.e., the choice, to intervene in the flow of actions, which grants them the possibility to modify or radically alter social structures, which may explain why revolutions and other radical political changes occur. Intervention is an exercise of power, and it "is a necessary feature of action that, at any point of time, the agent 'could have acted otherwise' either positively in terms of attempted intervention in the process 'events in the world' or negatively in terms of forbearance" (Giddens, 1979, 56).

In its broader sense, power implies the ability to "act otherwise," i.e., to intervene in the flow of action or refrain from doing so with the intent of influencing particular processes or a course of events. Power entails the ability to get things done or to alter pre-existing states of affairs or processes. As mentioned above, without the ability to exercise power, that is, "to act otherwise," agency ceases to exist. On the other hand, power in a narrower sense simply entails domination.

Nevertheless, power should not be confused with a resource. Resources are inherent in social structures and are drawn upon in production and reproduction of social structures by knowledgeable agents. As such, although power is present in all social actions, it is not a resource, but resources constitute the medium through which power is drawn and exercised.

As mentioned above, power is not restricted to specific types of action, but all social interactions involve power. Agency, in all social relations, assumes autonomy and independence to some extent. Even at their most dependent level, subordinates have resources through which they can influence and sway the actions of their superiors. This concept Giddens calls the *dialectic of control*. Employees withholding information from their supervisors, farmers leveraging their produce to bargain for a higher price, and workers refusing to provide manpower by way of a strike are examples of this concept.

Rules and Resources

Rules, from the structuration theory perspective, are generalizable procedures and schemes that human agents apply in the production and reproduction of social structures. Thus Giddens's (1984) definition of rules includes communication codes, linguistic rules, codes sanctioning morality, and other rules and norms governing the social interactions of agents. Rules can be articulated and explicit such as religious guidelines and civil, constitutional, and criminal laws, or they may exist as unarticulated, implicit, shared background knowledge such as semantic and grammatical rules.

Resources on the other hand are the capability to generate command over material and social objects, which in turn generates power. In their social reproduction, Giddens argues, all agents exercise power in one form or another through controlling two types of resources, namely, *authoritative* and *allocative resources*. Authoritative resources stem from the capability to coordinate the activities of social actors. Allocative resources, on the other hand, are derived from the control of material artifacts, such as command over objects and goods, and are derived from the dominion of humans over nature (1984).

SOCIAL STRUCTURES

Structuration theory defines structure as "generative rules and resources that members draw upon, but also thereby, change in their production of society" (1979). Contrary to the functionalist perspective where structures are descriptive patterns of social interactions, in Giddens's terms, structures are recursively drawn upon and instantiated through the social actions of human agency. Giddens (1984) identifies three types of structures in social systems: *signification*, *domination*, and *legitimation*.

It is important to note that although distinct, these dimensions are interlinked and must be studied both independently and in relation to one another. For example: while signification is structured through language, language use always mediates aspects of domination and has a normative force. Therefore, it is useless to analyze structures of signification without grasping their connections with domination and legitimation. Social action, the second pillar of the duality, is also broken down into three dimensions of communication, power, and morality, which will be discussed later in this chapter.

Structures and social interactions of humans are recursively interlinked via three modalities. Modalities are the modes of mediation that human agents draw upon in the production and reproduction of social structures. Modalities are modes of mediating between interaction and structure. Giddens identifies three such modalities: *interpretive schemes, facility*, and *norm*, which will be discussed in the next section.

Each structure is associated with particular social actions mediated through a modality.

Structures of Signification

In the context of social systems, signification structures are structures that signify meaning and understanding such as language. Interpretive schemes are the cognitive means through which actors communicate understanding and meaning in social interactions. In other words, interpretive schemes are a shared stock of knowledge that human agents draw upon to make sense of the actions and speech of other agents.

Structures of Legitimation

These structures are the moral constitution of social action. Legitimation structures are mediated through the shared morals, norms, and values of a society, and they institutionalize the rights and obligations of social actors. For instance, religion is a legitimation structure on the norms and values of which believers draw in social interactions to determine what is moral and just and what is not. For example, taking a life is a sin in Islam, but under certain conditions it is not only justified but is mandated, i.e., in the case of homosexuality, apostasy, or treason.

Structures of Domination

Last, domination structures are those of power, with the intent of exerting authority and dominion over other social actors. Patriarchy and slavery are examples of such structures. Facilities are the resources through which agents draw upon domination structures. Giddens identifies two types of facilities (resources): allocative and authoritative. Allocative resources are those capabilities that command control over objects, goods, or material life. Authoritative resources refer to control over people.

Modes of Mediation

Modalities are meaning generation processes that mediate production and reproduction of similar social practices across time and space. In other words, they link social action to patterns of social structure. Giddens (1984) notes that while the modalities facilitate reproduction of social patterns and practices, they also allow subtle changes and variations in practice that later enable changes in the very structures they were reproducing. This phenomenon is dubbed *duality of structure* by Giddens (1984) and will be discussed below.

Social actors draw upon stocks of implicit background and explicit foreground knowledge, as well as material and non-material resources, to mediate between social action and structures. These modalities are discussed next.

Interpretive Schemes

These are the implicit background knowledge or interpretive schemes that humans accumulate over time from their past experiences, socializations, customs, and traditions. Signification structures signify meaning and facilitate symbolic representation. These processes are made up of interpretive rules that represent shared stocks of knowledge and organizing regimes that guide social interaction. Communication, which is how actors interact with the structures of signification, imply tapping into shared interpretive rules that are the stock of knowledge human actors use to make sense of their own and another actor's communicative action.

Facility

Facility includes explicit foreground knowledge, as well as material and non-material resources. Explicit foreground knowledge is comprised of policies, procedures, rules of action, and explicit social and political norms (i.e., the constitution and civil and criminal codes of a country) that guide social actors in the process of social production. Material and non-material resources on the other hand refer to the social status, political position, charisma, special skills, etc., that some actors possess that can affect an action situation. Facilities are the basis by which material and non-material resources are allocated within social settings, and they are manifested through power interactions. Wielding of power by those human agents who are capable of drawing on facilities to allocate material and non-material resources in turn uses this modality to produce structures of domination.

Norms

Norms are those rules (religion, moral codes, etc.) and standards of morality that human agents sanction their actions based upon, and in that process, they produce social structures of legitimation. Norms are shared within a society where they enable understanding as well as sanction human interaction and thus give rise to structures of legitimation within that society.

The three dimensions of structure, social action, and modes of mediation are intricately interlined. As Lyytinen and Ngwenyama (1992) elegantly state, "While signification is structured through language, language use always mediates aspects of domination and has a normative-force. Therefore, it is useless to analyze structures of signification without grasping their connections with domination and legitimation" (23).

The Psychological Makeup of the Agent

Intervention in the ongoing flow of social life, i.e. agency, requires agents to continually monitor their actions and their consequences and respond by drawing upon implicit stocks of mutual knowledge. This concept is introduced by Giddens as the *reflexive monitoring of action* and defined as "the purposive, or intentional, character of human behaviour, considered within the flow of activity of the agent; action is not a string of discrete acts, involving an aggregate of intentions, but a continuous process" (1984).

Giddens argues that although that stock of mutual knowledge is not directly accessible by the consciousness of the agent, human agents are "purposive." This means agents not only have reasons for their actions, they can "routinely and for the most part without fuss maintain a continuing "theoretical understanding" of the grounds of their activity" (1984, 5). In other words, agents have reasons for their activities and if asked can discursively detail those reasons. This is a key concept to which we will return in later chapters.

SOCIAL ACTION: THE THEORY OF COMMUNICATIVE ACTION

In CST, *social action* refers to action that is oriented toward others against a social backdrop (i.e., in the society or organization). In TCA, Habermas (1979; 1984; 2000) argues that public speech can fall into one of the two categories of *strategic action* (being therefore oriented to success) or *communicative ac-*

Table 3.1. Action types and potential outcomes

Social Action	Action Sub-type		Orientation	Potential Outcome
Communicative	None		Achieving Understanding	Cooperation
Dramaturgic	None		Achieving Success	Influencing
Strategic	Open Strategic		Achieving Success	Influencing
	Concealed Strategic	Conscious Deception	Achieving Success	Manipulation
		Unconscious Deception	Achieving Success	Systematically Distorted Communication

Source: Adapted with some changes from Cukier, Ngwenyama, Bauer, and Middleton (2009).

tion (being therefore oriented to reaching mutual understanding). He makes a clear distinction between these two different categories of speech acts by stating, "Types of interaction can be distinguished according to the various mechanisms . . . I speak either of 'communicative action' or of 'strategic action,' depending upon whether the actions of different actors are coordinated by way of 'reaching an understanding' or 'exerting influence'" (1992, 70).

Action orientation refers to the basic goal or focus of the action type. Orientation is what ultimately the action type is set to achieve. Communicative action has the potential to obtain cooperation among social actors and can lead to conflict resolution and solidarity. Moreover, Habermas (1979; 1984; 2000) also distinguishes between conditions of conscious and unconscious deception in communication, recognizing that strategic action can potentially lead to a range of outcomes, some of which are antithetical to democratic discourse. Dramaturgical action is another goal-oriented action type that may be present in a discourse. Habermas defines this type of action as presentation of the *self* in a stylized manner (1984). Table 3.1 describes the various action types and their potential outcomes relevant to public communications.

Strategic Action

Orientation to success implies that social actors essentially act with the intention of achieving a desired outcome (Habermas, 1984). To reach these goals, actors primarily engage in activities that are expected to deliver success efficiently. Habermas dubs this action type *teleological action* and describes it as *purposive-rational*, or goal oriented: behavior directed at obtaining rational, measurable objectives, i.e., achieving success. Success is measured by how closely the actor has met his goals. Actors may engage in the arbitrary exercise of power and/or manipulation to attain their objective.

A form of teleological action is called *strategic action*. Following the rules of rational choice, strategic action focuses on influencing the behavior of opponents (other social actors) and transforming their behavior into conforming to the agent's preferred outcome. Actors engaged in strategic action essentially predict the behavior of other agents directed by a goal, and hence, try to manipulate the process. Strategic action is distinguished from other types of action in two fundamental ways: (1) strategic action focuses on influencing and manipulating human behavior, and (2) agents engaged in strategic action are conscious their opponents may also attempt to influence their behavior by engaging in counteraction. This trend, as discussed above, is described by Giddens (1979) as the *dialectic of control*. Actors engaged in strategic action recognize that "all forms of dependence offer some resources whereby those who are subordinates can influence the activities of their superiors" (Giddens, 1984, 16). While involved in strategic action, actors rely on their knowledge of the rules of the process to examine the goals that can be successfully reached and to similarly gauge their opponent's potential for counteraction.

Categories of Strategic Action

Strategic action may be openly admitted or covert depending on the conflict situation. In the case of *open* or *manifest* strategic action, at least one of the parties openly admits to using language in a way that indicates clearly their goal to reach success or to serve their self-interests, thus influencing the outcome. Strategic action stems from authoritative resources, to put this in Giddensian terms, thus there is an associated claim to power. Giving an order to a subordinate is one such example where the person in the position of authority openly attempts to influence her subordinate. Strategic action can also be *concealed* or *latent*, in which case Habermas, further divides this type of strategic action into the two categories of *conscious deception* and *unconscious deception*. In the case of conscious deception or manipulation "at least one of the parties behaves with an orientation toward success, but leaves others to believe that all the presuppositions of communicative action are satisfied" (2000, 169). Furthermore, manipulation means "at least one of the participants is deceiving the other(s) regarding the non-fulfillment of the conditions of communicative action which he or she apparently accepted" (Habermas, 1982, 264). Unconscious deception on the other hand is a more complex case of strategic action and leads to *systematically distorted communication*, which occurs when the internal organization of speech is interrupted. Systematically distorted communication occurs when one of the participants is deceiving themselves into believing they have adopted an attitude oriented to reaching mutual understanding, while they are actually behaving strategically.

While manipulation involves deception, systematically distorted communication is about self-deception. In both cases a border is crossed and the goal is no longer mutual understanding, but manipulation involves deliberately hiding an end from one or more of the interlocutors. But in systematically distorted communication, "interlocutors deceive themselves; they think they are in control of exchanges whose purpose is mutual understanding; in fact, they have ceded control" (Gross, 2010, 338). Systematically distorted communication is a powerful tool used by systems of domination and oppression and as such are important to examine.

Dramaturgical Action

Dramaturgy is the presentation of self in a favorable light to others, and thus it falls into the teleological (goal-oriented) action category (Habermas, 1984). "The concept of *dramaturgical action* refers primarily neither to the solitary actor neither to the member of a social group, but to the participants in interaction constituting a public for one another, before whom they present themselves. The actor evokes in his public a certain image, an impression of himself" (86). In other words, social agents can monitor public access to their intentions, thoughts, and desires, a system only they have privileged access to. Thus, the agent's action does not signify a spontaneous expression of the *self* but a stylized presentation with a view to the audience.

Communicative Action

Communicative action on the other hand, is oriented toward reaching mutual understanding where the driving factor is the force of a better argument. Habermas explains, "*Communicative action* refers to the interaction of at least two subjects capable of speech and action who establish interpersonal relations (whether by verbal or by extra-verbal means). The actors seek to reach an understanding about the action situation and their plans of action in order to coordinate their actions by way of agreement" (1984, 86). The process of reaching mutual understanding cannot be undertaken while trying to reach an agreement about something and exerting influence on one or more participants simultaneously. Thus, mutual understanding can only be reached via the power of rational argument and cannot be imposed strategically or otherwise by one party on the other (Habermas, 2000).

Orientation to understanding implies social actors seek to communicatively coordinate and reach an agreement with other communicating actors in their world. Although they are seeking a mutual agreement, it is critical to understand that such actors are also in pursuit of their own goals. The key difference, however, is that the actors coordinate their action plans based on a communicatively reached agreement and a common understanding of the conditions instead of direct exercise of power or manipulation of other actors. Communicative action is oriented toward reaching a common understanding among social actors. In this case, the desire to reach mutual understanding replaces the orientation to success. Communicative action is an *individual* action concerned with reaching consensus in a *group* via *cooperation*.

Mutual understanding is achieved via rational argumentation, negotiating a shared understanding of norms, values, and objectives, and defining shared expectations and assumptions. The success of communicative action is highly dependent on the spirit of the cooperation under which consensus is achieved and the extent to which individual plans of action are coordinated.

Communicative action is enacted by way of language and other symbolic interactions present in communication (e.g., body language). Social actors draw upon common interpretive schemes and a pool of shared background knowledge, assumptions, and beliefs to make sense of the world and reach a mutual understanding of their surroundings. Actors engaged in communicative activity presuppose a common language, media, and shared interpretive schemes. While engaged in communicative activity, social actors claim validity for the four criteria of ideal discourse, namely, *truth*, *legitimacy*, *sincerity*, and *comprehensibility*. In other words, theoretically speaking, communicative activity takes place in an ideal discourse situation.

Although the goal of communicative action is to reach consensus via mutual understanding, we can't overlook the possibility of conflict among participants. When conflict arises in a situation and the participants no longer agree on the truth, legitimacy, sincerity, and comprehensibility of a communicated message by an actor or actors, communicative action can no longer take place. Instead, Habermas argues, in situations of conflict, social actors either resort to discursive activity to restore the conditions of understanding or to strategic action to influence and coerce other actions to achieve success.

Validity Claims and Speech Acts

In order for human agents to understand communication, decode a discourse, and interpret meaning, they first decide on the orientation of the speaker. Every communication among actors implies, as noted, a set of four validity claims, namely, the truth, legitimacy, and comprehensibility of the utterance, and the sincerity of the speaker. "An engaged listener (or reader) will interrogate the speech (or text) to test the implied validity claims. When any of the validity claims are contested or found wanting, such speech (i.e., strategic communication) can be viewed as deviating from achieving mutual understanding and may be oriented towards open or concealed strategic action on the part of the speaker" (Cukier, Ngwenyama, Bauer, and Middleton, 2009, 178). These validity claims facilitate understanding communication but they also provide a general basis for critically examining speech, according to Cukier et al. This book will therefore use the four-part validity claim test developed by Cukier et al. to determine the orientation of speech acts. Chapter 5 will discuss this methodology in detail.

The Public Sphere

The *public sphere* is an arena of social life where private individuals gather to hold rational discussion about matters of public concern or common interest and to influence political action through that process. It is against this backdrop that structuration unfolds and will be studied as such in this project.

In other words, it is to discuss and identify societal problems and to influence political action through debate. The public sphere is a discursive arena in which private citizens as well as groups assemble to discuss matters of mutual interest and, where possible, to reach a common judgment. The public sphere encompasses a wide array of public institutions such as a parliament, political parties, mass media (mainstream and social), lobbyist and special-interest groups, and corporations, as well as clubs and gatherings where sociopolitical matters are discussed. Habermas, the most influential figure on the topic, defines the public sphere as an "intersubjective shared space" governed through principles of "communicative rationality" (1996, 361). While autonomous from both the state and the private sphere (the home), the public sphere, specifically in Western democracies, mediates between the state authority and the society and as such is the cornerstone of democracy since it empowers and organizes citizens to stand up to public authority. Therefore, a strong democratic state requires a public sphere of informal citizen deliberation that forms public opinion through rational debate and steers political systems critically.

Through his work, Habermas provides a sociopolitical history of the inception and transformation of the public sphere in late-seventeenth- and early-eighteenth-century Europe. Although the public sphere is considered a theoretical concept, the discursive arenas of social life such as France's salons, England's coffee houses, and Germany's *Tischgesellschaften* are considered physical manifestations of this sphere. However, after the emergence of the printing press, this arena slowly moved to the newspapers and other print media. Following that logic, one can extend that definition and draw the conclusion that with the emergence of analog (cassette tapes) and later digital media and the internet, the public sphere, although not completely but to a great extent, moved from print to the virtual world. My intention in this book is to show the public sphere and its manifestation in the virtual space and to analyze those discussions and debates that took place on the various social media platforms in the context of the Iranian Green Movement. The audiocassette tape, a popular form of analog media in the 1970s and 1980s, emerged as the medium of choice during the 1979 Islamic Revolution, an era sandwiched between print media and digital media domination.

Habermas's theories of the public sphere remain central to the discussion because his account is the most systematically developed critical theory of the concept to this date (Dahlberg, 2005; Dahlgren 2005; Fraser 1990). Additionally, Habermas's TCA, the concepts of which are intertwined with those of the public sphere, is central to this paper and as such this study will adopt a Habermasian approach to the principles of the public sphere.

The Concept of Communicative Rationality

The role of the public sphere is one of mediating between society and the sphere of the public authority or the *state* via *publicity*. Publicity refers to the *public* nature of the discourse taking place in the public sphere that shapes *public opinion* and permits the formation of political will. Public opinion is the tasks of criticism and control that citizens informally and formally through periodic public elections practice via the ruling structure of a political state. Central to the Habermasian public sphere is the concept of *communicative rationality*, which describes a rational critical discourse, also referred to as *argumentation*, where participants' actions are coordinated based on reaching mutual understanding rather than manipulation or domination oriented toward achieving success. Mutual understanding is achieved via rational argumentation, negotiating a shared understanding of norms, values, and objectives, and by defining shared expectations and assumptions. The result is a communicatively constituted public sphere where rationally formed public opinion can critically guide the political system. In other words, the Habermasian public sphere presupposes a form of communicative rationality: it is a reflexive and impartial space where arguments are critical and rational and validity claims are well-reasoned.

While Habermas and others often refer to the public sphere in a singular form, it is essential to understand the plural nature of the public sphere in that it is constituted of a shared collective of many different communicative spaces. As Dahlberg notes, "When talking of *the* public sphere, Habermas is not talking about a homogenous, specific public, but about the whole array of complex networks of multiple and overlapping publics constituted through the critical communication of individuals, groups, associations, social movements, journalistic enterprises, and other civic institutions" (2005, 112). Private citizens hence become public actors in the public sphere, exercising public reasoning and rational argumentation and standing up to public authority.

The Conditions and Principles of the Public Sphere

The public sphere includes the two vital organs of *information* and *political debate* such as print, broadcast, and social media as well as the institutions of political debate such as parliaments, public assemblies, literary and political clubs, and other public spaces where sociopolitical discourse ensues. These organs enable individual citizens and groups to critically express their opinion on all matters of general interest, shaping public opinion and thus influencing the political process. The public sphere essentially allows the establishment of a realm of critically debated and formed public opinion that ultimately stands up to the sphere of public authority (the state, corporations, special-interest groups, etc.). As previously discussed, the public sphere is a realm of open debate about all matters of public interest employing the tools of discursive argumentation for the purpose of reaching consensus and mutual understanding. Inherent in this definition are the principles of freedom of the press, speech, assembly, and political participation, which guarantee an individual's right to freely argue an opinion and participate in political debate and decision-making without fear or threats of reprisal and punishment. To further protect the rights and freedoms of citizens and groups from infringement by the state authority, the establishment of an independent judicial system is crucial. In most Western democracies, the judiciary is mandated with mediating the claims between individuals and the state as well as between various individuals. Iran, though, doesn't follow those principals, a dilemma which will be discussed in later chapters. The media is central to a thriving public sphere as it is the vehicle through which information is disseminated and public debate facilitated, and thus it will be discussed next.

The Role of the Media in the Public Sphere

The media assume a central role in the political conception of the public sphere as they have the power and the tools to shape public opinion and exhort social control. The primary function of the media is facilitating rational discourse and critical argumentation. In the absence of discursive argumentation, the institutions of the public sphere, i.e., the mass media, pose a threat to democracy, since they have the power to "select, shape and present messages and to strategically use political and social power to influence agendas and frame public issues without deliberation of citizenry" (Cukier et al., 177). The mass media mold public opinion, and in the absence of critical discourse, citizens have become spectators of media presentation, and their key role as the primary actors of the public sphere is reduced to objects of news, information, and public affairs. This is the "colonization of the public sphere" by the state, corporations, and special-interest groups (Habermas, 1991). To this extent, significant consideration must be devoted to a critical analysis of the roll of the mass media in the public sphere because "those who work in the politically relevant sectors of the media system (i.e., reporters, columnists, editors, directors, producers, and publishers) cannot but exert power, because they select and process politically relevant content and thus intervene in both the formation of public opinions and the distribution of influential interests" (Habermas, 2006, 419).

Furthermore, while the media is structurally independent, particular actors in the public sphere hold a powerful position when it comes to negotiating privileged access to the media. The political elite (politicians and political parties) are by far the strongest in that they supply a large share of media content (news and commentary). However, considering the high level of both material and organizational resources that representatives of functional systems (politicians, corporations, and lobbyists) and special-interest groups hold, they too enjoy privileged access to the media. Their position enables them to use professional techniques and employ corporate communication management methods to transform their social power into active political muscle, colonizing the public sphere for their political imperatives. As a consequence of this privileged access to the mass media, the actors of civil society are placed in a weaker position compared to politicians, lobbyists, and the advocates of special-interest groups.

Systematically Distorted Communication and Ideology in Totalitarian Regimes

In this section, I will sketch a genealogy to describe the relationship between systematically distorted communication, ideology, and hegemony implemented by totalitarian regimes, all taking place within the context of the public sphere. This will help us develop a richer understanding of the impact and implications of distorted communication in ideological regimes such as that of the Islamic Republic.

Ideology is a shared network of beliefs that ground self-deception and impede improvement yet remain unexamined. The self-deception involved in this practice is rooted in the justification of inequalities in power and in economic, social, and political life. Therefore, to preserve their gains, that segment of the society that benefits from such inequalities intervenes through the power of the state to substitute for the legitimacy that can only result from rational and critical debate in the public sphere. In other words, ideology can be thought of as a fake substitute for communicative rationality in the public sphere. Such power manifests itself not as a blatant imposition of force but as a barrier to critically interrogating and exposing ideological justifications in the public sphere.

> Structural violence is not manifest as violence; instead it blocks in an unnoticed fashion those communications in which are shaped and propagated the convictions effective for legitimation. Such a hypothesis about unnoticed yet effective barriers to communication can explain the formation of ideologies; they can make plausible how convictions are formed by which the subjects deceive themselves about themselves and their situation. Illusions that are afforded the power of common convictions are what we name ideologies (Habermas 1983, 184).

Thus, structural violence gives rise to ideologies, and ideologies are justified through systematically distorted communication. Moreover, systematically distorted communication is the linguistic manifestation of a regime such as the IRI that dominates through real and structural violence. Such regimes are dominated by an ideology, in this case a specific political reading of Shi'ite Islam.

Thus, in totalitarian regimes such as Iran, the physical and structural violence of the state dominating through ideology trumps the force of better argument (i.e., communicative action), increasing the potential for the political elite to engage in distorted communication. In turn, communication distortions impede freedom of speech and threaten the survival of the public sphere and by extension freedom of speech itself, which is central to this study.

PARTICULARIZING THE THEORY TO THE STUDY

My research will use this theoretical framework to choose which social and political structures were targeted for change by the leaders of the Green Movement, Mousavi, and Karoubi. To this end, I will study their communications, including campaign promises and protest messages, to understand the type of social action that was taken to achieve those goals. I will conduct a critical discourse analysis of the validity claims of those leaders regarding changing oppressive structures to determine the orientation of their action, i.e., success or mutual understanding. My analysis will look for three types

Table 3.2.   Code Table

Theoretical Concept		*Operationalized Definition*
Social structures: the rules and resources that human agents draw upon and also change in their production of society	Structures of signification: structures that signify meaning and understanding such as effective use of language Structures of domination: structures of power with the intent of exerting authority and dominion over other social actors Structures of legitimation: structures that reside in the moral constitution of social action	Those social structures targeted by Green Movement protesters such as women's rights, human rights, the economy, the election process
Social action: action that is oriented toward others	Strategic action: goal-oriented action aimed at achieving success Dramaturgical action: goal-oriented action aimed at presenting one's self in a favorable light to others Communicative action: oriented toward reaching mutual understanding	The type of action the leaders of the Green Movement engaged in while campaigning and during the protests

of structures as defined by Giddens, namely structures of signification, domination, and legitimation. The type of structures addressed in the Green Movement's communications and the orientation of social action taken will determine the outcome and thus help us understand the Green Movement, its goals, and its place in Iran's sociopolitical arena. Table 3.2 summarizes the concepts that guide my inquiry.

4

Critical Discourse Analysis

The Methodological Approach

AN OVERVIEW OF THE CHAPTER

In order to investigate the impact of the discourse of the leaders of the two major uprisings in the past four decades in Iran—namely, Khomeini on the Islamic Revolution, and Mousavi, Karoubi, and Rahnavard on the Green Movement, I used critical discourse analysis (CDA). CDA is a well-established critical method in the use of language in relations of power, and while there are various approaches to this methodology, I will be focusing on the Habermasian approach.

To address research questions 4 and 5 as well as the overarching research question, this investigation uses a CDA method based on Habermas's universal validity claims present in the *ideal speech situation*, namely, truth, legitimacy, comprehensibility, and sincerity (1984). Additionally, for practical reasons in this book I will rely on an operationalized approach to CDA based on the work of Cukier, Ngwenyama, Bauer, and Middleton (2009) that proposes a set of questions and speech elements for examining and revealing potential violations of validity claims in public discourse. Considering the empirical material for this book is in the form of both text (Khomeini) and videos (the Green leaders), I applied both descriptive and visual content analysis methods in order to code the data for interpretation. Visual content analysis (for the videos) is a methodology that is used to "systematically code, characterize, observe, and quantify the representations within the population of video clips meeting set criteria" (Rutledge, 2009, 67). An exploratory or descriptive and visual content analysis of the collected texts and videos helped identify the common themes in the material and extract the social structures targeted for change by the actors.

I will begin this chapter by outlining the key concepts and principles of Habermasian CDA. Next, I will define the corpus of data, including an outline of my reasons for selecting YouTube as the medium for this study. Lastly, I will discuss content analysis, data collection, and coding.

CRITICAL DISCOURSE ANALYSIS

As a means of analyzing discourse, critical social theorists have developed the CDA methodology. This study uses CDA to examine the discourse of those who led Iran's last two main uprisings. I will specifically focus on the validity claims of those leaders regarding two different yet interrelated structures of (1) patriarchy (i.e., women's rights) and (2) the economy. The corpus of empirical materials for this book were drawn from two distinct sources to cover the discourse of the leaders of these two events thirty years apart. *Sahifeh-Ye Imam* (2008), which is a collection of Khomeini's sermons, writings, and interviews before, during, and after the 1979 revolution, provided one set of data. Another set was the public speeches, interviews, and official campaign videos of the leaders of the Green Movement before and after the June 2009 elections, that is, the period of January 2009 to February 2011, at which point the movement had largely lost steam and the two leaders were under house arrest.

My critical interpretive strategy for this study was focused on examining the promises of improving women's rights and eliminating economic inequality made by the two Green leaders prior to and after the elections to reach and mobilize the electorate in order to assume the country's presidency, and implement change. Such an analysis provides a better understanding of what demands drove the Green Movement of 2009 and why the movement faltered. A similar strategy was applied to understanding Khomeini's discourse. Khomeini was instrumental in structuring the regime and its institutions within which the Green Leaders operated, thus understanding his discourse is key to understanding his vision for the Islamic Republic. While Khomeini's rhetoric mobilized different factions of Iranian society, including intellectuals, students, women, youth, clerics, and lay and religious citizens under the utopian umbrella of political Islam, Mousavi, Karoubi, and Rahnavard organized somewhat similar crowds in the name of Islamic Reformism, or in Mousavi's words "Imam's path." I aim to demonstrate how those leaders, thirty years apart, were able to appropriate the public sphere's discourse in order to appeal to such a wide spectrum of society to the point of a mass uprising.

Growing resistance to the Islamic Republic over the decades has led a sizeable segment of the society to look for an alternative that corresponds to their demands for freedom, social justice, and prosperity without the violence, cost (human and capital), and uncertainty involved in overthrowing yet another regime. One such alternative that emerged in the late 1990s was the Reform Front, which will be discussed in chapter 5. For over twenty years, the Reformists have been putting forth a message of change, arguing that economic prosperity, democracy, and freedom can be achieved by reforming the constitutional framework and political order from within, without a complete overthrow of the regime that Ayatollah Khomeini established. This message was articulated again in the 2009 presidential elections and reached its heights during the protests.

I am especially interested in critically analyzing the speeches of both Ayatollah Khomeini and the Green leaders to uncover their strategies of systematically distorted communication in the Habermasian sense. I conducted this research in an effort to find out what a critical interrogation of their political rhetoric would uncover and whether some of the inherent contradictions present since the inception of the Islamic Republic had found their way into the discourse of the Green Movement.

While traditional discourse analysis and interpretive approaches are rooted in traditional hermeneutics, CDA is rooted in the critical hermeneutics of Habermas, which is concerned with uncovering power relationships and the ways in which social structures undermine and inhibit the emancipatory interests of citizens. The goal of this critical approach is to assist citizens in emancipating themselves from ideological superstructures of society, such as patriarchy and economic domination, that inhibit their full participation in creating the kind of society they want. Within the context of the Habermasian theory of communicative action (TCA), CDA is a method of critical investigation into the use of language and its implication for human beings who wish to emancipate themselves from all forms of domination. In other words, CDA is a study of language that allows scholars with various backgrounds to adopt a social perspective in the cross-cultural study of media texts. It allows researchers to better understand the deep structure, systematic communicative distortions, and power-relations that underline communicative discourse.

Cukier et al. (2009) detail the fundamental principles for applying universal pragmatics to the analysis of discourse according to TCA as follows.

The reader or hearer assumes all speech is oriented to achieving mutual understanding but at the same time tests the validity claims present in the speech against the four principles of ideal speech. The assumption is that every discourse is communicative and yet redeemable if its implicit validity claims are thrown into question.

In the event any of the validity claims present in the discourse fail, the researcher must judge the intent of the discourse, which is done by interrogating the orientation and the objective of the discourse. In other words, should any of the validity claims fail, implying the discourse is no longer communicative, the analyst must then make a judgment call about the type of strategic action taken based on the objective of the discourse and the intention of the speaker. The discourse must be examined from the perspective of all four validity claims. For more theoretical discussion on the topic please see chapter 4.

While every discourse is open to critical interrogation, it is also redeemable based on the orientation of the speech (mutual understanding vs. success). Additionally, public discourse must be analyzed based on the orientation and intentions of the speaker and impact and implications of the speech, and thus we must pay special attention to the corpus of the argument. Therefore, in this methodology, while the strategy to understand the argument and analyze public speech is by parsing it at the level of the sentence, the final judgment about its orientation is made based on the entire argument. Furthermore, Habermas emphasizes, "It is possible, of course, for individual validity claims to be thematically emphasized . . . however, they are universal, that is, they must always be raised simultaneously, even when they cannot all be focalized at the same time" (1976, 160).

While Habermas lays out CDA in a conceptual framework through TCA, he does not offer a practical methodology for conducting empirical analysis of text and speech. In this book I have utilized an operationalized version of CDA developed by Cukier et al. (2009) based on TCA principles. Below, I will briefly outline the details.

OPERATIONALIZING THE METHOD

TCA establishes that implied in every communication are four sets of validity claims—truth, comprehensibility, legitimacy, and sincerity—that represent the context-independent and necessary conditions for critical interpretation and analysis of the discourse.

The *truth* claim is mainly concerned with misrepresentation and whether statements are factual or can be refuted. Truth claims generally deal with half-truths and omissions. The validity test for truth claims deals with biased arguments, false statements, omissions, and incomplete statements against which rational counterarguments cannot be formed, which could lead to manipulation (Van Dijk, 2006). To establish the validity of truth claims, the method tests whether an utterance corresponds to the "objective world" but argues that "this correspondence is not always directly observable and must sometimes be inferred. This requires a contextualized reading of the text and analysis of the argument (Ngwenyama and Lee, 1997) in which each text is analyzed in the context of the entire discourse and general standards of rational argument (logical consistency, completeness, and defensibility [cf. Toulmin, Rieke, and Janik, 1979]). "Contextualization allows a consolidated understanding of the specific texts (text element) within the discourse context, while the standards of logical consistency, completeness and defensibility allow for an analysis of the quality of argumentation" (Cukier et al., 2009, 180).

On the other hand, the *legitimacy* claim is focused on the conformity of the norms and social context embedded in the claims. In other words, legitimacy claims test the congruity between an utterance and its social context. Additionally, Habermas contends that actors can come to a mutual understanding only in the context of an *ideal speech* situation, which includes equal representation of all stakeholders, where everyone has an equal opportunity to participate in the dialogue. Therefore, an indicator of legitimacy in public discourse is the degree of representation of those in power and the silencing of dissenting voices. Thus, it is important to examine validity claims to determine which groups are marginalized or excluded from the discourse.

Sincerity deals with examining the consistency of the claim (i.e., whether what is said is what is meant) and action of the speaker. Sincerity, unlike the other three claims, must be inferred from the discourse of the speaker since we cannot observe intentions directly. The sincerity of the speaker is tested by examining inconsistencies between the speaker's speech and action. Particularly, sincerity of the speaker is tested by interrogating what the speaker says, how she says it, and what she does. This methodology pays "particular attention to emotionally charged adjectives and nouns, to hyperbole, to metaphors and to jargon, which can be used to invoke powerful associations, values and larger discourses" (Cukier et al., 2009, 181). Additionally, stylistic choices, e.g., wearing a chador, are of particular importance because they often have social and ideological implications and frequently signal a particular school of thought, opinion, or bias that, without being explicitly expressed, may have an impact on the hearer (Van Dijk 1991). Table 4.1 summarizes the general approach and guiding questions for this methodology.

CDA views the *comprehensibility* claim as the syntax and symbolic representation of language by investigating if what is said is audible, legible, and intelligible and whether or not the level of detail is too burdensome for the reader and/or hearer (Stahl, 2007). While the other three claims refer to the pragmatics of language, comprehensibility addresses syntax and semantics as necessary conditions for pragmatic analysis. Comprehensibility in public discourse is determined by such indicators as completeness of the symbolic representation, the presence of a shared language, and the utterance's

Table 4.1. Categories and principles of Habermasian critical discourse analysis.

Validity Claim	Criteria for Ideal Communication	Potential Distortion	Validity Test	Speech Elements for Empirical Analysis
Comprehensibility	What is said is audible (or legible) and intelligible	Confusion	Is the communication sufficiently intelligible? Is the communication complete? Is the level of detail too burdensome for the reader or hearer?	Completeness of physical representation; syntactic and semantic rules
Truth	The propositional content of what is said is factual or true	Misrepresentation	Is the evidence and reasoning provided sufficient?	Argumentation
Sincerity	The speaker is honest (or sincere) in what he or she says	False Assurance	Is what is said consistent with how it is said?	Connotative language; metaphors; jargon
Legitimacy	What the speaker says (and hence does) is right or appropriate in light of existing norms or values	Illegitimacy	Are competing "logics" (e.g., stakeholders) equally represented?	Use of "experts" and "authorities"; silences

Source: Cukier, Ngwenyama, Bauer, and Middleton (2009).

syntactical and semantic correctness. Information overload, and excessive use of a language difficult for the participants to comprehend, e.g., use of Arabic and hard-to-understand phrases by the clergy community, are all violations of the comprehensibility claim.

Cukier et al. (2009) combine qualitative along with quantitative techniques to develop a rigorous method and to remedy the common criticism of CDA's selectiveness. They lay out this methodology in the following four iterative steps.

1. Defining the corpus of data to be analyzed.
2. Content analysis and coding procedure.
3. Reading and interpreting the empirical observations.
4. Explaining the findings.

Steps 1 and 2 will be detailed in the next section, while 3 and 4 will be discussed in chapters 6, 7, and 8.

THE CORPUS OF DATA: FROM THE 1979 ISLAMIC REVOLUTION TO THE GREEN MOVEMENT

Since I was looking at two distinct yet related events decades apart, the data naturally came from two different sources and in different formats. Ironically, while the 1979 revolution is known for its reliance on the cassette tape as a medium of communication, the Green Movement was among the early pioneers of adopting social media.

The 1979 Islamic Revolution and the Discourse of Ayatollah Khomeini

Sahifeh-Ye Imam (2008), a comprehensive collection of Khomeini's speeches, sermons, letters, and decrees published in twenty-two volumes and translated through the official supervision of the Iranian government will be consulted for the purpose of this analysis. This text is of critical importance since it demonstrates the mode and style of Ayatollah Khomeini's communication, which has direct implications for the research in focus here. *Sahifeh-Ye Imam* includes Khomeini's speeches both on and off pulpit, letters, and official press interviews as far back as the early 1930s, many of which address the Ayatollah position on the political affairs of the time. As such, this text opens a window onto the leader's thought and his political and religious stance on issues such as the enfranchisement of women and freedom of expression. Special focus, however, is given to the period from the mid-1970s to the mid-1980s, the height of Ayatollah Khomeini's power. To further inquire into Ayatollah Khomeini's ideology and thought, I also consulted his other works, including *Islamic Government* (1970).

Khomeini recognized the power of the modern media of his time, embraced it to communicate his message, and continued this trend throughout the first years of the revolution. In the years and months leading to the Shah's demise, Ayatollah Khomeini communicated his sermons and messages to the nation using the telephone and audio tapes, which were disseminated through informal and traditional communication networks such as the Bazaar. While the Shah dominated "big media," that is, television and radio stations, Khomeini successfully resorted to "small media." According to Sreberny and Mohammadi (1994), Khomeini managed the most successful use of "small media" in revolutionary mobilizations to that point. Audio cassettes were so unique to the Iranian revolution and so successful in their role that they were dubbed "electronic *minbar*" (119).[1] To demonstrate the enormous length of the messages on the audio cassettes released, *Sahifeh-Ye Imam*, a transcribed embodiment of mainly Khomeini's spoken word, consists of twenty-two volumes—about a three-foot-high stack.

THE GREEN MOVEMENT AND THE POWER OF SOCIAL MEDIA

Similar to their mentor and predecessor Ayatollah Khomeini, Mousavi and Karoubi also embraced the power of the modern media of their time, i.e., social media, and more specifically, YouTube. Thus the corpus of data for this study of the discourse of the Green Movement comes from official campaign releases, state TV interviews, and speeches prior to and after the elections for the period of January 2009 to February 2011. In what follows, I will discuss YouTube as a medium of communication of choice in more detail.

YouTube as a Data Source

Bennett and Segerberg (2011) claim that "design of a social technology can greatly determine the kinds of actions that people may coordinate through it" (34), a view that is shared by many digital media communications scholars. Like Marshal McLuhan's famous claim that the medium is the message, my choice to study the Green Movement through YouTube videos over other forms of social media was based on the objectives of this investigation to explore social media as an alternative channel of communication in this political uprising. But first, I will discuss some statistics about the penetration and popularity of the internet as a new medium of political communication in Iran and worldwide.

According to the most recent reports, the number of internet users worldwide exceeded 3.7 billion in 2017 (www.internetlivestats.com/internet-users/), which represents more than half the world's population. In 2011, 50 percent of internet users had a mobile broadband connection; in 2012, video made up 50 percent of internet traffic; in 2013, developing countries (including Iran) had more than 50 percent of the world's mobile broadband subscribers; and in 2014, smartphones comprised over 50 percent of all mobile phones. Thus, while the internet is becoming considerably more accessible in the developing world, mobile and smartphone internet users are also on the rise, as is video traffic, all of which are directly related to this study.

The Internet Society estimates Iran's internet user penetration at 48.9 percent and on a steady rise for the past then years (Internet Live Stats, n.d.). Interestingly, in terms of the broadband internet Affordability Index, Iran scores in the top 40 (33rd out of 147 countries), higher than China, India, and neighboring Turkey and Pakistan. The popularity of social media in Iran began with blogging in response to increasing government pressure to restrict freedom of expression, especially of journalists.

> In light of this editorial censorship, many journalists who were willing to suffer the penalties associated with crossing the Red Line, especially the younger generation, felt marginalized and sought other mediums in which to report and share their opinions. They migrated to the Internet (Ctrl+Alt+Delete: Iran's Response to the Internet, n.d.)

On the internet, blogs provided an easily accessible yet powerful means of communication for individual citizens and quickly became an important platform for the voice of dissent unable to express itself via traditional forms of media. Over the years, that trend has shifted toward other forms of social media such as Facebook, Twitter, WhatsApp, and YouTube. Despite the encouraging trend of internet penetration and despite the popularity of mobile broadband internet, restrictive and discriminatory internet related laws from content censorship (Iran ranks number 1 in the world in terms of limit on content) to bandwidth limitations remain the biggest challenge in Iran (Internet Society, 2014).

While we know that Facebook, Twitter, blogs, YouTube, and various instant messaging platforms were used during the Green Movement protests to communicate the narrative of that political uprising to the rest of the world, my study focuses on YouTube videos. This decision was made, in part, because in the absence of traditional media sources, YouTube was widely used by protesters as an alternative platform of communication and dissent in the aftermath of the 2009 elections after the clampdown on domestic journalists, expulsion of independent foreign reporters, and tightening of control of the state media by the ruling elite. I situated my study within perspectives of social media that treat YouTube as a communicative tool that has proven to be popular among the crowd of the Green Movement. YouTube not only acted as a platform of communication for the protesters, it also allowed their narrative to be heard worldwide. Major media outlets such as CNN, BBC, and Al Jazeera began to frequently televise as well as upload YouTube videos online and thus disseminated the voice of Iranian dissent and the subsequent political uprising worldwide.

Another deciding factor in my choosing YouTube over other forms of networked social media such as Twitter and Facebook was the platform's inherent ability to become an alternative to traditional TV due to its rich communicative abilities, both audiovisual and textual. As noted, mass media in Iran is under the direct control of the regime and is at the service of the leadership elite. Because of the significance of mass media and its influence over the masses, the Iranian leadership has always kept direct control of television. Broadcast media are state owned in Iran, and the head of the radio and television organization is directly appointed by the Supreme Leader to ensure compliance with the overall state narrative.

Strict control of broadcast media further hindered freedom of expression during the Green Movement and left people with no choice but to look into other sources such as BBC Persian, Al Jazeera, and Voice of America[2] as well as internet sources for access to independent information, news, and commentary. It is worth noting that all the above broadcasting services are only available in Iran via satellite dishes, which are officially banned but nevertheless widely accessible to the public.

According to Arif (2014),

> YouTube, however, bridged this gap not only for citizens to have an alternative to TV media, but also gave them an opportunity to become producers of their own narratives at the same time. It was not only protesters who benefitted from YouTube as an alternative to TV media during the political uprisings, but also traditional media organizations such as Al-Jazeera also followed YouTube to get updated information and protest-related videos shot (14).

In other words, YouTube plays a counter-hegemonic role in authoritarian regimes such as Iran, where the mass media is colonized by the ruling class. Therefore, in the absence of independent broadcast media, studying YouTube videos will help us develop a better understanding of the 2009 political uprising in Iran.

Since this investigation involves political protests in an authoritarian regime intolerant of dissent in any shape or form, anonymity becomes an important aspect of online activism enabling protesters to engage in political communications without fearing for their safety. Iranian authorities routinely jail and otherwise punish online activists—for example, blogger Arash Sigarchi and cartoonist Atena Farghadani—for expressing views not sanctioned by the regime. Bennett and Segerberg (2011) argue the inherent anonymity of internet tools such as YouTube partly explain why online political activism is more popular in authoritarian regimes than in open societies.

It is easy to grasp why personalized networking is so appealing in authoritarian regimes such as Tunisia, or Egypt, where conventional political organization—particularly of the democratic reform variety—is often policed and punished. Joining online protest networks offers at least a measure of anonymity and safety in the numbers of people with mobile phones, access to Internet cafes, or friends with tech skills, often resulting in dense recombinant networks (41).

Understandably, YouTube's cloak of anonymity played an important role in the political communications of the Green Movement protesters because activists could upload videos of the uprising under anonymous profiles, thus keeping the dialogue alive while protecting their lives and their safety. This level of anonymity, however, is rather difficult to maintain on other popular social media sites such as Twitter and Facebook. This excerpt from an article in the *New Yorker* best describe web-censoring governments' frustration with YouTube:

Google has diverse presences in other Web-censoring countries. In China and Iran, where censorship is the norm, YouTube is completely blocked, but in Saudi Arabia a state agency filters pornographic and other "immoral" sites. From 2007 to 2010, YouTube was repeatedly blocked in Turkey for posting videos that "insulted Turkishness" and the country's founder, Kemal Ataturk. Eventually, a company in Germany asserted a copyright to those videos and took them down, and YouTube was unbanned. Google blocked the trailer for "Innocence of Muslims" in Indonesia, India, Jordan, Malaysia, Russia, Singapore, and Turkey after the governments of those countries requested removal of the video from YouTube. So the censorship that the site has accommodated, in various ways and to various extents, does not pose a dilemma for YouTube, per se. But it leaves possible security issues for any in-country staff, along with potential legal liabilities. Google would need exemption from country-specific laws in the window of time that exists between a potentially offensive video being uploaded and it being removed or restricted on the site. But, as Google stated in its letter to the Lahore High Court, it hasn't been offered that protection in Pakistan (Sethi 2013, 3).

Next, not only anonymity but the integrated and networked nature of YouTube also makes it an important focus in the study of social media's role in political uprisings. Arif (2014) describes YouTube's integrated and networked nature as the site's ability "to be accessed, viewed, commented, and disseminated via Facebook and Twitter by simply having access to smartphones, computers, and the availability of an Internet connection" (14). Furthermore, YouTube not only serves as an empowering tool of political communication, it also allows ordinary citizens to engage in reporting activities by further disseminating content online.

Additionally, YouTube's global reach and broad accessibility are important deciding factors: even in countries like Iran where the site has been banned since December 2006, citizens can download software such as VPN to bypass firewalls and internet filtering. Lastly, for the purpose of this investigation, YouTube proved to be an excellent source of archival data compared to other social media platforms that could be accessed and collected without raising user privacy concerns (as with Facebook), considerable expense (as with Twitter), or specialized software (required for blogs).

CONTENT ANALYSIS AND CODING PROCEDURE

This investigation is deductive in nature, meaning it involve1s testing an empirical situation, e.g., the 1979 Islamic Revolution and the Green Movement, against a theory or a set of theories, e.g., a structuration–TCA framework, thus validating or extending the conceptual framework (Blaikie, 2010). Content analysis is one of the qualitative techniques suited to conducting research based on deductive reasoning (Patton, 2002). Although less common in deductive qualitative research, the content analysis approach is increasingly being used in this field (Arif, 2014; Hazra, 2014; Pope, Ziebland, and Mays, 2006; Duriau, Reger, and Pfarrer, 2007; Ngwenyama and Nielsen, 2003), and as such is adopted for this inquiry.

While content analysis was developed within communication studies in the twentieth century, empirical inquiries into the content of communications dates back to the sixteenth century when the Church was concerned about the spread of non-religious propaganda by newspapers. Klaus Krippendorff (2004), a prominent scholar in the field, defines content analysis as "a research technique for making replicable and valid inferences from text (or other meaningful matter) to the context of their use" (18). Content analysis is a reliable, multipurpose, and rigorous technique that may be applied to many empirical situations from social identities associated with smartphones (Hazra, 2014) to the analysis of naturally occurring language (Markel, 1998), and from organizational culture and software process improvement (Ngwe-nyama and Nielsen, 2003) to video analysis of social movements (Arif, 2014). The content analysis approach is adaptable to "all kinds of communications—texts, images, interviews, and observational records" (Krippendorff and Bock, 2009, 2), which is why it was selected for this inquiry.

What distinguishes content analysis from other types of qualitative and interpretive message analysis is the extent to which it attempts to meet the standards of the scientific method, which includes satisfying the following criteria among others: *reliability*, *validity*, and *replicability*. Accordingly, reliability is "the extent to which a measuring procedure yields the same results on repeated trials" (Neuendorf, 2002, 12). Validity, on the other hand, "refers to the extent to which an empirical measure adequately reflects what humans agree on as a real meaning of a concept" (Neuendorf 2002, 12). Finally, replicability "is a safeguard against overgeneralizing the findings of one particular research endeavor" (Neuendorf 2002, 12). The above criteria testify to the scholarly rigor of the empirical measure, i.e., content analysis, as the chosen methodology for this study.

Berelson (1952) provides one of the first and more comprehensive definitions of the content analysis methodology, describing it as "a research technique for the objective, systematic, and quantitative description of the manifest content of communication" (18). Holsti (1969) emphasizes that content analysis is "any technique for making inferences by objectively and systematically identifying specified characteristics of messages" (14). From this perspective, audiotapes, photographs, video clips, and any other form of communication that can be made into text are amenable to the content analysis method. To that effect, Abrahamson (1983) also suggests "content analysis can be fruitfully employed to virtually examine any type of communication" (286), thus making content analysis an appropriate method of analysis for analyzing the videos included in this study. Additionally, more recently the historical definition of content analysis has been updated to include new modes of human communication such as information and communication technologies (ICTs), the internet, and social media, the latter of which is the most relevant concept to our subject. Earl Babbie's (2015) definition is one such example that attempts to incorporate new modes of human communication in order to keep the approach relevant in modern times: "Content analysis is the study of recorded human communications, such as books, websites, paintings and laws" (323). Definitions such as Babbie's are more comprehensive and appropriate for today's research projects, encompassing revolutionary new media of communication such as YouTube, Facebook, and Twitter.

While regular content analysis was applied to Khomeini's discourse, I adopted a *descriptive* content analysis approach to study the Green Movement.

Descriptive content analysis describes the content of and relationships among the variables in a message pool. Considering that the deductive nature of this study implies adopting a descriptive/explanatory approach, this method of analysis is appropriate to the study. In other words, I applied a descriptive content analysis approach to conduct a critical discourse analysis of the Green Movement political uprising in Iran through the lens of video clips. According to Arif (2014), "descriptive visual content analysis is not only the proper tool for finding commonalities of themes among the video clips of political protests under study, but it also provides a means of describing and contextualizing multiple angles and observations regarding these videos" (85). Qualitative discourse and visual analysis was essential for identifying, analyzing, and reporting patterns and significant themes emerging from the collected data of the Green Movement.

Units of Analysis

Selecting units of analysis is one of the most crucial initial decisions made by an analytical researcher. Neuendorf (2002) offers a functional definition for this concept.

[A] unit is an identifiable message or message component, (a) which serves as the basis for identifying the population and drawing a sample, (b) on which variables are measured, (c) or which serves as the basis for reporting analyses (71).

Carney (1971) on the other hand suggests units can be words, characters, themes, time periods, interactions, or any other result of "breaking up a 'communication' into bits" (52). Thus, in this study, each individual YouTube video is considered a unit.

In this book I propose to explain the 2009 Iranian political uprising through the lens of a Giddens-Habermas framework as described in the previous chapters. Thus, my study aims at finding and discussing the empirical observations of two of the concepts of the framework: various structures targeted for change, and different types of social action, within the data set of videos (the Green Movement) and texts (the 1979 Islamic Revolution).

Selection Criteria

For this book, I selected videos of official campaign releases, state television interviews, and other speeches from between January 2009 and February 2011. This time period was selected because presidential campaigning, unofficially, began around January 2009 and continued until the June 12 election date, when the protests began. Mousavi and Karoubi, the two leaders of the

Green Movement, were placed under house arrest on February 3, 2011, and banned from most communication with the outside world after they urged their followers to organize in support of the Arab uprisings in the region. Videos were selected specifically when validity claims were made regarding changing social structures.

A similar approach was taken in studying Khomeini's discourse from *Sahifeh-Ye Imam* for a period of two years from January 1978 to the end of 1979, although the majority of the claims were concentrated right before and right after the revolution.

Sampling

For the purpose of this inquiry, I have used *purposive* or *judgment sampling* (Neuendorf, 2002) to collect the most relevant and representative videos of the 2009 political uprising. According to Neuendorf (2002), this "type of sampling involves the researcher making a decision as to what units he or she deems appropriate to include in the sample" (88). Based on the guidelines provided by Neuendorf, I conducted a content analysis of Green Movement videos drawn at random from a keyword search of YouTube. I then coded the videos returned by the YouTube search engine in response to search queries both in English and Farsi using keywords such as "Green Movement" and "2009 Iranian presidential elections." The sample was collected during a period of two months in June and July 2014, and included videos had posted as early as the fall prior to the elections on June 12, 2009, continuing to the movement's anniversary a year later. A total of sixty-five videos were analyzed, and after I had eliminated those that were not relevant to the Green Movement, and duplicates, the final sample size included twenty-seven videos. Significant effort was put into developing meaningful keywords to retain more representative data, such as terms that incorporated the key actors (e.g., "Khamenei" or "Mousavi" or "Karoubi"), milestones (e.g., "Ashoura 1388" and "Silent March 1388"), and slogans (e.g., "where is my vote?" and "death to dictator").

YouTube was selected as the search engine of choice for this study for holding the largest number of videos available on the internet and also for being the platform of choice for posting videos of the movement. Next, only videos shot of the events in Iran were selected and the rest, including those of events held by the Iranian diaspora in support of the movement, were eliminated. This decision was made to keep the sample relevant and representative of those directly involved in the movement.

It is important to note the sample is affected by several limitations as described below.

As per Google's guidelines (Google is YouTube's parent company), You-Tube's search results are limited to returning no more than one thousand videos per query. To overcome this limitation, I ran multiple searches with my keywords using the sorting criteria available by YouTube as follows: Most Relevant (YouTube's default), View Count, and Ratings. Moreover, I thoroughly studied Ayatollah Khomeini's sermons, interviews, and addresses from *Sahifeh-Ye Imam* and selected claims relevant to the structures I was studying both before and after the revolution.

Despite my best efforts to access a larger collection of videos from different sources to gain a more comprehensive perspective of the movement through the lens of social media, YouTube essentially proved to be the most efficient and accessible choice. During my research, I came across a collection that the University of Southern California, Los Angeles, was putting together for their library and comprised of largely unpublished, unedited videos of the Green Movement. However, after lengthy email and Skype conversations, I was informed that "Iranian Green Movement Collection of Ephemera" was still being processed and not yet available for public access. Being in the processing stages, the raw data had not yet been stripped of the senders' information, release of which would violate privacy rights but more importantly threaten senders' security, considering that the majority lived in Iran. In 2014, the curator of the collection, Ali Jamshidi, informed me during a Skype conversation that while the collection's opening date was unknown, it was estimated to be no sooner than late 2015, which would have been too late for my purposes. I acknowledge, therefore, that my sample does not consist of all the relevant videos that might be examined in response to a "Green Movement" query, nor does it contain all the relevant videos that might be available in the future on the subject.

Despite the above limitations, I feel this sample accurately reflects a collection of videos accessible to and accessed by YouTube users. The data set is diverse, including videos of participating actors, significant milestones, and demands. I believe this sample represents the best possible survey of videos of the Green Movement currently accessible to the public.

Coding

I conducted the content analysis of the sample by carefully viewing each video and then coding them in Microsoft Excel (see appendix A). Each video was coded for instances of the *social structures* the actors aimed at changing (structures of signification, domination, or legitimation), based on the study's conceptual framework and the code table discussed in chapter 3. To narrow down the research and arrive at a more workable data set, I decided to select two instances of proposed change from each of the three main categories of social structures. For example, since the initial content analysis revealed the economy and women's rights to be two major structures targeted for change, those two instances of domination structures were selected for further analysis. That selection was based on the fact that both the economy and women's rights dominated the campaigns of both Reformist candidates. Once the instances of structures were decided upon, I conducted another round of content analysis, transcribing every instance of discussions, promises, and allusions to the selected topics from the videos. Next, since all the communications naturally occurred in Farsi, I translated everything to English. I am fully fluent in both Farsi and English and did my best to stay true to the message. However, I acknowledge that my work is not that of a professional translator and as such may not be perfect. Each utterance, or *empirical material*, was then given an identification code EM1 to EM52.

Once everything was translated to English, I conducted CDA on the empirical data and began coding for instances of violation of each of the four validity claims of truth, legitimacy, comprehensibility, and sincerity. The analysis was done on individual utterances as well as on the entire corpus of the data as detailed by Habermas to determine the impact and implication of the speech as well as the orientation of the speaker.

A similar approach was taken in order to conduct an analysis of Ayatollah Khomeini's discourse, except that in this case everything was already translated into English and so I conducted the coding and labeled the observations EM53 to EM105. However, please note that the texts are directly copied from the text of *Sahifeh-Ye Imam*, including interviews with journalists in which the reporter's name, location, and broadcasting station are named.

NOTE

1. Minbar has been translated to "pulpit."
2. The official external broadcast institution of the United States federal government, which has a Persian broadcasting section.

5

Participating Social Actors
of the Green Movement

AN OVERVIEW OF THE CHAPTER

The 1979 Iranian Revolution politicized many ordinary citizens and was the scene of active participation of social actors from Marxist and Communist groups such as *Fedayian e Khalgh* to liberal democrats such as the National Front and various Islamist groups which were discussed in detail in chapter 2—as well as women (most political factions had a chapter specific to women) and ethnic minorities, especially the Kurds and Turkmans (such as the *Kumelah Party of Iranian Kurdistan*, and the *Turkman People's* Party). Almost four decades have passed and there is an incredible body of scholarship dedicated to that phenomenal uprising and its sociopolitical actors by academics, journalists, revolutionaries, and activists of all political inclinations from across the world in a multitude of disciplines. Therefore, I will spare the reader a long list of political actors participating in the 1979 revolution and will focus instead on a more recent phenomenon: the Green Movement. For a list of relevant work focusing on the revolutionary actors, please refer to Ervand Abrahamian (1982); Charles Kurzman (1996); Sreberny and Mohammadi (1994); Keddie and Richard (2006); and Abbas Milani (2000) among others. Ayatollah Khomeini is the main social actor on whose discourse this book is focusing from that era. For more detailed background on this actor, please refer to chapter 2.

In this chapter, I will provide a brief overview of both the ideological orientation and the intellectual underpinnings of the different actors that participated in the Green Movement, including their goals, their roles, and their aspirations. This exploratory approach allows for a better understanding of the composition of the "Green Wave" and those in opposition to the movement, thus drawing a more comprehensive picture of the movement's power struggles.

The key actors of the Green Movement can be categorized into three groups: *civil society groups*, the *Islamic Reform Front*, and the *Conservative Bloc*. While civil society groups are by definition non-government organizations, Reformers and Conservatives are the political manifestation of the two ideological factions ruling Iran. Reformers represent the Islamic-Left, and the Conservatives the Islamic-Right, among each of which there are smaller factions. However, I should point out that "Left" and "Right" used in this context are different from the Western understanding of those designations and refer to the positions these factions claim with regard to social and economic issues, and they must be viewed within that contemporary context. Lastly, while some of the organizations and groups studied below may carry a party designation in their naming convention, party politics carrying clearly defined agendas in a Western sense are not permitted in Iran.

Studying the actors of the Green Movement, pro or con, also provides us with an overview of the Iranian political system and power distribution by mapping the organizations, foundations (*bonyad*), institutions, and affiliations of the country, leading to a richer understanding of the country's complex power structure. Although the official opposition groups of the 1979 revolution now reside in the Iranian diaspora—the *Islamic Mojahedin Khalgh Organization* (MKO) and an array of Marxist groups (e.g., the *Tudeh Party*, the *Communist Labor Party*, Fadayian factions, the *Democratic Party of Kurdistan*, Kumelah)—they had little to no role in the Green Movement and as such will not be studied here. These groups are largely remnants of revolutionary factions, the majority of which were violently crushed by Khomeinists in the post-revolutionary power struggle. Those members who survived the arrests, executions, long sentences, torture, and assassinations at the hands of Khomeini's men now largely live in forced exile.

IRANIAN CIVIL SOCIETY GROUPS

A diverse cross-section of Iranian civil society participated in the Green Movement. Women's rights groups (the *One Million Signatures Campaign*, the *Feminist School*, and the *Change for Equity Group*) and human rights organizations (the *Committee of Human Rights Reporters*, the *Defenders of Human Rights Center*, and *Human Rights Activists in Iran*) were notably active in the movement and therefore will be the focus. Student organizations (Islamic associations, *Tahkim-i Vahdat*), professional organizations (the *Lawyers Association*, the *Iranian Writers Association*) and trade unions (the

Teachers Guild, the *Vahed Bus Drivers Guild*) were among other prominent civil society groups that participated in the movement.

On the eve of the presidential elections in June 2009, a number of civil society organizations formed a coalition and published a manifesto titled "Iran's Civil Society Demands." The coalition presented their list of minimum demands to the representatives of the presidential candidates (Demands of the Coalition of the Iranian Civil Society Groups, 2009). The demands included

- recognition of civil society as a social force
- guarantees of freedom of association
- respect for independence and non-interference in the internal affairs of civil society groups
- review and reform of all laws and regulations that oversee the work of civil society organizations
- guarantees of freedom of speech, freedom of the press, and media diversity
- recognition of a right to the free flow of information
- capacity building and empowerment of citizens and associations
- ratification and execution of conventions on labor laws
- reform and review of Iran's discriminatory civil code
- membership on the Commission on the Discrimination against Women (CEDAW)
- respect for gender equality and gender justice
- response to professional demands
- protection of the environment (Razzaghi, 2010, 14)

Around the same time another significant alliance, *Convergence of Women's Movement to Convey Demands during Elections*, was formed to discuss women's rights issues and their struggles for equality and to put forward their demands (Convergence of Women's Movement to Convey Demands during Elections, 2009). In a published statement, the alliance detailed their demands for

- gender equality
- conformity to the International Women's Rights Convention's principles
- elimination of all forms of gender discrimination
- reform of discriminatory laws against women
- reform of divorce and family laws, which don't recognize a woman's right to divorce or to have custody of her children

The alliance included different chapters of the One Million Signatures Campaign, *Mothers for Peace*, the Feminist School, and the Change for

Equity Group, which are among the most prominent Iranian women's rights groups, among many others.

Clearly, there was a range of commonality among the above alliances comprised of a large number of active civil society organizations. It is safe to say that their demands remained unchanged when the post-election protests erupted, and women, youth, and human rights groups were among the most active participants in the movement. It is important to keep in mind the grave restrictions faced by these progressive civil society groups, both in their mandate and their activities, compared to other groups such as the Reformers, which will be discussed next. These advocacy organizations were frequently closed by the Islamic government, their publications banned, and their members arrested, jailed, or forced to flee and leave the country. Shirin Ebadi, Atena Farghadani, Narges Mohammadi, Mansour Osanloo, Nasrin Sotoudeh, Mohammad Seifzadeh, and many others were among the lawyers, journalists, and activists who suffered this fate. Those who managed to survive and remain in Iran faced continuous harassment, intimidation, and censorship even as they tried to stay within the legal, constitutional, and informal red tape of the Islamic Republic.

A majority of Iranian civil society groups participated and supported the post-elections protests. It is important to note that while many Greens supported the movement in hopes of a better life, change, equality, and greater liberties, they may not necessarily have supported the candidates, Mousavi and Karoubi. While both candidates enjoyed significant popular support, many Greens joined the protests simply to voice their dissatisfaction with the status quo, their outrage at the violence visited on the peaceful marchers, and essentially their disappointment with the established regime and the unfulfilled promises Khomeini made in 1979.

This gives us a general overview of what some groups within Iranian civil society were looking to achieve: improvements in the rights of women, children, and minorities; gender equality; fairness in labor relations; and above all, freedom of association and expression and for their right to be recognized and respected as a social force. These groups joined and at times participated in leading and guiding the direction of the movement to alter oppressive social structures such as marriage, custody, and divorce laws; restrictive labor union regulations; and other legalized forms of harassment.

THE REFORMIST FACTION

The Iranian Islamic Reform Movement is a coalition of political parties and organizations that brought forth the notion of reforming the system to embrace more freedom and democracy and to be more inclusive of all members of the society. Although rooted as far back as the late-1990s following the end of war with Iraq and Ayatollah Khomeini's death, the movement truly came to life in May 1997 to support the presidential candidacy of a little-known cleric, Mohammad Khatami, who later won the election in a landslide victory, collecting over 20 million votes (70 percent) more than the Conservative hardliner Hojatol Islam Ali Akbar Nategh Noori, former speaker of the Majlis. To commemorate that historical shift in the life of the country, the Reform Movement is often also called the 2nd of Khordad Front, which refers to the date of Khatami's landslide victory in the Persian calendar. Among the key figures of the movement have been Mohammad Khatami, Mir Hossein Mousavi, Abdolkarim Soroush, Hojatol Islam Mohammad Mousavi Khoeiniha, Saeed Hajjarian, and Akbar Ganji.

The Reform Movement argues that the Islamic regime can be reformed from within to accommodate more "openness," democracy, and freedom within the boundaries of Islam, essentially putting forth a different interpretation of Shi'ite jurisprudential doctrine than that of the establishment, which is largely based on Khomeini's writings. It believes in empowering civil society within the boundaries of the constitution, Islam, and pluralism; allowing for a more inclusive approach to political participation; engaging in dialogue with citizens as opposed to the established top-down approach; and respecting citizens' civil rights. The Reformers' reading of Shi'ite doctrine finds no discrepancies between Islam, civil rights, and democracy. It is equally important to note that the Reformers cite allegiance to Khomeini and "Imam's Golden Path," claiming to be following in his footsteps in steering the nation. In what follows I will briefly describe some of the chief principles upon which the religious Reform Movement stands.

THE THEORETICAL FOUNDATIONS OF THE MOVEMENT

The Reform Movement was the brainchild of a group of Islamic scholars loyal to Khomeini who actively participated in the construction of the Islamic Republic and the establishment of a religious state. Khomeini's death left the type of moral and authoritative vacuum that is often felt following the death of a charismatic religious leader, and this accelerated the disillusionment of some scholars with clerical authorities and their excessive interference in every aspect of life. Coinciding with the years following the end of war with Iraq, those same figures began deconstructing the sociopolitical aspects of Islam to make room for rational and democratic decision-making. Some of the main theoretical influencers of the movement, who later became known as the "religious intellectuals," were Abdolkarim Soroush, Mohammad

Mojtahed Shabestari, Hojatol Islam Kadivar, Hojatol Islam Yousofi Eshke-vari, Hamidreza Jalaeipour, and Alireza Alavi-Tabar (Jahanbegloo, 2012). The first three names on the list, however, largely dominate the Reformist political discourse for their attempts at reconciling political Islam with mo-dernity by introducing the concept of *religious democracy* and disputing the doctrine of Velayat-e Faqih (Guardianship of the Jurisprudent), which not surprisingly proved highly controversial (see for example Jahanbegloo, 2012; Adib-Moghaddam, 2006; Engeland, 2011). To facilitate a better understand-ing of the philosophical and theoretical foundations of the movement, I have provided a short overview of their works as follows.

Abdolkarim Soroush

Soroush, who in the early days of the 1979 Islamic Revolution was considered one of its most eloquent and prolific thinkers and especially in the face of opposition from Marxist intellectuals, is now considered one of the most in-fluential figures in the Reform Movement. He is a religious philosopher and is credited with having coined the term *religious democracy*, one of the founda-tional premises of religious Reformism (Holtan, 2005, 3). Soroush states that religious democracy means that the values of religion play a role in the public arena in a society populated by religious people (Soroush, 2003). He believes that democracy can take many shades and hues depending on a society's specific characteristics, hence there is more than one type of democracy, e.g., secular democracy, religious democracy, and so on. He asserts that embracing religion is not at conflict with democracy, but religious democracy is a perfect demonstration of how democratic principles can thrive in different cultural elaborations. He maintains that democratic values are not violated when faith is embraced by the state; only when religion becomes an ideology, belief is imposed, and disbelief becomes punishable by law is democracy in danger (Soroush, 2003). Soroush, who now lives in the United States, however, fails to develop a framework for the institutional schema of his proposed "religious democracy" (Esposito and Voll, 2001). Most of his arguments are abstract and don't address how in a religious democracy women's rights, freedom of religion and expression, and the rights of minorities are dealt with.

To further argue the compatibility of Islam and democracy, Soroush main-tains that while Shari'a (Islamic law) remains static and unchanging, the hu-man conception and knowledge of it (*ma'refat*) evolves over time, and since humans are in a constant state of change and flux, the evolution of theology and religious knowledge are also inevitable (Kamrava, 2008). The third theo-retical notion by which Soroush parts ways with traditional conservative phi-losophy is his belief in the de-ideologization of religion in society. While he maintains a firm belief in Islamic values and asserts they should be embraced, he also argues that we must let reason reign supreme and avoid ideologizing religion for political purposes.

Far from a champion of gender equality, Soroush's views on what is *essential* in Islam and what is *accidental* has radically influenced Islamic feminists and their interpretation of the role of a Muslim woman. Grounding himself in hermeneutics, Soroush claims that there are essentials (*zati*) in Islam, which are the elements that cannot be changed and without which Islam would lose its essence. Furthermore, Soroush puts forth a second set of elements that he calls accidentals (*arazi*), which are context dependent. Accidentals, he claims, are the results of Prophet Mohammad's time and place of birth as well as socialization in an Arab patriarchy.

> All history is contingent, including the history of Islam. My criterion for separating the essentials and accidentals of religion is the knowledge that things could have been otherwise. Things that could have happened otherwise are accidentals. For example, *tawheed* (oneness of God) is an essential because it could not have been otherwise (Soroush, 1996).

Based on that perspective, Soroush advocates the doctrine of "expansion of Prophetic experience" (Soroush, 1999) suggesting that "the Prophet is a human being and his experience is human, so are his disciples" (Soroush, 1999, 21). More specifically, Soroush indicates that it was merely accidental that the Prophet was born in the Arabian Peninsula and thus the language of Islam is Arabic, a fact that Soroush claims significantly shaped the conceptual framework of Qur'an (Soroush, 1999). If the Prophet had been born in Greece or Iran for example, his way of thinking and his language in passing the word of God to his people would have been instead vastly influenced by Greek or Persian culture. Therefore, Mohammad's birthplace of Arabia largely shaped Qur'anic rules on social issues that Soroush considers accidentals.

> If the Prophet had lived longer, and more incidents had befallen him . . . the Qur'an could be much more than this . . . If the accusation of adultery had not been levied on Ayesheh, would the first verses of the chapter Light (Qur'an 24:1–19) have been revealed? If the war of confederate tribes had not taken place would the chapter on it be revealed (Qur'an 33)? If there was no Abu-Lahb, would the chapter Abu-Lahab (Qur'an 111) have arrived? These are all unimportant historic events whose occurrence or non-occurrence would be the same. There is a record of them in the Qur'an only because these events took place (Soroush, 1999, 21).

It is Soroush's interpretation of Shari'a as "silent" rather than unchangeable that Islamic feminism has largely embraced in order to declare Islam

compatible with and supportive of gender equality (Soroush, 1999). Soroush's thesis on "expansion of Prophetic experiences" allows Islamic
feminists to argue that those verses of Quran, experiences of the Prophet's
personal life, and the Hadith that the Shi'ite clerics often use to determine
women's rights are essentially obsolete. They argue that those tools the
clerics use were only valuable in a certain time period and have lost their
relevance in modern times and are no longer applicable, thus advocating for religious thought to be reformed. For example, Shahla Sherkat,
Zanan's editor in chief, declares, "Since several articles of the Civil Code
are based on the Shari'a, then the Shari'a needs to be reinterpreted and
women should be involved in the process" (cited in Kian-Thiébaut, 1996).

For denying his role as one of the main architects of the "Cultural Revolution" of the early 1980s and for never fully acknowledging his close ties to
the regime he is now critical of, Soroush proves to be the most contentious of
these three thinkers (see Moosavi, 2007; Derayeh 2006; Jahanbegloo 2013;
Kurzman 1999). The Cultural Revolution Committee, to which Soroush was
directly appointed by Khomeini, saw the closure of universities for three
years in order to Islamicize them by putting in place a Shi'ite–friendly cur-
riculum and weeding out critical views.

Mohammad Mojtahed Shabestari

An Islamic theologian and philosopher, Mohammad Mojtahed Shabestari
similarly maintains that religion by nature has limited knowledge and rules
and thus is dependent upon additional sources. Mojtahed Shabestari argues
that Islamic knowledge (Quran and *Sunnah*) and Islamic jurisprudence (*fiqh*)
are not capable of responding to the changing circumstances of our era and
must be complemented with other modern sources. He asserts that for Islam
to survive, we must complement *fiqh* with modern science since answers to
many questions of the modern world cannot be found in the original sources
of Islam, questions such as where the legitimate basis of a political system
lies, whether capitalism is an acceptable economic system, and how far governments should interfere in individual lives and liberties.

Mojtahed Shabestari, in his book *A Critique of the Official Reading of Religion* (2000), applies modern hermeneutics to Shi'ite jurisprudence. Similar
to Soroush, he argues in favor of religious (specifically Islamic) compatibility with democracy and modernity. He suggests that divine providence has
already anticipated the separation of religious values and secular realities.
He thus vigorously defends modern concepts of democracy, civil society, human rights, and individualism, arguing they do not pose a threat to religious
values, and although they have not been specifically articulated in Quran

and Sunnah, Islam is in no way antithetical to the most important modern values of liberty and democracy. In response to the claims of a large body of Shi'ite jurists that essential and eternal values of Islam make the religion autonomous of any and all external sources, he maintains since modern concepts such as human rights are the product of human rationality and reasoning and evolve over time, they could not have been provided for in Quran and Sunnah (the tradition of prophet Mohammed), yet they do not contradict the divine truth of Islam for that reason.

Mojtahed Shabestari's second but more critical theoretical notion is the concept of *free choice*, by which he means that God created man free, and without free choice belief is meaningless. Therefore, he asserts, when it comes to political systems, a democracy is the form of governance most conducive to the fulfillment of religious beliefs.

> The logic of belief dictates that believers be aware of social and political realities, and themselves be responsible in political matters, so that they can consciously and freely search for their beliefs (Mojtahed Shabestari, 1998, 79).

Mojtahed Shabestari thus believes strongly in a religious democracy, asserting that democracy is necessary for the survival of Islam and that an Islamic democracy is a necessity for Iran.

Hojatol Islam Mohsen Kadivar

Hojatol Islam Mohsen Kadivar is an Islamic theologian, cleric, and university lecturer whose ideas stand in stark contrast to those of Ayatollah Khomeini regarding *Guardianship of the Jurisprudent (Velayat-e Faqih)*. Khomeini's theory of Islamic government details the principles of government by divine mandate (*Hokoomat e Velayi*) in which Shi'ite clerics, as the mediators between God and people, rule the Muslim nations (*Ummah*). At the top of the clerical hierarchy is the Supreme Leader who must be a *Mojtahed*, or Source of Emulation (*Marja' Taghlid*), which means he is an authority to interpret Islamic law and make legal decisions within those confines. Ayatollah Khomeini was Iran's first Supreme Leader, a title that was later bestowed on his successor Ayatollah Seyyed Ali Khamenei. Kadivar writes,

> Every member of society and every member of government is subject to the law. No one can be above it. Everyone has the same rights, yet the root of the faqih is inequality. He assumes he is above it . . . It is time for the Supreme Leader to be subject to the constitution too. After all, the Supreme Leader doesn't come from God! (Wright, 2008, 296).

Refuting the premises of Khomeini's doctrine of *Absolute Guardianship of the Jurisprudent*, which provides the theoretical foundations of the Islamic Republic, Kadivar proposes that such rule has led to government by appointment instead of representative governance on principles of republicanism as the constitution implies. He deems government by divine mandate (Velayat e Faqih) unnecessary and false.

> The principle of Velayat e Faqih is neither intuitively obvious, nor rationally necessary. It is neither a requirement of religion (Din) nor a necessity for denomination (Mazhab). It is neither a part of Shiite general principles (Osoul), nor a component of detailed observances (Forou') It is, by near consensus of Shiite Ulama, nothing more than a jurisprudential minor hypothesis (Subani, 2013, 271).

In 1999, the *Special Court of Clergy (Dadgah-e Vizheh Rouhaniat)* sentenced him to eighteen months in prison for criticizing the institution of the Supreme Leadership under charges of dissemination of falsehoods, disturbing the public opinion, and spreading propaganda against the Islamic state. He currently lives in the United States to avoid persecution in Iran. In the 2009 elections, Kadivar supported the candidacy of Mir-Hossein Mousavi and sided with the Green Movement when the protests had been suppressed. He became a key member and adviser of *Jaras* (the *Green Path of Hope*), a policy-making council for the internet organization of the movement, from July 2009 to October 2011 (Kadivar, n.d.).

Together Soroush, Mojtahed Shabestari, and Kadivar in large part formulated the theoretical underpinnings of the Reform Movement by opposing the absolutist theology of the current establishment and challenging the clerical hegemony. By utilizing indigenized forms of scholarship such as hermeneutics and Western philosophy and sociology, together they represent a modern Iranian Islamic discourse that attempts to guard the spiritual and cultural values of Islam while attacking ideologizing theology and totalitarian Islam. They claim objective secularism and a religious democracy are a real political possibility for Iran and its only way out of its current disenchanted state. While Soroush emphasizes the evolving nature of theological knowledge, Mojtahed Shabestari and Kadivar underline its limited and varying essence.

It is however important to remember the form of democracy that these Iranian religious scholars advocate implies separation of religion from government, not politics. While they oppose institutionalized Islam, they are in favor of embracing religious values in the public arena. Largely considered Islamic political revisionists by their secular counterparts (Nikfar, 1999; Moosavi, 2007; Ghobadzadeh, 2013), these Iranian religious intellectuals remain either silent or vague on many crucial questions. For instance, they have been repeatedly questioned by their secular peers to no avail how their interpretation of political Islam would guarantee democratic values such as freedom of expression and the rights of women, minorities, and non-believers.

The Reform Movement was founded on a particular interpretation of Islam that argues democracy and religion can peacefully coexist. On another note, Reformists put forward such modern concepts as human rights, civil society, and individuality, which Islamic teachings are largely silent on, and argue that those concepts too are not in conflict with Islam since they were developed over the course of time as the product of human reasoning. As such this movement advocates reforming current laws to accommodate the necessities of modern life within the boundaries of Islam.

The topic of Guardianship of the Jurisprudent is, however, approached with much caution by the Reform Front for a variety of reasons, above all for fear of persecution. Arguments such as those of Kadivar's and any criticism of the institution of Supreme Leadership is severely punished and at the same time puts the Reform Front at the risk of being accused of disloyalty to the regime and to the revolutionary ideals. Khatami, Mousavi, Karoubi, and many others have always maintained their loyalty to the Supreme Leader and to the principle of Velayat e Faqih. However, over the years and especially after the 2009 elections, many prominent Reformists (i.e., Abdolkarim Soroush, Ataollah Mohajerani, Akbar Ganji, Mohsen Kadivar, Mojtahed Shabestari, Yousofi Eshkevari, etc.) left the country and only once in the safety of a Western democracy most openly stated their disagreement with the principles of Guardianship of the Jurisprudent, which is critical to the survival of the regime.

PLACING THE MOVEMENT ON A POLITICAL SPECTRUM

It is important to note that the Reform Front is not a homogenous community. The Reform umbrella houses a large spectrum of social, political, and professional affinities. In the following sections I will describe the chief organizations under that umbrella.

Majma'-I- Rouhanyun- I- Mobarez

Otherwise known as the Combatant Cleric Society,[1] Majma'-I- Rouhanyun-I- Mobarez is the most powerful group within the Reform camp. Its former leader and founding member Hojatol Islam Mehdi Karoubi, speaker of the house from 1989 to 1992 and 2000 to 2004 and head of powerful *Bonyad-e Shahid (Martyr's Foundation)* from 1980 to 1992, was also one of the contesting candidates of the 2009 presidential elections and a leading figure of the Green Movement who is currently under house arrest for his role in the movement along with the movement's other leader, Mousavi. The organization houses a broad spectrum from radical elements in favor of "export of the revolution" and enemies of the United States such as Hojatol Islam Mohtashami Pour, minister of intelligence from 1985 to 1989, and Hojatol Islam Mousavi Khoeiniha, leader of the 1979 U.S embassy take over in Tehran, to more liberal voices represented by former president Hojatol Islam Khatami (current chairman of the organization; Buchta, 2000). In the 2009 presidential elections, however, the party backed Mir Hossein Mousavi's candidacy. Karoubi had left the organization four years earlier due to factional differences.

Sazeman-I- Mojahedin-I- Enghelab-I- Islami

Also known as the Organization of the Mojahedin of the Islamic Revolution,[2] Sazeman-I- Mojahedin-I- Enghelab-I- Islami was originally founded in 1979 but was later dissolved and then reactivated in 1988. Behzad Nabavi is a founding member of the organization, and currently Mohammad Salamaty serves as its secretary general. Both men served in Mir Hossein Mousavi's cabinet during his premiership from 1981 to 1989 as minister of heavy industries and minister of agriculture, respectively. The organization's leadership and members are exclusively religious laypersons largely educated in technical fields (Buchta, 2000).

Jebheh -I- Mosharekat-I- Islami -I- Iran

Also known as the Islamic Participation Front of Iran, Jebheh -I- Mosharekat-I- Islami -I- Iran is an organization known for its openness to all reform-oriented forces and is formed from a broad alliance of clerics, religious laypersons, Islamic-oriented labor forces, and religious women's activist groups (Buchta, 2000, 15). Among those who served as the Secretary General of the organization are Mohammad Reza Khatami, former President Khatami's brother, and Mohsen Mirdamadi, former Premier of the oil-rich province of Khouzestan and founding member of the elite *Islamic Revolutionary Guard Corps* (IRGC). Saeed Hajjarian, chief political strategist of the Reform Movement who is permanently paralyzed due to an assassination attempt, and Hamidreza Jalaeipour, a religious intellectual, are among other prominent members of this organization. Mosharekat emphasizes a more liberal reading of Islam and advocates an open market economy, political liberty, and normalization of a foreign policy to pull Iran out of its isolation. This organization too endorsed Mir Hossein Mousavi's candidacy in the 2009 elections.

All three groups firmly advocate *Khat-e Imam*, which literally means the political line of Khomeini, but recently have been moving away from the social and cultural hardline of that era, allowing more liberal voices to gain prominence. While Mir Hossein Mousavi has never officially belonged to any of the above groups, he has been an ardent supporter of the movement although his position as prime minister was abolished by a constitutional amendment in 1989.

The alliance of these diverse groups under the Reform umbrella revolves around the two imperatives of *Islamism* and *preservation of the Islamic Republic regime* through reform—as is evident in the faction's name. I will briefly discuss the two trends below.

Religious Affinity

One common trend here is that of the religious nature of the Reform Movement bringing all these various groups together. While some movement members may privately believe in secularism, the movement has never openly embraced the concept. On the contrary, the Reform Movement's figureheads, from intellectuals to its leaders such as Khatami, Hajjarian, Mousavi, and Karoubi, have always maintained their faith and their belief in a government grounded in Islamic theology. It is important to note that Reformers don't just embrace private faith, but similar to their conservative counterparts, they believe in a political system informed by Islamic traditions, being convinced that Islam is a political religion and not simply a spiritual guide. What differentiates this group from their conservative counterparts is their particular reading of Islam and of religion in general that is somewhat more lenient and more in tune with modern times. Looking back at the history of these prominent members of the Reform Movement, one can observe their religious nature. Many now reside in democratic nations such as the United States, Canada, and Western Europe and away from the regime's repression, yet a majority such as Soroush and others maintain their religious beliefs, so fear of the repression of the regime cannot be a factor here.

Preserving the Regime

A second common trend binding the groups under the Reform umbrella is an ardent desire to preserve the regime. The Reformers argue that should the political elite fail to implement limited reforms, the continuous dissatisfaction and defiance of certain sociopolitical strata will cause an upheaval similar to that of 1979, putting the future of the regime in danger (Kamrava, 2008). However, while the movement firmly believes in the necessity of systemic reform, the extent of those reforms are confined within the boundaries of Islam and the constitution of the Islamic Republic as advocated by the leader of the revolution, Ayatollah Khomeini. In one of his last official speeches, Mir Hossein Mousavi stated in no uncertain terms: "I have come to save the Regime" (Keyhan, 2009), while in a gathering with post-secondary students in the province of Mazandaran, Mousavi asserted, "We have the Islamic Republic regime and won't say a word more than Imam [Khomeini] has commanded us. Therefore republicanism has to be accompanied by Islamism and it hurts the country if either one of those is undermined" (Mousavi: I don't dare ask Khatami for his help, 2009), as well Khatami has asserted that "the Islamic Republic is an achievement of our revolution and we all have to safeguard it" (Safeguarding and strengthening the Islamic Republic is a duty for all of us, 2014). On another occasion Khatami also stated, "We are not looking to overthrow the regime and our goal is to safeguard the regime" (Khatami: Many mistakes are made in the name of the regime, 2010).[3]

In other words, the Reform Movement is considered by its secular opponents as the regime's "pressure safety valve," implying that this group has heard the voice of dissent and dissatisfaction among large classes of Iranian society and is trying to remedy that with superficial reforms. It is imperative to keep in mind that Khatami and the others are almost all regime insiders who were crucial to the establishment of the regime and are naturally keen on preserving it. However, contrary to their conservative counterparts, the Reformers believe further oppression of those disenchanted by the regime will only threaten the survival of the regime. Reforms are this movement's remedy to restrain dissent and discontent and guarantee the longevity of the Islamic Republic. By way of example, this movement does not challenge the attire and headscarf imposed on women and has never publicly acknowledged universal gender equality or equality for religious and other minorities.

Therefore, it is important to remember the movement as a whole did not advocate secularism or overthrow of the regime. On the contrary, the Reformist discourse is a religious discourse that attempts to preserve the system by reforming the current laws and institutions of the regime to incorporate more modern concepts such as democracy, women's rights, civil rights, and transparent governance. In other words, the Reformers see the crisis of legitimacy that the system is facing and are putting forward a solution to save it.

REFORMERS AND THE GREEN MOVEMENT

The Green Movement was largely formed in response to the disputed election results of 2009. Mousavi and Karoubi, both Reform Movement candidates, disputed the election results that declared incumbent president Mahmoud Ah-madi Nejad the winner by a landslide shortly after the polls closed. They asked their supporters to join in and voice their concerns and allegations of election fraud in a peaceful march of silence on June 15 (three days after the elections), in which hundreds of thousands of people marched the streets of Tehran and other major cities. The movement was dubbed the "Green Movement" by both domestic and later foreign media largely due to the green symbols carried by Mousavi supporters. Following Western branding and political campaigning strategies, Mousavi's camp had already used the color green to set itself apart from its opponents. The significance of this choice of color will be discussed at length in later chapters. Prominent Reformist politicians almost entirely threw their support behind the Green Movement both before and after the elections when the protests erupted. Reformists such as Ataollah Mohajerani (Khata-mi's minister of culture and Islamic guidance), Ali Abtahi (Khatami's chief of staff), Emadeddin Baqi (Reform strategist), and others staffed or endorsed Karoubi's presidential campaign. Although a founding member of the Re-form Movement and considered the Reform Movement's endorsed candidate, Mousavi had maintained his independent candidacy during the campaign but welcomed support from all factions (Mousavi: I Have Come Independently, 2009). Despite Mousavi's insistence that he did not belong to any one Re-formist group, Mousavi's presidential platform was closely defined based on Reformist principles. His candidacy was formally endorsed by Khatami—who withdrew at the early stages of the race in his favor (Khatami Drops His Presi-dential Candidacy in Support of Mousavi, 2009)—and Alireza Beheshti (son of Ayatollah Mohammad Beheshti, a former head of the judiciary who was as-sassinated in 1981), Mohammad Mahmoud Robati, and many others from his past administration formed his campaign staff. Once the election results were announced and protests erupted, many prominent members of the Reform Front supported the Greens and were among those arrested and imprisoned.

COMPLEXITIES OF THE IRANIAN POWER STRUCTURE

Despite their religious affinities, and despite their devotion to the regime, the *Conservative Bloc* continuously accuses the Reformers of treason and disloyalty to revolutionary ideals and has dubbed their brand of Islam "American-style Islamism," implying impure intentions and diluted faithful-ness. Khatami's election in 1997 was considered by many a major turn in the history of the Islamic Republic and facilitated the flourishing of the post-revolutionary discourse of reform that had begun a few years earlier. How-ever, during Khatami's two terms as president[4] the movement was largely incapable of delivering on its promises of transparent governance, a more open political space, individual freedom, and a thriving civil society, among other things. Suffice it to say that in 2005, at the end of Khatami's second term, Mahmoud Ahmadi Nejad, Tehran's little-known mayor and a Conservative Hardliner, was elected by a large margin over the Reform candidates.

The Reform Movement's failures throughout the eight years of Khatami's presidency are largely attributed by the movement elite to structural factors within the system. While the Reform Front largely occupied the executive and legislative branches, Conservative Hardliners still wielded considerable influence by controlling some of the most powerful institutions of the state. Kamrava (2008) describes some of the chief strongholds of the Conservative Hardliners as follows.

> The office of the Faghih (Bonyad-e Rahbari), the Judiciary, many publications and the state-controlled radio and television network (IRTV), and many of the economic foundations (Bonyads) in charge of the commanding heights of the economy (31).

The following is an overview of some of the structural roadblocks incorporated into the fabric of the Islamic Republic to ensure the clerical Conservative Hardliners' supremacy and grip on power. In the next few pages I will argue that the Supreme Leadership (Vali e faqih) and the principle of Absolute Guardianship of the Jurisprudent (Velayat e Motlagheh Faqih) are stipulated in the constitution to ensure concentration of power in the hands of the traditionalist Right. Consequently, the Guardian Council, the Assembly of Experts, the Special Court of the Clergy, the Judiciary, and countless other foundations (*Bonyad*) and institutions are the political manifestations of the structural need to preserve the institution that acts as the beating heart of the Islamic government envisioned by Ayatollah Khomeini and to ensure the balance of power continues to remain with the Hardliner clerics.

The Supreme Leader

The doctrine of the Supreme Leader draws its legitimacy from the principle of Velayat-e Faqih, a concept developed by Ayatollah Khomeini during his exile (from 1964 to 1979). Khomeini argued that the purpose of the Islamic state was to prepare the Ummah (Islamic nation) for the reappearance of the 12th Shi'ite Imam, Mahdi, who disappeared in 941 CE (Jones, 2011). In essence, Velayat-e Faqih means Guardianship of the Jurisprudent, or the rule of clerical authorities. Khomeini held the view that a just, and pious, religious leader "who surpasses all in knowledge" of Islamic law (a Marja', or Source of Emulation; Khomeini, 1970) must be at the helm to ensure that decisions and policies are consistent with Shari'a. Jurists (*Foqaha*; plural form of *Faqih*), according to this view, are the only sources of divine legitimacy after the prophet and the imams and are responsible for maintaining the Ummah in a fit condition to hasten the reappearance of Imam Mahdi (Khomeini, 1970). Khomeini became Iran's first Supreme Leader after the 1979 Islamic Revolution.

On June 4, 1989, Hojatol Islam Ali Khamenei succeeded Grand Ayatollah Khomeini after his death and became Iran's second Supreme Leader. The Iranian constitution required at the time that the Supreme Leader be a *Marja' Taqlid* (Source of Emulation), but since Khamenei was not, the constitution was amended to accommodate that and to legitimize his moral and religious supremacy.

To explain the significance of this move, we have to first explore Shi'ite hierarchical clerical ranking. The Usuli Twelve Imam Shi'ites, the dominant group among the Shi'ite Muslim, believe in *Ijtehad*, which means the use of critical reasoning in deriving new rules of *fiqh* from Quran and Sunnah, which are the main sources of law in Islam. A distinguishing pillar of Usuli doctrine is *Taqlid* (imitation), i.e., adhering to the religious rulings in matters of worship and personal affairs of someone regarded as a higher religious authority during the absence of the 12th Imam, Mahdi. That higher authority is called a *Marja' Taqlid* (Source of Emulation), or *Marja'* for short (Momen, 1985). To reach the level of Marja' and be a legitimate source of religious and moral authority, a cleric's knowledge of *fiqh* and *Usul* must have surpassed that of a *Hojatol Islam* and the cleric must have been accorded the rank of *Ayatollah* or *Mojtahed*. A select few astute Ayatollahs with expert opinions are then elevated to the rank of Grand Ayatollah, or Marja'. An absolute requirement of becoming a Marja' is to publish a *Resaleh*, a book in which the jurist addresses the vast majority of daily Muslim affairs from marriage to worship and taxes and so on, which is referred to by those who emulate him (*Moghalid*; Momen, 1985). Following a deceased Marja' is forbidden in Usuli Shi'ite tradition. Grand Ayatollahs Khomeini, Behbahani, Tabatabayi, Mirza Shirazi, Ha'eri e Yazdi, Bayat e Zanjani, Sane'i, and Montazeri are among the past and present Marja's in Iran that have also had a hand in shaping Iran's political landscape. For more detailed discussion of the subject, please see Momen (1985).

For a jurist to reach the rank and the religious authority of a Grand Ayatollah that legitimizes his *Marja'iat*, his scholarship has to be approved by other established senior Marja's. In Khamenei's case, although the political establishment promoted him from a mid-ranking Hojatol Islam to a Marja' practically overnight, many senior religious authorities in the seminaries rejected his legitimacy, often silently but sometimes openly. Grand Ayatollahs Hossein Ali Montazeri, Mohammad Shirazi (not to be confused with Mirza Shirazi), Hassan Tabatabayi

Qomi, and Yasoubedin Rastgar Jooybari are among the Shi'ite authorities that disputed the legitimacy of Khamenei's Marja'iat, citing his lack of religious scholarship, including not having written a Resaleh (Pike, 2009). Eventually those elements within the clerical system that were not supportive of Khamenei's ultraconservative agenda were either silenced by the establishment through house arrests, public attacks, or forcible defrocking (Montazeri was placed under house arrest and forced to remove his white turban signifying him as a cleric), or they chose to be silent themselves. In understanding the role of Supreme Leader Khamenei, Mehran Kamrava (2008) explains,

> Whether elected or appointed, an overwhelming majority of the country's political figures, only wield technical, administrative power in certain well-defined areas of activity, in all of which ultimate authority rests with none other than the Leader, *Valiye Faqih* and his narrow inner circle. Even many of the policy making purviews of these politicians are limited and are subject to final approval by the Leader, especially in key areas such as the economy, foreign and national security policy and the like (32).

Since he lacks the status of a Marja' and is thus incapable of acting as a source of Taqlid, Khamenei sees himself as especially beholden to the conservative faction of the clerical hierarchy and acts accordingly. Kamrava (2008), Buchta (2000), and others argue that both by design and by structural path dependence, the current political system in the Islamic Republic is fractured along multiple lines of authority, all of which ultimately lead to the same institution and to the person of the Supreme Leader. However, despite naive observations by some Western powers, the Islamic Republic is not a monolithic dictatorship ruled by a single totalitarian minded clergy.

The Guardian Council, the Assembly of Experts, the Judiciary, and the Special Court of the Clergy are among the most effective instruments of silencing non-conformists, including those of the Reform Movement and the Green Movement. I will briefly describe those institutions in an effort to offer some insight into the intricate power structure of the Islamic Republic.

The Judiciary and the Special Court of the Clergy

It is especially important to note that while Article 156 of the constitution stipulates an "independent judiciary," this branch of the government is under the paramount control of the Supreme Leader, who directly appoints the head of Judiciary, who in turn appoints the prosecutor general and the head of the Supreme Judicial Council. According to Article 162 of the constitution, the prosecutor general and the head of the Supreme Judicial Council all must be "Just Mojtahids" who are appointed to serve for a period of five years. The Ministry of Justice, the head of which is appointed by the president and approved by the parliament, is only a division of the legal framework and largely acts as the administrative body of the judicial branch of the government according to Article 160. Therefore, in reality, Vali-e Faqih (the Supreme Leader) has direct oversight on how the judicial branch of the government is run, which gives the Conservative Right an effective instrument to oppress those they find in opposition to their views, including the Reformists.

Emadeddin Baqi (2003), a prominent Reformist thinker and a political prisoner, also argues that the Special Court of the Clergy, established by Ayatollah Khomeini in March 1987 to "protect the dignity of the clergy and the seminaries" (Kamrava, 2008, 31), is an especially effective instrument in the Right's efforts to silence the none-conformist clerics on the left. While under the judiciary's umbrella, the Special Court of the Clergy is solely accountable to the Supreme Leader and is independent of the regular judicial framework. This court has prosecuted and punished a considerable number of clerics associated with the Left for their sermons, writings, and speeches. Figures such as Abdollah Noori (interior minister during Khatami's first term as president), Hassan Yousofi Eshkevari, and Mohsen Kadivar are among those clerics summoned before this court and punished for their views. Sentences range from jail time, house arrest, and defrocking to lashes, fines, and publication bans.

Grand Ayatollah Montazeri was by all accounts the most prominent dissident cleric in the history of the Islamic Republic and the Special Court of the Clergy. A close ally of Khomeini's during the revolution, he was designated to be his successor, however that all changed in 1989 once news of the mass executions of political prisoners after the Iraq war in late summer and early autumn of 1988 at Khomeini's undisputed directive surfaced. Montazeri wrote a letter to Khomeini, which was latter obtained and made public by the BBC, vehemently condemning the massacres and also criticizing Khomeini's *fatwa* (religious decree) against Salman Rushdie, stating, "People in the world are getting the idea that our business in Iran is just murdering people" (Wright, 2000, 20). That letter is said to have sealed Montazeri's political fate: Khomeini strongly condemned Montazeri's words and a few days later removed him from his position as the successor and stripped him of his title of "Grand Ayatollah." His lectures and sermons were removed from state publications, and all references to him were banned. Montazeri spent the next twenty years under house arrest in his home in Qom until his natural death on December 19, 2009, which ironically occurred during the Green Movement. For his views on human rights, women's rights, religious minority rights (such as Baha'is), and civil rights, and for his support of the Green movements and the regular harassment and the grave punishment he took for taking a stand, Grand Ayatollah Montazeri is considered the spiritual father of the Green Movement.

The Guardian Council and the Principle
of Approbation Supervision

The Judiciary is not the only branch of government standing in the way of the Reformers and by extension the Greens. While the Reformers managed to gain a majority in parliament and the city councils and some other elective assemblies during Khatami's presidency, the Hardliners managed to weaken the legislation they passed through the Guardian Council. The Guardian Council of the Constitution (Shoray-e Negahban-e Ghanoon-e Assi), or "Guardian Council" for short, is an appointed yet powerful assembly mandated by the constitution. The council is charged with interpreting the constitution of Iran, supervising elections of, and approving candidates to, the presidency and the Majlis, and "ensuring . . . the compatibility of the legislation passed by the Islamic Consultative Assembly [i.e., the Majlis] with the criteria of Islam and the Constitution." Six of the twelve members of the assembly must be just clerics appointed by the person of Vali-e Faqi. The remaining six are Muslim jurists, expert in various areas of law and the constitution and nominated by the head of Judiciary, who is in turn appointed by Vali-e Faqih, and elected by the Majlis (Article 91 of the constitution). As a result, the Guardian Council is typically occupied by Hardliners following the Supreme Leader's agenda.

The principle of Approbation Supervision (*Asl-e Nezarat-e Estesvabi*), allows the Guardian Council, an appointed assembly, to basically overrule or veto any legislation passed by the elected assembly, the parliament, on the grounds that it violates Islam or the constitution.

For example, when Khatami introduced what came to be known as the "Twin Bills" to the Majlis, the first bill was to expand the president's executive powers, allowing for intervention to prevent and reverse actions by the Judiciary that were in direct violation of the constitution. The second bill, introduced at the same time, was aimed at curbing the Guardian Council's powers by limiting the scope of principle of Approbation Supervision when it came to vetting and eliminating candidates. Expecting resistance from the Guardian Council, Khatami famously said, "The Guardian Council can either say a bill is against Islam or the constitution. The bill I'll present is part of the constitution and it is definitely not against Islam (Moaveni, 2002)."

Needless to say, despite Khatami's threat of resignation, the Guardian Council rejected both bills. By tactically undermining the president and the legislative Majlis, which at the time was predominantly occupied by Reformers, the Conservatives successfully caused the many Reformist policy agendas to grind to a halt and blocked any kind of reform that would loosen their grip on power.

Observing the failure of the Reform Movement is important because the Greens, or at least their prominent leaders, were Reformists planning on continuing on the path that started with Khatami's election and that became known as the "Reform Era." However, the above structural limitations clearly demonstrate that the ruling conservative elite will not tolerate defiance of official state doctrine, and over the years they have successfully silenced those who disagree through various provisions in the constitution. While eliminating outsiders has been an agreed-upon and routine policy of this regime from the outset, the Reformers (while considered "insiders" by all accounts) and their ideas have also been the target of elimination through such institutions as the Special Court of Clergy, the Guardian Council, and so on. Hamid Reza Jalaeipour, a prominent Reform thinker, says, "The principal problem that the Reform Movement faces is that its opposition accepts neither its methodology nor its modes of operation" (Kamrava, 2008, 33). The Reform Movement is admittedly committed to "gradualism" as a methodology for reforming the system from below, however, their opponents are not hesitant to change the rules of the game and to resort to brutal tactics to maintain the status quo. Lastly, due to their position as regime insiders loyal to the principles of Islamic governance, the Reformers' discourse not only puts them at odds with the Conservatives, it also puts them at odds with the secular discourse, and while they may be successful at gaining some sympathy from the latter, they fail to garner enough support to face the full force of the former, leaving them to their own devices.

This observation leads to a couple of conclusions: one, the evidence suggests that the political system of the Islamic Republic at its core will not tolerate defiance from mainstream conservative doctrine even if it is by the "brothers" of yesterday and the "Reformers" of today. Second, violence and brutality have been a major tool for keeping the opposition in line since the birth of the Islamic Republic, whether on the roof of *Refah* School, in the mass execution of political prisoners, or in the assassination of exiled opposition leaders. Therefore, history is indicative of why the hardliners was not hesitant to use those same tactics to cripple the Reformers and by extension the Greens by the same means. Lastly, the above tactics perhaps partly explain why the Green Movement protests were crushed swiftly and brutally.

THE CONSERVATIVES

Kamrava (2008) argues that the religious Right's emphasis since the beginning of the revolution has been on the interpretation, preservation, and strengthening of those notions of Shi'ite *fiqh* that legitimize and rationalize the conservative clergy's tight hold on power. Typically, the conservative religious Right avoids theoretical and doctrinal change unless political

Table 5.1. Disaggregating the Right

Traditionalists		Modernists	
Radical Right	Traditionalist Clergy	Islamic Councils	Modernist Right Thinkers
Hey'at-e Mo'talefeh; former Fadayian-e Islam members; traditionalist Bazaaris; former and present Basij members; Former Hojjatiyeh Society members; and the loosely organized Hezbollah groups	Politically influential conservative clerics based in Tehran, Qom, and the provinces affiliated with Howzeh Elmiyyeh; the Imam Khomeini Education and Research Institute; the Assembly of Experts; and the Jame'e Rouhaniyyat-e Mobarez group. Includes most Friday Prayer imams, and the "Supreme Leader's representatives" in various organizations	Active on university campuses and among certain professional groups. They are largely formed to ensure their members' conduct complies with Islam and the regime ideology	Lay and clerical scholars and thinkers generally supportive of the Islamic Republic system, though some call for modifications in its *modus operandi* and certain institutional features—for example, senior clerics such as the late Grand Ayatollah Montazeri and lay Conservative thinkers such as Professor Davari Ardakani

circumstances prove those changes absolutely necessary. Naturally, the religious Conservatives on the right have been reluctant to acknowledge and respond to some of the consequences of modernity and globalization, such as civil rights, pluralism, etc., which are considered problematic by this faction. Despite external pressure, however, it is argued (Kamrava, 2008; Buchta 2000) that there is very little chance the religious Right will change course in the near future in a way that will bring meaningful change to the Iranian political arena. The post-election events of 2009 in which the government forces brutally crushed the Green Movement protests are the most recent and tangible proof of this argument.

Although there are close connections between the traditionally conservative, high-ranking Shi'ite theologians and Grand Ayatollahs and the most powerful office, namely the Office of the Supreme Leader (*Beit-e Rahbari*), the religious Right is not a homogenous faction. Kamrava (2008) argues that while the common purpose of preserving the doctrinal and institutional legacy of Ayatollah Khomeini has led to a symbiotic relationship between the current political system and religious conservatism, the conservative theological current includes a diverse array of doctrinal and political persuasions. Table 5.1 summarizes the various persuasions of the conservative Right based on Kamrava (2008) and Buchta (2000).

At its broadest level, the Right can be divided into a traditional–modern spectrum. Within this broad spectrum four general categories can be distinguished: an extreme Radical Right, Traditionalist Right clergy, Islamic Councils, and modern Right thinkers. In terms of engaging in an intellectual discourse, of the four groups, only the Traditionalist Right clergy and modern Right thinkers engage in a meaningful production of ideology. I will detail each category further below.

The Traditionalist Right

By and large, the Traditionalist Right clergy produce the doctrinal output that forms the backbone of the Islamic Republic's official ideology and discourse, which once considered and approved internally is then transmitted to larger society through various organs and arms such as the Hezbollah groups. Alireza Alavi-Tabar calls the political outlook of the traditionalist clergy on this side of the spectrum "*Shari'at*-Centric" (Kamrava, 2008, 85) with *fiqh* as the primary resource within which solutions to contemporary social, political, and even economic problems are uncovered. They advocate safeguarding traditional institutions of family, Bazaar, private ownership, and ritualized forms of worship. Most importantly though, this group is a loyal advocate of the concept of Velayat-e Faqih. Ayatollah Mohammad Taqi Mesbah Yazdi is one of the most vocal and combative theologians behind the traditionalist conservative religious current.

Hey'at-I- Mo'talefeh Islami

Also known as the Coalition of Islamic Associations, Hey'at-I- Mo'talefeh Islami is a religious professional association and has been led by a number of high-profile clerics and lay people on the right such as former presidents Hashemi Rafsanjani, and Ahmadinejad, and speaker of the parliament Ali Larijani among others. Hey'at- e Mo'talefeh links the traditionalist ruling clerics to their single most important historical backers, namely the Bazaar merchants (Buchta, 2000, 15).

Jame'-I-Rouhaniyyat-I-Mobarez

Also known as the Militant Clergy Association (not to be confused with the Reformist Combatant Clergy Association), Jame'-I-Rouhaniyyat-I-Mobarez is the most influential group within the Traditionalist Right, which counts among its most senior members Supreme Leader Ali Khamenei, former speaker of the house Ali Akbar Nategh Noori, and also Hashemi Rafsanjani. The Military Clergy Association's sphere of influence goes further: the two power centers of Shoraye Negahban (the Guardian Council) and Majles-e Khobregan-e Rahbari (the Assembly of Experts, which is in charge of electing the Supreme Leader and approving constitutional amendments), are largely dominated by the members of this group. This group also has at its disposal a countrywide network of guilds and religious professional associations (such as Hey'at- e Mo'talefeh). Deriving their legitimacy primarily from Islamic-theocratic components of the 1979 revolution and Khomeini's doctrine of Velayat-e Faqih, the members of this group favor a theocratic sociopolitical model, and for them the dominance of Islam takes clear precedence over the people's collective will.

Modernist Conservatives

Islamic Councils (Anjoman—I—Islami)

As mentioned in table 5.1, the Islamic Councils are largely active on university campuses and to a lesser extent in professional associations such as the Engineers Association and in the state bureaucracy. Their primary task is to ensure the compliance of civil society with the regime's official doctrine, which includes monitoring non-conformist professors and students, as well as reporting dissenting views, these associations produce little or no doctrinal output and instead act more as the guardians and enforces of the official orthodoxy.

Modernist Right Thinkers

It is important to note the distinction between the modern Right and the Reformers. The modern Right are aligned with the overall jurisprudential underpinnings of the Islamic Republic. However, according to Kamrava (2008), they "advocate modifications to some of its [the Islamic Republic's] specific features and, if possible, criticize the conduct of its officials" (85). This group does not question the doctrine of Velayat-e Faqih, unlike the Reform camp. Dr. Reza Davari Ardakani, professor of philosophy at the University of Tehran, is by far the most notable lay conservative thinker and advocate of this group. The late Grand Ayatollah Montazeri was perhaps the most prominent spokesperson for this group.

Conservatives and Dissent

Clearly, conservative actors were in absolute opposition to the Green Movement or any type of dissent in general and thus broke up the protests swiftly, brutally, and effectively. The *Islamic Revolutionary Guard Corps* (Sepah-i Pasdaran-i Enghelab-i Islami; IRGC), a military powerhouse charged with guarding Iran's Islamic system and founded at the onset of the revolution at the request of Khomeini, and the Basij militia, a paramilitary volunteer and auxiliary force subordinate to the IRGC, are essentially the oppressive muscles of the Conservatives. Basij and the IRGC essentially provided the boots on the ground to beat, disperse, and intimidate the protesters during the 2009 protests. Those arrested were often beaten and tortured before being prosecuted and sentenced by the same judicial system that, as described above, is basically an executive arm of the institution of the Supreme Leadership. This is essentially how the oppressive machine of the Islamic Republic responds to any type of dissent.

CHAPTER SUMMARY

This chapter addresses research questions 1–3 in order to answer my main research inquiry. In other words, in this chapter the key categories of stakeholders in the Green Movement along with their aspirations and power dynamic are identified. While three distinct actors participated in the Green Movements, civil society groups were clearly the less influential of the three.

Reformers, the main leaders of the group who triggered the events, while considered insiders and still holding considerable power and influence within the government, were essentially overpowered by the ruling Conservatives. The former wields power and asserts its hegemonic domination through various institutions and organizations, the most important of which are the institution of the Supreme Leadership and the Judiciary, followed by smaller more targeted ones such as the Guardian Council and the Special Court of the Clergy. The increasingly powerful IRGC and the Basij militia provide the Conservatives with the manpower required to break up protests.

NOTES

1. Not to be confused with the conservative Militant Clergy Association, described in the next section.
2. Not to be confused with *Sazman-i-Mojahedin-i-Khalgh* (MKO), which is an opposition group in exile.
3. All translations from the original text in Farsi are the author's
4. The Iranian constitution limits presidential candidates to two terms in office.

6

Analysis of the Public Discourse
of the Green Movement

AN OVERVIEW OF THE CHAPTER

In this chapter, I will conduct a critical analysis of the political discourse of the two Reform candidates during the 2009 elections. The focus here is on proposed changes to the three different structures of signification, domination, and legitimation. Studying the data reveals that the majority of the changes proposed by the two candidates fell into the category of structures of domination. Thus, patriarchy and the economy were selected for this book for their significance and their domination of the 2009 election discourse. I will start with the Green Movement for it is the more recent phenomenon and apply the methodology in detail to establish the groundwork. The revolutionary discourse of Ayatollah Khomeini will be discussed in the next chapter.

Studying the Green Movement first reveals some of the structural hurdles and discriminatory laws inherent in the constitution and political organization of the Islamic Republic, the regime established by Ayatollah Khomeini three decades prior. Examining the events in reverse chronological order will help facilitate a better understanding of Khomeini's rhetoric and the political structures he helped put in place. Those structures provide the backdrop against which the Green Movement occurs. In other words, we will study the government and the laws Khomeini put in place while also demonstrating the methodology step by step before we examine the rhetoric that led us here.

STRUCTURES OF DOMINATION: PATRIARCHY

Women in Iran have a long history of participating in sociopolitical movements. The women's movement in Iran started in the late-nineteenth century
and in particular during the Iranian Constitutional Revolution (see chapter
2), when women participated in street protests. During the 1979 revolution,
Iranian women also were a strong presence since the uprising created a sense
of participation and civic responsibility across both gender and class. In the
marches that led to the revolution, women from different social backgrounds
were strongly present and active agents of revolution. There were professional women without scarves and women from traditional backgrounds
wearing the black veil (*chador*) and women from lower- and middle-class
families with their children walking shoulder to shoulder with men, hoping
that the revolution would bring for them improvement in their economic,
social, and, most importantly, legal status.

Furthermore, both modern and traditional women played an active role in the
revolution. While modern and professional women (e.g., university students,
nurses, doctors, journalists, lawyers, engineers, and workers in the public and
private sectors) were more visible, toward the end of the former regime some
of them began to wear light scarves (*hijab*) as a gesture of defiance against the
regime. However, in the aftermath of the Islamic revolution, women were the
first group to be neglected and oppressed by the new elite in power.

After the 1979 revolution, the Islamic government established by Ayatollah Khomeini, naturally, adopted a more conservative view of women and
their legal and political status in the society. This view, informed by Shi'ite
doctrine and championed personally by Ayatollah Khomeini, promoted an
image of women as mothers, wives, and homemakers both through policy and
propaganda. Citing the Shari'a, discriminating laws were encoded in the very
first draft of the new constitution limiting a woman's choice and activities
with policies such as forced hijab, barring women from seeking high political and judicial offices, and reversal of a number of initiatives taken under
Mohammad Reza Shah.

In 1967, following White Revolution initiatives, the Shah created the
Ministry of Women's Affairs, introducing family protection laws that year
and family courts in 1975. The Family Protection Act restricted polygamy
and granted women equal access to divorce and legalized abortion in certain
circumstances. Shari'a law has designated the age of consent for marriage
for women as nine, but prior to 1967, the Iranian Civil code had amended it
to fourteen, and finally the Family Protection Act raised the age of marriage
to eighteen for women. However, as one of his very first orders of business
after the revolution, Ayatollah Khomeini reversed the Family Protection Act

and dissolved the family courts, denouncing these measures as being in direct contradiction of Qur'an's directive (Khomeini, 2008) and calling down the fury of God upon those implementing and administering such laws.

But perhaps no measure was as symbolic of religious persecution of women as forcing them into veiling (hijab*)*. On March 6, 1979, less than a month after the collapse of the old regime in a speech in the holy city of Qom, Ayatollah Khomeini introduced the subject of mandatory veiling.

> Islamic ministries should not have a sacrilegious atmosphere. Uncovered women should not come to Islamic ministries. Women may come but they should don Islamic covering (2008, 6:286).

Two days later in mass demonstrations staged to celebrate International Women's Day on March 8th, women across Iran reacted, strongly opposing Khomeini's comments. Among their chants were "Liberty and equality are our undeniable rights," "We will fight against compulsory veil," "Down with dictatorship," "In the dawn of freedom, we already lack freedom," and "Women's day of emancipation is neither Western, nor Eastern, it is international."

Following further demonstrations and sit-ins, the regime retreated. The prime minister of the interim government, Mahdi Bazargan, announced that Ayatollah Khomeini's statements were misunderstood and that compulsory veiling was not on their agenda (Tabari, 1980). However, once the dust settled, a few short months later veiling for women holding government positions became mandatory. The trend continued to all segments of the society until women were no longer able to appear in public without hijab. The penalty for doing so, according to the constitution of the Islamic Republic of Iran, is seventy-four strokes of the lash. The situation is best described by this slogan adopted by Hezbollah, as club-wielding Khomeini supporters said to women, "Ya rusari ya tusari [Cover the head or a blow to the head]." Compulsory hijab is in effect to date.

WOMEN'S RIGHTS AFTER THE 1979 ISLAMIC REVOLUTION

Despite continuous and systematic persecution, women fought back against religious oppression through education and by organizing and actively fighting for their cause and developing one of the most visible and successful campaigns of Iranian civil society particularly after the war with Iraq ended in 1988. Since the revolution, due to a variety of socioeconomic factors beyond the regime's control and despite their original intent, young Iranian women have become highly educated. In September 2012, women made up more than 60 percent of all university students (Sahraei, 2012). The war with Iraq

(1980–1988), which sent many men to the front and left women as the primary breadwinners, limitations placed on women's employment and most other activities outside the home, and the activities of many women's rights groups were among those factors contributing to current higher levels of education among women. It certainly seems like the regime's male-centric policies indirectly pushed women to the only venue available to them: the universities. Additionally, because of the limited number of spots available in universities, students must pass a rather difficult entrance exam called *Konkoor* to enter the university, which also indicates that these young women are getting in on their own merit and not based on any affirmative action. Higher education for women over almost four decades has naturally introduced changes to the largely traditional fabric of the Iranian society. It is commonly understood that higher education among women tends to be a contributing factor in such social shifts as women's larger share of the labor force, their significantly higher age of marriage, fewer children, and higher rates of divorce.

While higher education has paved the way for some advances for women, the institutionalized gender discrimination embedded in the policies and laws of the country continue to oppress women and hinder their cause considerably. Iranian family law does not recognize a woman's right to file for divorce or to take custody of her children in most cases. Additionally, by law, polygamy and temporary marriages (*sigheh*) are a man's religious and legal right in which his wife doesn't have a say; the age of consent is basically non-existent; and in order for a married woman to enroll in higher education, travel outside the country, or seek employment, her husband's explicit and legal consent is required. Under Shari'a, upon which the Iranian legal and punitive system is built, a woman's life, her *diyeh* (blood money), and her testimony are equal to half that of a man. It was only in 2017, following the petitions of high-profile women in the West including late Stanford University professor Maryam Mirzakhani that legislation was introduced to recognize the right to citizenship of children of Iranian women married to non-Iranian citizens, but as of August 2017, that legislation had not yet been passed. To battle systematic social and institutional discrimination against women in the name of religion and convention, a number of women began to organize to work and change the system from within. The women's movement gave birth to action groups like the One Million Signatures for the Repeal of Discriminatory Laws Campaign (or the Campaign for Equality) and education and awareness-raising groups like the Feminism School and Women's Cultural Center discussed in chapter 5. Women's rights activists come from all walks of life; ordinary citizens, lawyers, journalists, authors, filmmakers, scholars, and artists are all moving toward the same goal: to lobby the government, the Majlis, and the courts for more equality and to educate and raise awareness. Shirin Ebadi (former judge, lawyer, and Noble Peace Prize laureate), Mehrangiz Kar (lawyer, scholar, and author), Nasrin Sotoudeh and Narges Mohammadi (lawyers), Parvin Ardalan (journalist and activist), Rakhshan Bani Etemad (filmmaker), and Mahboubeh Abbasgholi Zadeh (journalist and activist) are on the long list of women's rights activists in Iran.

Unsurprisingly, the Islamic government has been systematically cracking down on the movement and taking harsh measures such as long jail sentences, torture, exile, lifelong bans on public activity including a woman's right to practice in her own profession, erratic arrests, and physical and emotional harassment. The subject of women and their rights has come up in almost every presidential election, especially since 1997, and it is always considered controversial, but depending on the faction in power, there are periods of more intense oppression and periods when activists have more room to maneuver. In the 2009 elections both Mousavi and Karoubi made women's issues including women's rights a theme of their platforms. Considering that Ahmadi Nejad had introduced a number of bills that further marginalized women and discriminated against them, women's groups threw their support behind the two Reformist candidates.

Both candidates campaigned heavily on women's rights and promised to introduce change and expand their freedoms, facilitate wider participation of women in the society and in the labor market, and to hire more women in their administrations. Their vows to alter this social structure naturally drew significant support from women's rights activists, ordinary citizens, students, and youth.

CRITICAL DISCOURSE ANALYSIS:
CLAIMS ABOUT WOMEN'S RIGHTS

In this section I will apply the principles of CDA to examine the validity claims of two Green movement leaders, Mir Hossein Mousavi and Hojatol Islam Karoubi, as well as Ms. Zahra Rahnavard, regarding the struggles of women and its political implications. To this effect, the four validity claims of truth, sincerity, legitimacy, and comprehensibility will be tested as described by Habermas (1984) and operationalized by Cukier et al. (2009).

Empirical Analysis of Truth Claims

Truth claims are concerned with factual accuracy, biased and incomplete statements, and logical consistency (see table 6.1 summarizing validity claims of truth). Upon closer examination of the truth claims regarding women and issues of gender discrimination, several logical inconsistencies are revealed in the discourse of the two leaders. It appears they both treat gender discrimination as a phenomenon external to the system and not as something stemming from the structural foundations of the Islamic regime.

> Mousavi: There are many things that under the name of Islam and securing family values, but in reality influenced by discriminatory gender views and legal issues, have created serious hurdles for women in society (empirical material[EM]8).

This argument, and other similar ones (both EM1 and EM15), however, are logically inconsistent for several reasons. In actuality, what creates "serious hurdles for women" are discriminatory laws of the country that are written in accordance with Shi'ite doctrine (*fiqh*) and Shari'a. The above statement reduces the structural and systemic gender discrimination upon which the Islamic Republic's legal and constitutional framework is founded to a certain interpretation of Islam. A quick look at some of the articles of the Iranian penal and civil codes, however, refutes this argument and leaves little room for interpretation. Article 300 of the Iranian Penal Code states that the value of a woman's life is half that of a man's, while Article 102 asserts women must wear full Islamic hijab in public (Penal Code of the Islamic Republic of Iran, n.d.). Moreover, men can divorce their wives at any time if they choose to, but women can only file for divorce under certain strict conditions (Civil Code of the Islamic Republic of Iran, n.d.). Similarly, Karoubi's account of Khomeini's stance on women (EM15) in politics conflicts with reality. While Khomeini did not object to women running for parliament, he refused to allow them to run for the office of the president or to be appointed a judge (Articles 115, and 162 of the constitution; Constitution of the Islamic Republic of Iran, n.d.). In fact, as per Khomeini's mandate in 1979 after the revolution, all female judges were removed from the bench. Table 6.1 summarizes validity claims of truth.

Furthermore, there are other assertions by both candidates that are factually untrue. Mr. Mousavi repeatedly suggests that women have found a voice under the Green umbrella (EM7, EM14), and are able to organize due to the diverse and tolerant nature of the movement. However as previously discussed, women were already organized years before the Green Movement; the One Million Signatures campaign in fact was established in 2006. It is equally untrue to claim women's rights groups enjoy some sort of a safe haven and are immune from punishment because they have gathered under the Green umbrella. The Islamic regime arrested and imprisoned many women's rights activists such as Noushin Ahmadi Khorasani, Mahboubeh Abbasgholi Zadeh, and Nasrin Sotoudeh, among others. Some of them, such as Narges Mohammadi, Shiva Nazar Ahari, and Bahareh Hedayat, were still serving those sentences at the time this book went to publication.

Table 6.1. Empirical analysis of truth validity claims regarding women's rights

Claims Regarding Changing Structures	Source	Guiding Questions to Identify Validity Claims of Truth	Evidence of Distortion
Unidentified woman: one of the most important topics in social justice is the issue of gender equality. Discussing that first and foremost our girls and boys must feel safe.	EM1	T1. Is this argument logically consistent?	It is unclear how gender equity and the youth feeling safe are related.
Rahnavard: Why shouldn't our women be safe in our society? Why are so many women killed? Why are so many women killed under the pretense of honor? Although, honoring the codes of chastity is not harmful if they are bound by law.	EM1	T2. Is this argument true or false?	"Codes of chastity" and "honor" are harmful to women since they oppress women.
Mousavi: Considering the turn of events in the past year, women and youth have a new understanding of themselves and a renewed sense of identity. Their worldviews and thoughts have changed. Therefore, a certain pain is felt that is related to this renewal of identity. Because our governing, legal, and traditional structures are incompatible with this newly born identity. We have to study this issue.	EM7	T3. Is this argument factually true?	Women's and youth movements date much further back than the Green Movement of 2009.
Mousavi: There are many things that under the name of Islam and securing family values, but in reality, influenced by discriminatory gender views and legal issues, have created serious hurdles for women in society.	EM8	T4. Is this argument logically consistent?	The hearer or reader is left to decode what "many things" and "serious hurdles" are and how those influences come into play.

(continued)

Table 6.1. (continued)

Claims Regarding Changing Structures	Source	Guiding Questions to Identify Validity Claims of Truth	Evidence of Distortion
In response to a question about the One Million Signatures Campaign and noting the Green human chain formed last year from Tajrish Square to Railroad Square as symbol of reconciliation and national unity. Mousavi: I consider that day a great representation of the Green Movement. In previous years we have put forth "reconciliation" as our motto, which was a good motto for our national unity that will solve and even brings forward our problems. Some benefit from not reconciling. Currently in different formats including the families of political prisoners, different groups and movements have been created that didn't have the possibility to organize prior to the Green Movement. The women's movement is of those movements too.	EM14	T5. Is this argument factually true?	This statement is false since women were already organized, as previously discussed, prior to the Green Movement.
Mousavi: Some women used to participate in certain activities under the umbrella of the One Million Signatures Campaign that were even criminalized maybe because they were conducting those activities apart from each other.	EM14	T6. What evidence has been provided to support these arguments?	These groups were penalized because of their demands and not because they were organized separately. No evidence is presented to the contrary.

Mousavi: But due to the colorful and diverse nature of the [Green] Movement, today they are part of the extensive Green mass movement without the presence of suspicion against this group.	EM14	T7. Is this argument true or false?	The assertion that there is no suspicion against these groups is false since the government was cracking down on them under various charges.
Karoubi: I will say this bluntly here, Imam [Khomeini] was very sensitive to moves that would demotivate people from participating in the elections and would readily oppose them. At a point in time, it hasn't been forgotten, that it was said that women shouldn't participate and don't get elected into the *Majlis*. Imam readily said that women must participate in the elections and be able to get elected to the *Majlis*.	EM15	T8. Is this argument logically consistent?	It is unclear who/which group suggested women should not be elected and in what context.

To sum up, when the standards of Habermas's truth claims are applied, there is evidence of communication distortion. Logical inconsistencies attempting to frame institutionalized discrimination embedded in the constitution and various penal and civil codes as merely the interpretation of a certain group are one such distortion. Additionally, there are statements made that are simply inaccurate and untrue but play to the heart of the Green leaders' attitude toward the women's movement. Mousavi's repeated attempts to frame the longstanding struggle of women for their rights as a movement formed under the Green umbrella is a factually incorrect assertion made for political gain.

Empirical Analysis of Sincerity Claims

Sincerity implies consistency between what is expressed in the communication and the underlying intent. In examining the data, I paid particular attention to the congruity between what was stated in the political communications of the Green leaders and what was assumed. In other words, did they actually mean what their message implied to the audience or not. In table 6.2 I have summarized validity claims of sincerity.

One subject that consistently comes up in the movement's discourse is gender equality and discriminatory practices against women. In (EM1) for example, three women, Zahra Rahnavard (Mousavi's wife), Fatemeh Mo'tamed Aria (a well-known actor), and an unidentified woman talk about gender discrimination and its manifestations in Iranian society such as needing their husband's, father's, or a male guardian's consent for everything from staying in a hotel while traveling to receiving medically required surgery.

In that video, an official campaign release, Zahra Rahnavard openly and passionately protests the gender inequality present in society and demands change.

> Rahnavard: All forms of discrimination must be eliminated in society. We are against all forms of discrimination. Discrimination disrupts human growth. Now gender discrimination is one of its forms . . . there has to be a new reading of the role of women. Women are saying we are present, we have expectations, and we still want to take part in deciding our destiny (EM1).

Similarly, Mousavi in (EM6) asserts, "There are no differences between men and women when it comes to freedom and working toward achieving democracy, and everyone must march together on this path." Along the same lines, Karoubi's campaign video (EM19) makes a point of mentioning that "Karoubi considers solving women's problems an important and critical goal of his government and will try to execute the 6th Majlis bill for Iran to join the [UN's] Convention on the Elimination of All Forms of Discrimination against Women."

Table 6.2. Empirical analysis of sincerity validity claims regarding women's rights

Claims Regarding Changing Structures	Source	Guiding Questions to Identify Validity Claims of Sincerity	Evidence of Distortion
Rahnavard: All forms of discrimination must be eliminated in society. We are against all forms of discrimination. Discrimination disrupts human growth. Now gender discrimination is one of its forms . . . there has to be a new reading of the role of women. Women are saying we are present, we have expectations, and we still want to take part in deciding our destiny. "Rahnavard, Rahnavard, stands for equality of men and women."	EM1	S1. Is what is said consistent with how it is said?	Ms. Rahnavard states this while wearing full Islamic cover, which is contradictory to the concept of gender equality.
	EM3	S2. Does this communication elicit an emotional response?	Gender equity is a highly charged and coveted concept in Iranian society
Mousavi: There are no differences between men and women when it comes to freedom and working toward achieving democracy, and everyone must march together on this path.	EM6	S3. What is missing or suppressed in the discourse?	Iran's laws discriminate against women and limit their freedom. Despite this, the speaker pledges to uphold the law to its fullest extent.
Mousavi: Women's problems in our country won't be solved unless they become a national problem, and there should be no segregation between men and women. Gender segregation is the root of discrimination, which renders the problem unsolvable.	EM6	S4. Is what is said consistent with what is implied?	The speaker is silent on what he means by "gender segregation" and "discrimination."
Mousavi: We cannot have a free and just society unless we solve women's problems.	EM6	S5. Is what is said consistent with what is implied?	The audience is left to decode what exactly are women's problems from Mr. Mousavi's perspective and how they should be solved.

(continued)

Table 6.2. *(continued)*

Claims Regarding Changing Structures	Source	Guiding Questions to Identify Validity Claims of Sincerity	Evidence of Distortion
Mousavi: The faith of the Green Movement is tied to the women's movement in the future, and I don't think the Green Movement can achieve its goals without being accompanied by women every step of the way. The opposite is true too, meaning if we fail to make political change, women's conditions won't change either.	EM10	S6. Is what is said consistent with what is implied?	What are the goals of the Green Movement regarding women?
Mousavi: The Green Movement is after justice and freedom and the execution of the law, and if we achieve those, other issues stemming from those will be solved too. The reason we are facing actions that are causing us pain is because our conditions are not aligned with the constitution and human dignity and honor.	EM12	S7. Does the text elicit an emotional response?	The language associated with adherence to the law invokes positive emotions and attributes "pain" and problems to unlawfulness.
Karoubi: We published our third campaign promise during the month of Farvardin, which was about civil rights. Civil rights bound by the constitutional framework. Regarding women, regarding ethnicities, regarding the various religions that exist in Iran, regarding universities, regarding prisons that people come to get into, the pointless restrictions they place on people's lives and the bitter incidents [they have caused], pointless nuances, interfering in the private lives of families, which Islam has so advised [against], civil rights in general bound by the constitutional framework or those principles of the constitution that are left vague.	EM16	S8. Is the user engaging in jargon?	What are the "principles of the constitution that are left vague"?

Female Voice-Over: Karoubi considers solving women's problems an important and critical goal of his government and will try to execute the 6th *Majlis* bill for Iran to abide by the [UN's] Convention on the Elimination of All Forms of Discrimination Against Women. He has plans to encourage and support non-governmental women's organizations and groups, and he plans to have at least one female minister in his cabinet.	EM19	S9. Is what is assumed consistent with what is implied?	Considering the speaker is fully aware of the legal and constitutional restrictions Iranian women face, and considering there already are women in the cabinet, is this appointment really going to help women's cause?

On the surface, these statements could be interpreted to imply gender equality in the Western sense of the term. However, closer examination of these claims reveals a number of contradictions in the discourse. First, despite extensive research, I was not able to find any communication by either of the leaders that would detail their definition of the concept of "gender equality." In my work I recognize the UN's definition of gender equity, which refers to

> the equal rights, responsibilities and opportunities of women and men and girls and boys. Equality does not mean that women and men will become the same but that women's and men's rights, responsibilities and opportunities will not depend on whether they are born male or female (United Nations, n.d.).

However, Iranian laws have a different view of gender relations, one that is in stark contrast to the UN's. Despite claiming equity, both candidates repeatedly pledge to uphold the law and abide by the constitution, the very same code that institutionalizes gender discrimination in the country.

Speaking of his campaign manifesto on civil rights, admittedly the first of its kind in the history of the regime, Karoubi lists a multitude of rights his government will address but only as long as they are "bound by the constitutional framework or those principles of the constitution that are left vague" (EM16). Often when Karoubi uses the phrase "civil rights" (including when referring to the rights of women), he immediately qualifies it by adding the phrase "bound by the constitutional framework" (EM16, EM18). On more than one occasion Mousavi emphasizes the same adherence to the constitution and the law. For example he says, "The Green Movement is after justice and freedom and the execution of the law" (EM12), and in a campaign speech on women he says, "The reason we are facing actions that are causing us pain is because our conditions are not aligned with the constitution and human dignity and honor" (EM12).

Phrases such as "gender equity" and "eliminating discrimination" have powerful associations for the segment of the society who formed the Green Movement and thus these phrases were used by the leaders to reinforce a vague notion of equity. Such terms elicit strong emotions and garner popular support despite the evidence that the situation has little chance of changing.

Furthermore, what is missing in the discourse of the Green leaders is a concrete and practical roadmap to achieve more equality for women. Neither candidate provided any kind of detail on the actual laws they would target to amend nor the policies they would put in place to further women's rights. We won't know for example if Mr. Mousavi was going to amend the law to make it easier for women to apply for divorce. Or was Mr. Karoubi going to propose to change Article 102 of the penal code and lift mandatory hijab since he alludes to its ineffectiveness when it comes to enforcing religion (EM17)?

We don't know this because their discourse is distorted on the concept of gender discrimination.

Examining those statements leaves us doubtful. The law, and the constitution, are the sources of institutional discrimination against women in Iran. It is Iranian law that states a woman's life is worth half that of a man, that recognizes polygamy as a man's right, that mandates punishment of women who refuse to sexually submit to their husbands, that denies a woman equal access to divorce and even bars them from entering a stadium to watch male sporting events. Both candidates also repeatedly declared devotion to Khomeini, his school of thought, and his ways. On many occasions Mousavi went on the record to say his goal was to take the country back to the "Golden age of Imam." But one of Khomeini's first orders of business was to overturn the Family Protection Act that banned polygamy, reduced the age of consent for girls to nine, and more as discussed at the beginning of this chapter. It was Khomeini who mandated forced hijab, which large numbers of women protest, to this date. One cannot achieve equality by promoting submission to laws that are deeply discriminatory or by attesting devotion to a leader who has established a regime on the notion that women should be subservient to men.

To further demonstrate that women's rights are on their agendas, both candidates go further than words and employ more visual signals. Mousavi was the first candidate in the history of the Islamic Republic to be accompanied by his wife, Zahra Rahnavard, while campaigning. Rahnavard, who holds a PhD in political science, served as chancellor of Alzahra University (a women-only college) in Tehran from 1998 to 2006 and as a political adviser to former president Mohammad Khatami. Karoubi soon followed suite with his wife Fatemeh Karoubi. Rahnavard, by far the more outspoken of the two, soon came to be viewed as a symbol of gender equality and women's rights as is evident in this popular slogan chanted by young women (EM3): "Rahnavard, Rahnavard, stands for equality of men and women."

Curiously, both women always appear in public in full Islamic attire or chador (long, traditional hijab), which emphasizes their dedication both to this religious yet oppressive concept and to the core values of the Islamic Republic. Chador has always been the cover of choice of the great majority of the clergy, including Khomeini, and although currently not enforced in public, it has been mandatory for many government employees since the revolution. Therefore, while the presence of these women in the campaign may signal progressive attitudes toward women and their rights, it was misleading. This is a clear case of engaging in goal-oriented *dramaturgical* action which is parasitic on communicative action and thus hampers the actors' ability to reach mutual understanding. This concept will be discussed further in the next sections.

Yet the women's chador-clad presence speaks volumes to the many con-tradictions and conflicts present in the makeup of the Green Movement. This is not to limit a woman's choice of clothing and step on religious rights, but because dramaturgy is the presentation of *self* in a favorable light to the public, it is designed to be seen by others in an attempt to improve one's self-image (Habermas, 1984). What a person, especially an individual in a position of power and influence, chooses to wear is testament to their reli-gious and ideological beliefs, particularly in the highly ideological context of Iranian politics. Clearly the candidates seek to signal equality and respect for women's rights through the image of having their wives present on the campaign trail. However, the presence of their wives' wrapped in chador also reinforces the very beliefs and institutional values that have objectified and oppressed women and trampled over their rights for decades. Let me make this very clear: I consider chador oppressive not because I don't recognize a woman's choice to her religious attire; I consider it oppressive because it is forced on many women, and it is advocated as the best option to protect a woman's chastity. In other words, chador is used as an ideological tool that further objectifies and sexualizes women and polices their bodies.

Moreover, further research reveals more contradictions in the discourse of Ms. Rahnavard regarding hijab and a woman's right to choose. She has writ-ten a book titled *Beauty of Concealment and Concealment of Beauty* (1987) in defense and justification of chador and forced hijab. She defends forced hijab according to "just and proper religious orthodoxy" and calls its abolition by Reza Shah a "tragedy," and an "imperialist" plot.

As soon as this lofty and exalted flag of Islam and nobility fell down from the hands of the people, it was replaced by ignominy, dishonor, unlimited freedom, villainy, cruelty, ostentation, depravity, debauchery and loss of complete free-dom and independence. May God break the hand of the Western and Eastern system of oppression that has thrown us for the fast fifty years in the abyss of ignominy of the isolation from our exalted Islamic Self! (Rahnavard, 1987)

In an interview on June 16, 2009, in the midst of the protests, she supports the mandatory veiling of Iranian women in an interview with the BBC, add-ing she would not change that law: "It has always been in Islam that women have the veil, and it is written in the Koran—tell Muslim women to cover themselves" (Profile: Zahra Rahnavard, 2009). Views such as the above are in sharp contrast to the spirit of the women's rights movement and to women's ownership of their bodies and their rights to choose.

In summary, there are inconsistencies in the discourse of the Green leaders, especially on the topic of gender discrimination and its political implications. While equality and women's rights were important issues in the 2009 elections, the evidence shows that perhaps there were different interpretations of the notion. There is a gap in the communication of this concept, because although discriminatory practices in society and the establishment are acknowledged, the evidence is not encouraging that real change would have actually happened if either of the two men had become president. Thus, when we examine the sincerity of those claims, the data point to distortion in communication.

Empirical Analysis of Legitimacy Claims

Analysis of legitimacy in this section is centered on conformity between an utterance and the norms of its social context. Additionally, I will discuss evidence of actor participation and focus on examining which stakeholders are included or excluded from the discourse. Studying the data reveals further evidence of communication distortion when the legitimacy of one of the main promises of both Mousavi's and Karoubi's campaigns is examined, namely, appointment of female cabinet members. Appointing women to their respective cabinets and other high political offices are one of the promises both candidates repeatedly make.

In a speech on the status of women in the society, Mousavi asserts, "In my opinion, women must be present in the cabinet" (EM5). At another point he says,

> We have a large number of female university students who seem to face enormous problems once they want to enter the labor market. They feel discriminated against in this respect. We similarly have huge problems when it comes to domestic women. Part of the solution is women should be present in high-ranking decision-making (EM4).

Rahnavard also echoes the same view: "A government that is run without women executives will definitely be a harsh one" (EM1).

Karoubi similarly voices his plans "to encourage and support non-governmental women's organizations" and pledges "to have at least one female minister in his cabinet" (EM19). Table 6.3 summarizes validity claims of legitimacy.

A content analysis of both candidates' campaign videos shows young men and women holding signs that read "Female Cabinet Members." One of Karoubi's official campaign video releases consists of interview-style questions put to him by his campaign advisors and would-be cabinet members. Ms. Jamileh Kadivar[1] is a member of that team and upon further research I learned that she was also his advisor on the status of women, all of which signaled women's political participation. However, what is left unaddressed in the discourse is the divisive and discriminatory nature of the Islamic Republic

Table 6.3. Empirical analysis of legitimacy validity claims regarding women's rights

Claims Regarding Changing Structures	Source	Guiding Questions to Identify Validity Claims of Legitimacy	Evidence of Distortion
Mousavi: When people's incomes shrink, when they don't have employment prospects, you can be sure these youth that see no light at the end of the tunnel, turn to drugs and foul behavior [bad akhlaghi] and these types of crimes will spread. But when in a society clear [economic] goals are stated, and there is hope for the future, which was the case during the war era despite all the hardship, I think all this foul behavior could be drastically reduced.	EM22	L1. What is missing or suppressed in the discourse?	The speaker is reducing the multitude of factors underlying high crime rates, widespread drug addiction, and moral and social problems to a single economic factor.
Mousavi: I have described this [economic conditions] as turning a society based on higher values into a commercial society. In a commercial society everything becomes utility-based and monetary-based. Cultural values turn into market values and economic values where everything has a monetary price—even human values are given a monetary value. There comes a point, for example, where a person bribes a member of the parliament with $5 million tomans to buy their vote. This is a consumerist society. The current situation with this way of looking at society and with false promises, and superstitions and such are far from the [value-based] era we went through [at the beginning of revolution].	EM24	L2. What information is suppressed or left out?	What led to this drastic change in socioeconomic conditions is left out.

Mousavi: On one hand we export crude oil and on the other hand imported consumer goods are flooding our market at the cost of destroying our domestic production.	EM25	L3. What information is suppressed or left out?	The argument doesn't discuss the fact that President Ahmadi Nejad would not have been able to accomplish this had it not been for the support of Iranian powerhouses (the House of Leadership, IRGC, etc.)
Karbaschi (video continues from previous section, showing Karbaschi's tears): In the position of the president, are you determined to use any tool at your disposal, even your reputation, for this purpose? Karoubi: I will definitely do this. First of all, I'm not a hero, first of all. Second, we have, as you know, a certain record and that I'm not dependent on fake heroism. And I will truly go into my own preview of what is working as the country's president and solving problems, and I am willing, as your honor has seen, I, to free a prisoner, when I was the *Majlis* speaker, I'd make a phone call to a colleague and he'd tell me you don't have to do this yourself, tell your office to call, you don't have to tell me, people's problems, people's lives, people's dignity and authority are really important to us.	EM48	L4. Is all relevant information communicated without distortion or omission?	The communication doesn't explain why the Speaker of the House should call to free a prisoner. Who is the prisoner? What about legal avenues?

(continued)

Table 6.3. *(continued)*

Claims Regarding Changing Structures	Source	Guiding Questions to Identify Validity Claims of Legitimacy	Evidence of Distortion
Female voice-over: Are you still asking yourself why Mehdi Karoubi is running for president? Maybe you remember in the last election Mehdi Karoubi promised that if he gets elected president, he will set a salary of 50,000 tomans a month for all Iranians eighteen or older. Esma'il Gerami Moghadam: Is this the continuation of your last plan, when you stated 50,000 tomans a month will be given to all Iranians eighteen or older . . . Is this a continuation of that plan and a more complete version of it? If this is the case please explain a little. Karoubi: This time around I think it is more comprehensive, it's better, meaning we have made it more detailed and clearer. Female voice-over: This plan, of course, was mocked by the other incumbents and was considered impossible. But after the elections many economists agreed with it and experts reviewed and completed it. Today this plan has been completed under "assigning oil revenue shares to people," and is ready for execution.	EM50	L5. Who are the experts or economists? Who is excluded?	The communication does not divulge who the expert economists approving this plan are. Additionally, the opponents of this plan don't have a voice in the discussion.
Female voice-over: Karoubi has other economic plans too, including exempting small businesses from taxes and reinforcing the private sector in the fields of production, commerce, and services through tax exemption and through partnership with private and public banks.	EM52	L6. Who is marginalized or excluded?	The critics of this economic plan are excluded from the debate.

that disenfranchises and discriminates against many groups. The question I pose here is What select group of women can run and get elected to political office? Below I will explore the answer.

The laws governing the executive branch require all cabinet ministers to, among other things, be religiously observant, be loyal to the regime, and have no criminal record. Therefore, by default many women are excluded, including the Baha'i minority, human rights activists with a prison record, regime critics, and those who don't observe strict religious codes such as chador. These women are all social actors with an interest in this particular discourse who are excluded from it. Therefore, upon unpacking the message, "women" in the discourse of the Green leaders doesn't mean all capable and qualified women as it implies—it means a select group of women, insiders to the regime, advocating and perpetuating the IRI's official ideologies, or women, in other words, who will extend regime hegemony and coopt the flourishing women's movement in typical hegemonic fashion.

Moreover, further content analysis of the videos of both candidates reveals a striking yet concealed trend: women who get an official voice on the video either as speakers, interviewers, or ordinary citizens asking questions are all depicted in full and proper Islamic hijab: covered from head to toe with the exception of parts of the face. However, when the cameras pan to show the masses of supporters, the women, and especially the younger ones, are dressed in more fashionable and modern styles that include loose and permissive hijab. This observation along with the above evidence of distortion leads us to the conclusion that only a select group of women who subscribe to the religious and political notions of the regime are given a voice in this discourse and the rest of the interested parties, who hold different views, are excluded, though their votes are welcome! Those such as Nasrin Sotoudeh, Shadi Sadr, Atena Farghadani, and many more are excluded from political participation despite their qualifications, interest, and capabilities. Therefore, when Karoubi and Mousavi speak of women's political participation, there is a silent footnote excluding many women from that activity.

Additionally, although both camps assert women must be present in their respective cabinets, the two candidates offer no other tangible plans. But since President Khatami in 1997, every government has had female advisors or ministers. President Ahmadi Nejad's cabinet was actually the first in the history of the IRI to include a woman: Marzieh Vahid Dastjerdi, as health minister. That same government, however, managed to pass one of the most oppressive and marginalizing amendments to the family laws that among other things made polygamy even easier for men and petitioning for divorce even harder for women. Therefore, while it is important to place women in high political offices, their mere presence is not enough, it is simply a cooptation tool. Once again, the critical details such as the above are left unaddressed, leaving the door open for interpretation and maybe even wishful thinking by women who are already oppressed and in desperate need for change. They leave the door open for misleading the public and for dishonesty by alluding to what the public wants to hear without having the intention, ability, or executive power to achieve it.

To summarize, holding the political discourse of the Green leaders up to a Habermasian validity claim of legitimacy, one can see evidence of distortion. Interested actors in the women's movement—activists, community leaders, and advocates—are largely excluded and their voices are suppressed. Moreover, history shows that simply appointing women to cabinet or other political positions available to them by law (as previously discussed) is not enough to improve their status or eliminate discrimination because they become mere tools in the political apparatus to reinforce and reproduce patriarchal notions.

Empirical Analysis of Comprehensibility Claims

While comprehensibility claims can be assessed in a variety of ways, in this section I have focused on clarity, and completeness, specifically to ensure the communication is without omissions that are important to its meaning. Since at the time of the Green Movement the Majlis was in the midst of debating a bill that would ease the conditions of polygamy and temporary marriage for men even further, the topic often came up during the 2009 elections. Table 6.4. demonstrates this matter in more detail.

When asked, Mr. Karoubi openly states, "Polygamy will destroy lives in our society for certain" (EM17). Similarly, Mousavi asserts that he is "against the polygamy bill" (EM2). Such assertions imply to the audiences that should either man be elected president, they would amend this law. However, as discussed in chapter 3, even if the president were to introduce bills to, for instance, amend the laws sanctioning polygamy, his limited authority in face of powerhouses such as the Guardian Council and the person of Supreme Leader makes such a bill impossible to pass even with a likeminded Majlis. Therefore, even if either man intended to change the laws discriminating against women once elected president, his chance would have been slim to none. Khatami and the twin bills he introduced, described in chapter 4, are perfect examples of well-intentioned and progressive bills that never saw the light of day since they were quashed by the guardian and the Expediency Councils. However, those realities are routinely omitted from the discourse while on the campaign trail to attract support from groups and individuals sensitive to this cause and prone to vote for a likeminded candidate. Moreover, a closer look at the data reveals a pattern of using confusing and unclear language that is at times difficult for the audience to decode. Claims such as "The issue of

Table 6.4. Empirical analysis of comprehensibility validity claims regarding women's rights

Claims Regarding Changing Structures	Source	Guiding Questions to Identify Validity Claims of Comprehensibility	Evidence of Distortion
Mousavi: "I am against the polygamy bill."	EM2	C1. What is left out of this communication?	The communication omits the fact that the president is very limited in terms of bills passed by the *Majlis* and the Guardian Council.
Mousavi: The issue of women in our country is both extensive and multidimensional. There are certain discriminations and disenchantments, both from a legal perspective, and from the executive perspective. Also from an employment perspective. We have a large number of female university students who seem to face enormous problems once they want to enter the labor market. They feel discriminated against in this respect. We similarly have huge problems when it comes to domestic women. Part of the solution is women should be present in high-ranking decision-making.	EM4	C2. Is the level of detail too burdensome for the audience?	There are too many messages left for the audience to decode such as "extensive and multidimensional," "certain discriminations," and "disenchantments."
In response to a question about the Green Movement's strategy regarding some Friday Prayers clerics on women's cover, recent earthquakes, and also the resurgence of Islamic Guidance Crews Mousavi: Certain events are happening in society and certain decisions are being made that instead of solving problems, they are after creating conflict. For example, our	EM11	C3. Is the communication sufficiently clear?	The speaker does not explain what he means by "diversion from truth." Which truth?

(continued)

Table 6.4. *(continued)*

Claims Regarding Changing Structures	Source	Guiding Questions to Identify Validity Claims of Comprehensibility	Evidence of Distortion
country is prone to earthquakes and parts of Tehran are on the quake line, which certainly is very dangerous and we have to stop it and the government is better off taking care of this, instead of mixing it with a dream or a deed like women's cover . . . this is diversion from truth to keep people busy with such discussions and create division. Even the purpose of Islamic Guidance crews is not really for rectifying scantily covered women, they are largely meant to create diversion in minds.			
Mousavi: They want to keep our minds busy.	EM13	C4. Is this utterance complete and intelligible?	Who is "they"? To what end do "they" want to keep our minds busy?
Karoubi: We published our third campaign promise during the month of Farvardin which was about civil rights. Civil rights bound by the constitutional framework. Regarding woman, regarding ethnicities, regarding the various religions that exist in Iran, regarding universities, regarding prisons that people come to get into, pointless restrictions they place on people's lives and the bitter incidents [they have caused], pointless nuances, interfering in the private lives of families that Islam has so advised [against], civil rights in general bound by the constitutional framework or those principles of the constitution that are left vague	EM16	C5. Is this utterance complete and intelligible?	The speaker leaves the audience wanting to know what he means by "those principles of the constitution that are left vague"

Jamileh Kadivar: Do you think forced hijab for women is a wise idea? Has it worked? You are a cleric after all, do you think, based on Islamic principles and religious teachings, is it right to force hijab? Karoubi: I think we have to do two things. One thing is to remove the aggressive way because those haven't worked and in many cases, they were counterproductive	EM17	C6. Is the communication clear and without confusion?	Mr. Karoubi does not provide a clear answer to the question
Jamileh Kadivar: What about polygamy? Karoubi: Polygamy will destroy lives in our society for certain	EM17	C7. What is left out of the communication?	The communication omits the fact that the president is very limited in terms of bills passed by the *Majlis* and the Guardian Council
Female Voice-Over: If he [Karoubi] is victorious in the presidential elections, he intends to create an organization for the defense of human rights and civil rights and intends to study and correct the behavior of governmental and national security institutions on a regular basis	EM18	C8. Is the communication complete?	What is this plan for correcting the behavior of those organizations? How will conflicting interests be handled?

women in our country is both extensive and multidimensional" (EM4) and "There are certain discriminations and disenchantments, both from a legal perspective, and from the execution perspective" (EM4) are vague and leave room for interpretation without really revealing the speaker's message. Further, Mousavi indicates, "They want to keep our minds busy" (EM13) and he also says, "Even the purpose of Islamic Guidance crews is not really for rectifying scantily covered women, they are largely meant to create diversion in minds" (EM11). The reader or hearer is however left to ask, Who are "they"? What is their position and power over the matter? Why are "they" trying to "create diversion in minds"? Diversion from what facts? And of what "truth" is Mr. Mousavi talking about?

On the topic of clarity, it is important to note that Mehdi Karoubi especially has a convoluted and at times confusing speaking style. He often leaves his thoughts unfinished and starts another one in the middle of the first (EM15, EM16, EM17), and his communications often defy syntactic and grammatical rules: "My first thing to do, my first manifesto, the manifesto that I published in [the month of] Bahman, my first manifesto was to revive [the center for] planning and management, which unfortunately got dissolved" (EM46).

As you can see, it is often difficult to understand and follow Karoubi grammatically and semantically. He often goes off topic and evades answering the questions put to him.

> Jamileh Kadivar: Do you think forced hijab on women is a wise idea? Has it worked? You are a cleric after all, do you think, based on Islamic principles and religious teachings, it is right to force hijab?
>   Karoubi: I think we have to do two things. One thing is to remove the aggressive way because those haven't worked and in many cases, they were counterproductive (EM17).

The topic of forced hijab has been a source of contention and defiance between Iranian women and the government since its enforcement after the revolution and thus is of considerable importance. Additionally, considering the candidate has made a point of including this excerpt in his official campaign communications, it is safe to assume that his intention is to convey where he stands on the topic of forced veiling. However, he goes off track, and at the end of the clip the audience is left waiting for an answer, for a clear stance. On another note, in Karoubi's campaign particularly, we notice the presence of dramaturgy again. Karoubi is a member of the clergy; he holds the rank *Hojatol Islam* and wears the robe that signifies both his status and his Shi'ite religious orientation. In other words, he presents himself as *rouhani*, or a member of clergy and one who is running for political office, which implies he believes in the ideology of political Islam, which defies the principles of separation of church and state. On another note, his communications imply he will address the issue of women's rights and will work to improve their status, but we the audience never know where exactly he stands on the issue. We can conclude based on his wife's appearance and his presentation of his "self" that his definition of equity is not aligned with the benchmark we discussed above. But the confusion and the distortion occur because he appears to be advocating women's rights and we don't know what those rights according to Karoubi are.

Evidence of communication distortion are present when the data is tested for comprehensibility validity claims. Confusing and unclear concepts, and at time convoluted and grammatically incorrect sentences, hinder understanding and conveyance of meaning.

CRITICAL DISCOURSE ANALYSIS: CLAIMS ABOUT THE ECONOMY

As in most elections, especially in developing countries, the economy and economic development are one of the most important points on any campaign platform. Through control of allocative resources, the economy also becomes an important structure of domination. In the following pages, I will examine the validity claims of the Green leaders on economy.

Empirical Analysis of Truth Claims

Mir Hossein Mousavi served as the Iranian prime minister from 1981 until an amendment to the constitution abolished that office in July of 1989, a month after Ayatollah Khomeini's death. His premiership coincided with the eight-year Iran-Iraq war during which he gained popular acclaim for his stewardship of the economy, including implementing a ration system to distribute food supplies and other essentials. From 1989 when his position was eliminated until 2009 when he registered to run as a Reformist candidate, he was generally absent from political life. Naturally, in his campaign he often referred to his tenure as the "war-time prime minister" and to his supposedly admirable management of the economy. I show the validity claims of truth in table 6.5.

What appears as a communication distortion while testing those assertions is the notion that the economy was in better shape in the 1980s than it was in 2009:

Mousavi: I have described this [economic conditions] as turning a society based on higher values into a commercial society. In a commercial society everything

Table 6.5. Empirical analysis of truth validity claims regarding economic development

Claims Regarding Changing Structures	Source	Guiding Questions to Identify Validity Claims of Truth	Evidence of Distortion
Mousavi: I have described this [economic conditions] as turning a society based on higher values into a commercial society. In a commercial society everything becomes utility-based and monetary-based. Cultural values turn into market values and economic values where everything has a monetary price—even human values are given a monetary value. There comes a point, for example, where a person bribes a member of the parliament with $5 million tomans to buy their vote. This is a consumerist society. The current situation with this way of looking at society and with false promises and superstitions and such are far from the [value-based] era we went through [at the beginning of revolution].	EM24	T1. Is there an ideological claim that is unexamined?	The claim that the post-revolution era, while Mr. Mousavi himself was prime minister, was a value-based era is not examined.
Mousavi: I have come to advocate for the poor [mostaz'afan]. Those whose backs are breaking under the pressures of inflation, and flawed economic policies have targeted their dignity.	EM30	T2. What evidence has been provided to support these arguments?	No evidence is presented by the speaker that his economic policies will in fact improve the economic conditions of the poor.

becomes utility-based and monetary-based. Cultural values turn into market values and economic values where everything has a monetary price—even human values are given a monetary value. There comes a point, for example, where a person bribes a member of the parliament with $5 million tomans to buy their vote. This is a consumerist society. The current situation with this way of looking at society and with false promises and superstitions and such are far from the [value-based] era we went through [at the beginning of the revolution] (EM24).

The discourse of Mir Hossein Mousavi reinforces the idea that the economic hardships of society are solely the result of President Ahmadi Nejad's flawed policies. His discourse typically compares the economic conditions of the revolutionary era and the eight-year period of the war[2] with Iraq—— during which not coincidentally he ran the economy, with that of the past four years under Ahmadi Nejad, without any reference to the years in-between (EM22): "I have come to advocate for the poor (mostaz'afan). Those whose backs are breaking under the pressures of inflation, and flawed economic policies have targeted their dignity" (EM30).

The fact of the matter is that while the economy suffered under president Ahmadi Nejad, Hashemi Rafsanjani and Mohammad Khatami, both backing Mousavi's campaign in 2009, had each served two terms (eight years) prior to that, and economic underdevelopment and unemployment had always been the number-one issue on the agenda, but to no avail. Therefore, while it is expected that a political candidate will draw attention to his achievements and competencies (EM22, EM30), attributing the current difficult economic conditions solely to Ahmadi Nejad's policies is only half true. The economic hardships of 2009 essentially stemmed from thirty years of the Islamic Republic's policies, four years of which (at the time) occurred under President Ahmadi Nejad. Considering both Khatami and Rafsanjani were known to be Mousavi's political allies at the time, and remembering that questioning the system is considered crossing a red line, it is conceivable that Mr. Mousavi intentionally omits some facts and only presents part of the truth. The data I have gathered, however, doesn't indicate much variation from truth validity claims on the part of Karoubi on this subject.

Empirical Analysis of Sincerity Claims

When it comes to testing sincerity validity claims, Hojatol Islam Karoubi's communications indicate distortion, especially through statements that are typically made for no other reason than to elicit emotional responses. In table 6.6, I summarize the validity claims of sincerity and show also that Karoubi's speaking style is the less clear and more ambiguous of the two.

Table 6.6. Empirical analysis of sincerity validity claims regarding economic development

Claims Regarding Changing Structures	Source	Guiding Questions to Identify Validity Claims of Sincerity	Evidence of Distortion
Mohammad Najafi: One of the most important issues regarding higher education of the youth is the expense of that education. Both those who study in state universities, and some of them have to go far away from home to other cities, and covering their expenses is difficult for those in private universities whose primary concern is covering their tuition and expenses. Karoubi: *I see how education affects people and families, and how difficult this burden is on them.*	EM45	S1. Does the communication elicit an emotional response?	Mr. Karoubi's response implies he feels the people's pain without offering any evidence to his assertion. Additionally, he is not responding to the question asked.
Gholamhossein Karbaschi: And I pointed out that you know the poverty line better than us because you frequently specially deal with veterans and martyrs (God's heavens be upon them). In any case, when this election and the political discussions are over, at least 12 million of our population will be poor. What are you going to do for them as a cleric president? [He says this while choking up.]	EM47	S2. Does the communication elicit an emotional response?	Mr. Karbaschi's tears and Karoubi's allusion to Karbaschi's emotional state imply to the audience their level of concern for the poor but the communication does not really offer a solution to the problem.

Karoubi: When Mr. Karbaschi remembers things, he unwillingly gets affected, and becomes upset. The other day too in a meeting which they came to my office and had a meeting, he got upset again. [He says all this as the camera zooms in on Karbaschi's face and his tears.] The answer is the same, you are sure I alone can't say, I have to think about it and sit on it first, the solution is with all the factions who want to work with me, and even those who may not work with us but they still feel for these issues. Let's sit down and think, I am ready to spend all my energy for things like this . . .

Karbaschi (jumping in): I'm sure you are like that, all I want to say is, in the position of the president, let's set all considerations aside. Talking about the poor and justice is easy. But feeding off their share and not doing anything for them in the name of "we will be a world hero," saying things that end up putting more pressure on people, and not doing anything for them is not the decent thing to do.

Karbaschi: In any case our main problem is the United States. If we can't enter the international political club and if we can't solve our problems, these issues, these problems' consequences will put more pressure on the people, Mr. Karoubi. When you mention "our people's dignity," our people's dignity is their stomachs should be full. Poverty is befitting our leaders, but they have to strive, at any price, so people are not poor.

EM49

S3. Is what is implied consistent with what is stated?

Mr. Karbaschi was charged and jailed for embezzlement while he was the Mayor of Tehran.

(continued)

Table 6.6. *(continued)*

Claims Regarding Changing Structures	Source	Guiding Questions to Identify Validity Claims of Sincerity	Evidence of Distortion
Female voice-over: Are you still asking yourself why Mehdi Karoubi is running for president? Maybe you remember in the last election Mehdi Karoubi promised that if he was elected as the president, he would set a salary of 50,000 tomans a month for all Iranians eighteen or older. Esma'il Gerami Moghadam: Is this the continuation of your last plan, when you stated 50,000 tomans a month would be given to all Iranians eighteen or older, and . . . it was also a solution for many unemployment challenges—is this a continuation of that plan and a more complete version of it? If this is the case please explain a little. Karoubi: This time around I think it is more comprehensive, it's better, meaning we have made it more detailed and clearer. Female voice-over: This plan, of course, was mocked by the other incumbents and was considered impossible. But after the elections many economists agreed with it and experts reviewed and completed it. Today this plan is completed under "assigning oil revenue shares to people," and is ready for execution.	EM50	S4. Is the communication clear and complete?	The plan's comprehensiveness and advantages are open to debate.

Karoubi's communications and campaign videos are also designed to appeal to the electorates' emotional side more than to provide factual value.

Mohammad Najafi: One of the most important issues regarding higher education of the youth is the expense of that education. Both those who study in state universities and some of them have to go far away from home to other cities, and covering their expenses is difficult, or those in private universities whose primary concern is covering their tuition and expenses.

Karoubi: *I* see how education affects people and families, and how difficult this burden is for them (EM45).

The above conversation, which is highlighted in Karoubi's official campaign release, offers very little in terms of a solution to the problem of the expenses associated with higher education. Rather, Karoubi's response, and his mannerisms and body language in the video basically give the appearance of sympathy and nothing more.

Similarly, the same campaign release highlights Karbaschi's[3] tears and displays of emotion when discussing the poor without actually offering a solution to their economic ordeal (EM47, EM48, EM49). Moreover, in response to Karbaschi's question "What are you going to do for them as a cleric [*rouhani*] president?" (EM47), we hear,

Karoubi: When Mr. Karbaschi remembers things, he unwillingly gets affected, and becomes upset. The other day too in a meeting when they came to my office and had a meeting, he got upset again. [He says all this while the camera zooms in on Karbaschi's face and his tears.] The answer is the same, you are sure I alone can't say, I have to think about it and sit on it first, the solution is with all the factions who want to work with me, and even those who may not work with us but they still feel for these issues. Let's sit down and think, I am ready to spend all my energy for things like this (EM47).

Not only does the above argument elicit an emotional response, it is incoherent, vague, and more importantly doesn't address the question. The response is merely designed to imply to the audience that Karoubi is on the side of the poor, or *Mostaz'afan*, which coincidentally was also one of Ayatollah Khomeini's favorite buzz words.

Similar arguments of distortion could be made about Karoubi's highlighted "oil shares" plan to give everyone over the age of eighteen 50,000 Tomans. The plan is described as "better" and more "complete" but the audience is not given any details or provided with any evidence to support this argument. Why is the plan better? What are some of the criticisms it received and how are they addressed? How is this plan different from Ahmadi Nejad's *Yaraneh*, or "subsidy," plan already in place that similarly offers cash sums to families?

To sum up, Karoubi's communications are often convoluted and ambiguous, and they focus on prompting emotional responses and appealing to emotional sentiments rather than offering evidence to support the argument—all of which points to communication distortion and evidence of insincerity.

Empirical Analysis of Legitimacy Claims

In criticizing economic conditions, as previously discussed, Mousavi often targets President Ahmadi Nejad and attributes the shortcomings and the pressures felt by the people to his mismanagement. By doing this, Mousavi is essentially separating the concept of *Dowlat* (the government) from *Nezam* (the system), and by doing so he avoids crossing the red line that tolerates criticism of the institute of presidency but not of the system. In reality, however, Ahmadi Nejad's mismanagement is a symptom and not the cause of economic underdevelopment. Similarly, drug addiction, crime, and in general "foul behavior" (EM22, EM35) were present before the revolution, and although they have intensified in recent years, they are not simply the result of President Ahmadi Nejad's economic policies. In fact, Iran has long had one of the world's highest addiction rates (Navai, 2014). This is by no means to absolve President Ahmadi Nejad of the atrocities of his government, I am simply unpacking a highly charged message. Furthermore, Mousavi observes, "On one hand we export crude oil and on the other hand imported consumer goods are flooding our market at the cost of destroying our domestic production" (EM25).

While that argument has merit, what is left silent in this argument is the fact that President Ahmadi Nejad is not solely responsible for this trend, especially considering the fact that the IRGC is increasingly involved in the economy, particularly imports and exports (Ilias, 2009; Wehrey et al., 2009). In light of the IRGC's increasing grip on the nation, the issue is not only far beyond Mr. Ahmadi Nejad but also far beyond the office of the president. Basic interpretive and critical understanding of argumentation tell us that when, in a society, "everything becomes utility-based and monetary-based" and when "cultural values turn into market values and economic values where everything has a monetary price—even human values are given a monetary value" (EM24), the issue goes far beyond mismanagement and ill-advised economic policies. This utilitarian and commercial view of life as per Mr. Mousavi (EM22, EM24) tells a tale of social and cultural paradigm shifts that are out of the scope of this book and not merely the result of the previous president's economic policies, no matter how destructive they may have been. However, one conclusion that can be drawn is the fact that criticizing the president is tolerated but discussing the IRGC's economic domination is considered crossing the red line, which carries severe consequences and is thus naturally avoided by the candidates.

Additionally, the crises of the economy, drugs, crime, morality, etc. that Mir Hossein Mousavi rightly speaks of are systemic issues far beyond the office of the president. It is the system and the injustice woven into the structure of the government that not only hand selects candidates such as Ahmadi Nejad, who has little experience running a country, but also elevates them to the point that Supreme Leader Khamenei asserts utmost support for him even in the face of a protesting public (Ahmadian, 2013; Kamali Dehghan and Borger, 2011). Let's not forget that Ahmadi Nejad rose from the ranks of the IRGC to be mayor of Tehran and then to become the country's two-term president. There are several executive and legislative layers of government that act as checks and balances to maintain the status quo of the executive branch and to avoid decisions that might, for example, damage domestic production (EM24, EM40). But if those decisions are executed as easily as the candidate suggests, then we are facing a systemic issue that involves more authorities, institutes, and levels of government than just the executive branch. Table 6.7 summarizes validity claims of legitimacy.

Corruption is evident, although not at the first glance, in the discourse of Mousavi: "There comes a point, for example, where a person bribes a member of the parliament with $5 million tomans to buy their vote. This is a consumerist society" (EM24).

The above tells the story of a corrupt system more than it describes lack of morals among the public. It tells us that the Iranian parliamentary members, and perhaps other officials, are corrupt and can be bought. Similar references can be found concealed in Karoubi's rhetoric. In response to a question by Karbaschi that asks him if he is willing to use all his powers to help the poor, Karoubi states,

> I will definitely do this. First of all, I'm not a hero, first of all. Second, we have, as you know, a certain record and that I'm not dependent on fake heroism. And I will truly go into my own preview which is working as the country's president and solving problems, and I am willing, as your honor has seen, I, to free a prisoner, when I was the Majlis speaker, I'd make a phone call to a colleague and he'd tell me you don't have to do this yourself, tell your office to call (EM48).

Why would the speaker of the house need to make a phone call in order to free a political prisoner? Why are peaceful political activists held in prison in the first place? Why would the system's regular legal channels be bypassed by those who are meant to implement the law unless the system were corrupt

Table 6.7. Empirical analysis of legitimacy validity claims regarding economic development

Claims Regarding Changing Structures	Source	Guiding Questions to Identify Validity Claims of Legitimacy	Evidence of Distortion
Mousavi: When people's incomes shrink, when they don't have employment prospects, you can be sure these youth who see no light at the end of the tunnel turn to drugs and foul behavior [bad akhlaghi] and these types of crimes will spread. But when in a society clear [economic] goals are stated, and there is hope for the future, which was the case during the war era despite all the hardship, I think all this foul behavior could be drastically reduced.	EM22	L1. What is missing or suppressed in the discourse?	The speaker is reducing the multitude of factors underlying high crime rates, widespread drug addiction, and moral and social issues to a single economic factor.
Mousavi: I have described this [economic conditions] as turning a society based on higher values to a commercial society. In a commercial society everything becomes utility-based and monetary-based. Cultural values turn into market values and economic values where everything has a monetary price even human values are given a monetary value. There comes a point, for example, where a person bribes a member of the parliament with $5 million tomans to buy their vote. This is a consumerist society. The current situation with this way of looking at society and with false promises and superstitions and such is far from the [value-based] era we went through [at the beginning of revolution].	EM24	L2. What information is suppressed or left out?	What led to this drastic change in socioeconomic conditions is left out.

Mousavi: On one hand we export crude oil and on the other hand imported consumer goods are flooding our market at the cost of destroying our domestic production.	EM25	L3. What information is suppressed or left out?	Mousavi doesn't discuss the fact that President Ahmadi Nejad would not have been able to accomplish this had it not been for the support of Iranian powerhouses (the House of Leadership, IRGC, etc.).
Karbaschi (video continues from previous section, while showing Karbaschi's tears): In the position of the president, are you determined to use any tool at your disposal, even your reputation, for this purpose? Karoubi: I will definitely do this. First of all, I'm not a hero, first of all. Second, we have, as you know, a certain record and that I'm not dependent on fake heroism. And I will truly go into my own preview of what is working as the country's president and solving problems, and I am willing, as your honor has seen, I, to free a prisoner, when I was the *Majlis* speaker, I'd make a phone call to a colleague and he'd tell me you don't have to do this yourself, tell your office to call, you don't have to tell me, people's problems, people's lives, people's dignity and authority are really important to us.	EM48	L4. Is all relevant information communicated without distortion or omission?	The communication doesn't explain why the Speaker of the House should call to free a prisoner. Who is the prisoner? What about legal avenues?

(continued)

Table 6.7. *(continued)*

Claims Regarding Changing Structures	Source	Guiding Questions to Identify Validity Claims of Legitimacy	Evidence of Distortion
Female voice-over: Are you still asking yourself why Mehdi Karoubi is running for president? Maybe you remember in the last election Mehdi Karoubi promised that if he gets elected president, he will set a salary of 50,000 tomans a month for all Iranians eighteen or older. Esma'il Gerami Moghadam: Is this the continuation of your last plan, when you stated 50,000 tomans a month will be given to all Iranians eighteen or older . . . Is this a continuation of that plan and a more complete version of it? If this is the case please explain a little. Karoubi: This time around I think it is more comprehensive, it's better, meaning we have made it more detailed and clearer. Female voice-over: This plan, of course, was mocked by the other incumbents and was considered impossible. But after the elections many economists agreed with it and experts reviewed and completed it. Today this plan has been completed under "assigning oil revenue shares to people," and is ready for execution.	EM50	L5. Who are the experts and economists? Who is excluded?	The communication does not divulge who the expert economists approving this plan are. Additionally, the opponents of this plan don't have a voice in the discussion.
Female voice-over: Karoubi has other economic plans too, including exempting small businesses from taxes and reinforcing the private sector in the fields of production, commerce, and services through tax exemption and through partnership with private and public banks.	EM52	L6. Who is marginalized or excluded?	The critics of this economic plan are excluded from the debate.

and unresponsive? Finally, there is yet another concealed truth that speaks to this argument in the above sentence, and that is the manner in which the story is told. Karoubi refers to his phone calls to free political prisoners on several occasions in his campaign video (EM43). Considering this is an official campaign release and of public record, and considering the matter of fact manner in which the assertion is made by him and received by his interviewers, one is left to conclude that this is an accepted practice, a norm and not at all out of the ordinary in the IRI.

Empirical Analysis of Comprehensibility Claims

When it comes to examining the comprehensibility of Mousavi's economic plans, what is missing from the conversation is an actual economic plan laid out by the candidate. Table 6.8 summarizes validity claims of comprehensibility.

While Mousavi criticizes the current difficult economic conditions and the increased poverty faced by large numbers of people (EM33), he fails to detail his own platform.

> Mousavi: We ask, during these past years, what great mission have you accomplished considering you spent $300 billion. Twenty-five percent inflation means the downfall of social security. Twenty-five percent inflation means addiction, foul behavior. Twenty-five percent inflation is like a tax the rich charge the poor. This is what the "handout" economy (eghtesad sadagheyi) has inflicted on us (EM35).

In the above statement and others like it (EM33, EM34, EM36, EM40), Mousavi is not off base in pointing to a variety of ills that plague the Iranian economy. However, what makes his communications unclear are, at times, the burdensome level of detail (EM35, EM40) as well as his failure to lay out his own alternative plans. Karoubi's campaign, on the other hand, provides more detail than his counterpart's when it comes to proposing an economic development plan such as his oil share plan (EM50), strengthening the private sector (EM42, EM44, EM52) and small businesses (EM52), attracting foreign and domestic investment (EM42, EM43), and reinstating the Office of Planning and Management (EM46).

However, as detailed in the previous section, Karoubi's conversations are frequently convoluted, his sentences are broken and incomplete, and it is often difficult to follow Karoubi grammatically and syntactically (EM43, EM44, EM46). Moreover, although Karoubi's campaign offers more detail regarding his economic plans, Mousavi frequently limits himself to criticism and drawing comparisons with the post-revolution and Iraq-war era thirty years before when he was in charge of the economy.

Table 6.8. Empirical analysis of comprehensibility validity claims regarding economic development

Claims Regarding Changing Structures	Source	Guiding Questions to Identify Validity Claims of Comprehensibility	Evidence of Distortion
Mousavi: Wealth distribution is in our religious beliefs, and [my] economic policy does not mean, obviously, that we would take money from one person's pocket by force and put it in another's. Our argument is that our collective economic policies should be designed in such a way that don't cause wide economic class gaps, and the middle class prospers so we can help the poor. But when over 50 percent of society collapses into the lower classes, it is impossible for the government to help the poor. Which is what is happening now.	EM28	C1. Is the communication sufficiently clear?	Mr. Mousavi is not explaining his actual economic policy. How is he planning to improve the economic situation for the middle classes? The poor?
Mousavi to a roaring crowd: Iran's destiny is not poverty.	EM33	C2. Is the communication complete?	The speaker remains silent on the factors contributing to the country's poverty.
Mousavi: We ask, during these past years, what great mission have you accomplished considering you spent $300 billion. Twenty-five percent inflation means the downfall of social security. Twenty-five percent inflation means addiction, foul behavior. Twenty-five percent inflation is like a tax the rich charge the poor. This is what the "handout" economy [eghtesad sadagheyi] has inflicted on us.	EM35	C3. Is the level of detail too burdensome for the audience?	Too many unexplained numbers and figures can obscure meaning.
Mousavi: What employment outlook do our 3 million university students have? It is easy to kickstart a project, it is easy to kickstart a project, [repetition is intentional]— securing the outcome is difficult.	EM36	C4. Is the communication complete?	It is not clear what the speaker would do to improve unemployment.

Mousavi: When I was in the North, the discussion was that while the rice produced by Iranian farmers is left in the warehouses, Pakistan's and India's basmati rice is being sold at a lower price in the Rasht markets. On top of that they were also discussing oranges, saying our oranges are left unpicked on the trees and imported oranges such as Egyptian and so on are in the market, and this is causing our fruited farmers to go bankrupt. They were talking about tea fields. I went to a tea farm where there were both tea farmers and tea specialists, and I was in those green gardens, and they showed me there how the fields are shrinking and talked about the problems they were facing. They were saying while over 180,000 metric tons of Iranian tea are left in the warehouses . . . our own markets are flooded with imported tea, and this has eliminated the possibility of healthy competition and growth. The same problem appeared when I went to Kerman. Fruit farmers there were also telling me that their oranges are left [in the warehouse] while importing oranges is increasing. Then I went to the silk industry, there I said the silk industry at some point was critical to the Safavid economy. Shah Abbas was one of the major silk merchants in the country who would both use silk imports to Europe for political purposes and also use it to find a way to preserve Iran's interests in the face of the Ottoman threat.

EM40

C5. Is the communication sufficiently clear?

While the utterance details problems associated with economic policies, he fails to present his own policy to rectify the situation.

(continued)

Table 6.8. *(continued)*

Claims Regarding Changing Structures	Source	Guiding Questions to Identify Validity Claims of Comprehensibility	Evidence of Distortion
Karoubi: Our second manifesto . . . was about oil shares . . . as we can see the large and unprecedented revenues that was at the disposal of the current honorable government in the past few years, hopefully they can explain what changes they have produced for our society with this unprecedented revenue where we sold oil at $100 and $120 [a barrel]—it's obvious how much the revenue levels were. Inflation, unemployment, the high cost of living, and recession are things that people are fully familiar with. They don't need opinion polls and central bank benchmarks, which are their rights, they see their lives and how much they have changed. Therefore, the oil shares as we detailed, which we are not going to get into how we're going to deal with them.	EM41	C6. Is the communication intelligible and without confusion?	The language and syntax are unclear and convoluted
Karoubi: And another more important issue, which is very very important to me, us, the government should oversee, the government shouldn't take over, the government should not interfere in the private sector and create limitations for them so much. The government should accommodate them, the government should create security for them so they can bring their capital in with confidence and don't continue to take them outside [the country] and don't run away. This is the first point. Second,	EM42	C7. Is the communication sufficiently clear and complete?	Despite the simple language, the speaker fails to offer a concrete plan that details how to accomplish, for example, attracting foreign investment. The hearer or reader is left to decode that message.

we have many Iranians . . . we truly have many many interested many Iranians all around the world who are willing to come and invest here and develop our economy: the government earns more taxes, earns more revenues, [the government] won't be reliant on oil so much, won't use up and sell and spend its capital so much. Next, partnership with the foreign economies, and foreign investment, again we attract them and bring them in. First off, professionals will come in, technology will come in, management will come in—we transfer our management to them, they transform their management to us, in all of this we will fully uphold our national interests, our principles.

Karoubi: And if I spend time, my own shortcomings, create crisis-making and dump it on this or that person, please note what hurdles are the private banks facing in our country? They have even gone to the verge of getting arrested. In a country like this that certain high ranking individuals or legitimate powerhouses have to intervene and prevent a certain bank CEO's arrest. Can investment be done in something like this? Is there security? If we want economic development, if we want high inflation to not exist, if we want sometimes we have to increase inflation we have to make it up, we have to couple it with extra revenues so we can make up for the inflation.

| EM43 | C8. Is the communication sufficiently clear and intelligible? | The language and syntax are unclear and convoluted. Additionally, in this communication, no solution is offered in only questions are posed. |

(continued)

Table 6.8. (continued)

Claims Regarding Changing Structures	Source	Guiding Questions to Identify Validity Claims of Comprehensibility	Evidence of Distortion
Karoubi: If we want everyone to be employed, we have no other way than to re-enforce the private sector and enter them into the job market. Naturally, we will oversee and we will take care, we have to do it so misuse doesn't happen, and that in itself doesn't create a new problem for us. And this is a very simple thing to do and it is regularly and frequently practiced.	EM44	C9. Is this utterance complete and intelligible?	The language is convoluted, sentences are broken, and the intended message of the speaker is unclear.
Morteza Alviri: if you become the president, what do you think the first thing to do, to set this train in motion to get to the higher goal so in any case we could have an economically developed country, is going to be? Karoubi: My first thing to do, my first manifesto, the manifesto that I published in [the month of] Bahman, my first manifesto was to revive [the centre for] planning and management, which unfortunately got dissolved.	EM46	C10. Is the communication complete and intelligible?	Language is convoluted and difficult to understand. The speaker does not explain how his response is relevant to his objective of economic development.

STRUCTURES OF SIGNIFICATION AND LEGITIMATION

The data I have gathered shows very little sign of the two leaders attempting to address the structures of signification and legitimation. The most obvious structure of legitimation the data points to is the presence of each candidate's spouse at public election gatherings and Ms. Rahnavard's outspoken and active participation in her husband's campaign. As discussed in the previous section, this is the first time since the revolution that candidates have been not only accompanied by their wives but the women have been visibly active, have spoken in support of their respective campaigns, and have been celebrated by the electorate. This is a clear attempt at breaking the norms of a society in which women are largely excluded from political participation and discouraged from displaying such public expressions of opinion. Both candidates break this social and political norm, which lends a hand to legitimizing women's public and political participation and their right to decide their own destinies.

NOTES

1. Jamileh Kadivar is a Reformist and former member of the parliament. She was Karoubi's campaign advisor on women's affairs. Furthermore, she is Hojatol Islam Mohsen Kadivar's sister and wife of Ataolah Mohajerani, Khatami's former minister of guidance and culture who supported Karoubi's candidacy.

2. There was a small window between the revolution and the beginning of the war with Iraq (February 1979 to September 1980).

3. Gholam Hossein Karbaschi was mayor of Tehran from 1989 to 1998 when he was arrested, convicted, and imprisoned for fraud and embezzlement. He belongs to the Reform Front, and his prison ordeal was largely considered political maneuvering by the Hardliner Conservatives (*New York Times*, 1999).

7

Analysis of the Public Discourse
of Ayatollah Khomeini

AN OVERVIEW OF THE CHAPTER

In this chapter, I will conduct a critical analysis of the political discourse of Ayatollah Khomeini during the 1979 Iranian Revolution. While the previous chapter established the methodological procedure step by step, in the interest of space, I have eliminated those details and simply focus on demonstrating the discourse analysis. However, please bear in mind the same methodological process was followed to analyze Ayatollah Khomeini's rhetoric as in the previous chapter. A similar trend as before reveals that Ayatollah Khomeini's discourse was largely focused on the structures of domination. The significance of the analysis of the discourse of the leader of the revolution is twofold: first, it helps us trace some of the grievances of the Green Movement back to the 1979 revolution by revealing the unfulfilled nature of those calls; second, and perhaps more importantly, it allows for a mapping of the sociopolitical structures founded on Ayatollah Khomeini's vision of an Islamic theocracy.

Considering democracy, women's rights, and freedom of expression were among the most significant demands of the protesters and thus dominated the revolutionary discourse, including that of Ayatollah Khomeini, they were selected here for examination. In the following sections I present my analysis of some of the primary claims of Ayatollah Khomeini regarding those three fundamental categories prior to and after his assuming power.

STRUCTURES OF DOMINATION: PATRIARCHY

As per our discussion in previous chapters, women's rights were at the forefront of revolutionary demands. Women contributed extensively to the revolutionary process, from taking part in street demonstrations, protests, and sit-ins to participating in guerilla organizations and attacks in such groups as Fadayian Khalgh and the Mojahedin Khalgh. Considering women's active presence in the revolution, Ayatollah Khomeini, a highly conservative and religious man, was naturally questioned about his own stance on women's rights and their role in an Islamic Republic.

Empirical Analysis of Truth Claims

Examination of Ayatollah Khomeini's truth validity claims reveals above all their ideological nature. He consistently makes biased claims regarding women's rights in Islam based on his own ideological interpretation of Islam, claims that remain unexamined and closed to rational scrutiny by opposing views. He offers very little evidence for his claims other than his own word. Khomeini repeatedly affirms that women are free (EM53, EM56, EM57, EM59, and EM61–64, to give a few examples) and that they are equal to men (EM54, EM62, EM64), though he never fully explains what he means by the highly charged word *freedom*. Remember, freedom was one of the main demands of the revolution, thus for the revolutionary crowd the word carried a significant weight when used by a charismatic religious authority such as Ayatollah Khomeini. Table 7.1 summarizes validity claims of truth.

These inconsistencies in the rhetoric of the Islamic leader point to incomplete utterances and half-truths. As an example, while he insists on women's equality to their male counterparts and their so-called freedom, he also states that women, while free in matters of *Taghlid*, are not allowed to leave the house without their husband's permission (Khomeini, 1967, 2:272). The legal ramifications of this fatwa are that Iranian women currently need their husband's permission to work or to apply for a passport and leave the country, which essentially restricts the freedom of physical movement (a guaranteed human right) of half the Iranian population. Additionally, Khomeini also believed in restricting a woman's choice in clothing and policed her body by forcing hijab on her, further restricting her choices.

On another note, while his revolutionary discourse speaks of freedom and equality, a look at his reaction to the 1967 Family Protection Law enacted by the Shah points to a blunt contradiction, leading one to believe he was concealing his true sentiments under a cloak of half-truths.

Table 7.1. Empirical analysis of truth validity claims of Ayatollah Khomeini regarding women's rights

Claims Regarding Changing Structures	Source	Guiding Questions to Identify Validity Claims of Truth	Evidence of Distortion
A delegate with Amnesty International: From an Islamic point of view, to what extent would women be allowed to participate in the construction of an Islamic government? Ayatollah Khomeini: Women play a significant role in building an Islamic society; Islam promotes women to where they can realize their humanistic values in the society, and more beyond the boundaries of being simply an object, and along with such growth, they can assume responsibilities in constructing an Islamic government.	EM53	T1. Is there an ideological claim that is unexamined?	Islam's promotion of women's rights is a value-based assertion. Additionally, women's realization of "humanistic values" is an emotionally charged statement that is associated negatively with objectification.
In an Interview with Russell Kerr, a member of the British House of Commons and member of the Labor Party. Shah's critic for human rights violations. Russell Kerr: Your enemies claim that the rights of the women in the Islamic government will be violated, the present rights that the women have gained during the Shah's rule will be revoked. Of course, I do not personally believe in it. What is your opinion? Ayatollah Khomeini: The women are free in the Islamic government; their rights will be identical with those of men. Islam emancipated the women from the captivation of men and put them on an equal footing with men.	EM54	T2. Is this argument logically consistent? T3. Is this argument factually true? T4. Is there an ideological claim that is unexamined?	T2. This utterance regarding women's freedom conflicts with some of Ayatollah's views regarding women, including not leaving the house without their husband's permission. T3. In reality, Islam as interpreted by Khomeini does not recognize equal rights for women. T5. The claims about Islam and human rights are unexamined.
Ayatollah Khomeini: The propaganda carried out against us aim to misguide the people. Islam has guaranteed all the human rights and issues.	EM55	T5. Is there an ideological claim that is unexamined?	The claim that Islam has provisions for all human rights is highly ideological and contested.

(continued)

Table 7.1. *(continued)*

Claims Regarding Changing Structures	Source	Guiding Questions to Identify Validity Claims of Truth	Evidence of Distortion
Professor Kirk Croft of Rutgers University: Which changes, in your opinion, are necessary to be made in the current status of women in the Iranian society? How do you think the Islamic government will change the status and situation of women? For example, the employment of women in governmental jobs or in different occupations such as medical practices, engineering, etc. and also some occasions including divorce, abortion, the right to travel and the compulsory observance of veil (chador). Ayatollah Khomeini: The disinformation campaign of the Shah and those who are employed by him have distorted the issue of freedom of women in a way that people think that Islam has come to merely confine the women to the four walls of their houses. Why should we be against women's education? Why shouldn't women hold governmental positions? Why should we be against women's traveling? Women are free in all these affairs as men are. There is no difference between men and women. That is right, women should have hijab [Islamic dress code], but their hijab should not necessarily be a veil [chador]. They can choose any kind of clothes that covers them. We cannot and Islam does not want us to make dolls of women. Islam intends to preserve the dignity of the women and make them efficient and serious human beings. We will never let the men to use women as a doll	EM56	T6. Is this argument factually true?	In reality, women did not have that choice, their choices were highly limited, and disobedience was punishable by law. Additionally, that alone is evidence that women are not free "in all these affairs as men are" and that there in fact is a huge "difference" between the two, in practice.

for their caprices and whims. Islam prohibits abortion and women can procure the right to take divorce in their marriage contract. No law or school has given as much freedom and respect to women as Islam has.

In an interview with the reporters of Iranian Keyhan and Etela'at Dailies.

Question: What will be the role of the women in the Islamic government? Will they, for instance, participate in the state affairs? For example, will they become minister or members of the parliament, if they demonstrate their competence?

Ayatollah Khomeini: The Islamic government will decide about these issues. It is not an appropriate time to express ideas about these issues now. Like men, women too will play a role in the construction of the Islamic society of tomorrow. They will enjoy the right to elect and the right to be elected. In current the struggles in Iran, women's contribution is similar to that of the men. We will grant all sorts of freedoms to the women. Of course, we will stop corruption and in this regard there will be no differences between men and women.

| EM57 | T7. Is this argument logically consistent? | This utterance conflicts with the view that human beings are born free, rendering blanket statements such as "granting" or "taking away" freedom problematic. The speaker assumes the legitimacy to grant or limit individual freedom. |

The law that has recently been passed by the illegal Majlis under the name of the Family Protection Law in order to destroy Muslim family law, is against Islam and both its originators and its implementers are guilty before the *shariat*. Women who are divorced in family courts should consider their divorce as null, and if they re-marry they are committing adultery. Whoever marries these women knowingly is also an adulterer, and should be punished according to *shariat* by whipping. The children of these men and women are illegitimate and are not entitled to inheritance (Paidar, 1997, 174).

As discussed in chapter 6, the Family Protection Law in 1967 and subsequent amendments in 1975 limited a man's unilateral prerogative in matters of divorce, custody, and polygamy, granting women more say in such affairs. Khomeini, however, was vehemently against granting such rights to women, leaving one to question not just the accuracy of his assertions but their sincerity as well. In other words, his insistence that Islam has guaranteed all human rights is an ideological and biased assertion far from the realities of women's lives in Iran.

Empirical Analysis of Sincerity Claims

As expressed in the previous chapter, sincerity claims deal with the congruity of what is stated by the speaker and what is assumed by the audience. In other words, sincerity claims test whether the speaker is attempting, even if subconsciously, to mislead the audience by implying one thing while concealing his intentions. In an analysis of the sincerity claims of Ayatollah Khomeini, we find, much as we did with the leaders of the Green Movement, no clear explanation of what Khomeini means by gender equality and discrimination against women and what the "rules" of Islam are and how they apply to each sex differently. Additionally, much like Karoubi, Khomeini tends to qualify his assertions on equality, freedom, and so on with ambiguous phrases such as "Women are free to choose their own activities and destiny as well as their mode of dress within Islamic standards" (EM58), or when he says that Islam puts men and women on equal footing but "of course there are certain rules which apply only to men and others which apply only to women, but this does not mean that Islam discriminates against women" (EM62). Such utterances give the appearance of coveted notions such as equality while in reality they restrict the concept by making it contingent on conditions, i.e., "Islamic standards," that are never fully clarified.

Phrases such as "We want a woman to be a person like other people, a human being like any other human being, to be free as others are free" (EM64) lead us to ask whether Khomeini might be intentionally misleading the public. Considering some of his views on women's rights as explained in the previous section, is he concealing those views from his supporters? Table 7.2 summarizes validity claims of sincerity.

Table 7.2. Empirical analysis of sincerity validity claims of Ayatollah Khomeini regarding women's rights

Claims Regarding Changing Structures	Source	Guiding Questions to Identify Validity Claims of Sincerity	Evidence of Distortion
Elizabeth Targood, a reporter with The Guardian: Will the Islamic laws be put into effect? And what difference will they make in daily life, compared to the current laws? May Ayatullah precisely explain whether women could choose between Islamic and Western dress freely, under the banner of Islam? Ayatollah Khomeini: Women are free to choose their own activities and destiny as well as their mode of dress within Islamic standards.	EM58	S1. Is what is said consistent with what is implied?	The statement implies that women will be free to choose, however, the phrase "Islamic standards" is left unexplained and is dependent on one's interpretation of Islam.
A delegate from Amnesty International: From an Islamic point of view, to what extent would women be allowed to participate in the construction of an Islamic government? Ayatollah Khomeini: Women play a significant role in building an Islamic society; Islam promotes women to where they can realize their humanistic values in the society, and more beyond the boundaries of being simply an object, and along with such growth, they can assume responsibilities in constructing an Islamic government.	EM59	S2. Does the text elicit emotional an emotional response?	Women's realization of "humanistic values" is an emotionally charged statement that is associated negatively with objectification. However, the speaker doesn't explain his understanding of objectification. Are women not wearing a hijab objectified, for example?
A German reporter: How the freedom of women in the future government will be? Will they have to leave schools and stay at home or will they have the chance to continue their educations? Ayatollah Khomeini: What you have heard about women and other issues are all propaganda spread by the Shah and the biased people. Women are free; they are also free in regard to education and they are free in other things as men are. It is now that neither women nor men are free.	EM60	S3. Is what is said consistent with what is implied?	The speaker is silent on what he means by "freedom." He does not offer the audience his understanding of the freedom of women.

(continued)

Table 7.2. *(continued)*

Claims Regarding Changing Structures	Source	Guiding Questions to Identify Validity Claims of Sincerity	Evidence of Distortion
Georgia Gayer of L.A. Times: With regard to social issues, how do you envisage the presence of the women in the universities or their working in the society? Will you impose any restriction that currently does not exist in the society, on them? What is your opinion about the family planning and coeducation in the universities?	EM61	S4. Does this communication elicit an emotional response?	Concepts such as "moral decadence" are highly charged. They invoke negative emotions and negatively associates women's (and men's) freedom with moral decadence.
Ayatollah Khomeini: Women will be free in the Islamic society and there will be no restriction on their admission to the universities, working in the offices and being elected to the houses of the parliament. What will be restricted is moral decadence in whose regard both men and women are treated equally; it is unlawful for both. The family planning will depend on the government's decision.			
Ayatollah Khomeini: This regime has disseminated propaganda to the effect that were Islam to come to power, women, for example would have to remain at home with the doors locked to prevent them from getting out! Such falsehoods they spread about Islam . . . of course there are certain rules which apply only to men and others which apply only to women, but this does not mean that Islam discriminates against women. Both women and men are free to attend university, both are free to vote and stand as parliamentary representatives.	EM62	S5. Is what is said consistent with what is implied?	The speaker is silent on what his understanding of discrimination or gender equality is, thus leaving the audience free to read other interpretations (including the conventional, liberal understanding) into it.

Text	Code	Question	Analysis
Ayatollah Khomeini: Islam does not oppose any of the manifestations of civilisation and is not against any one particular group of you. When it first appeared, Islam took women by the hand and made them equal with men. Even though women were regarded as nothing at the time the Prophet of Islam began his teachings. Islam gave women strength. Islam put women on a par with men and made them equal with men. Of course, there are certain rules which apply only to men and others which apply only to women, but this does not mean that Islam discriminates against women.	EM63	S6. What is missing or suppressed in the discourse?	The Ayatollah is surpressing his own views and interpretation of Islam of the role of women here. Additionally, he leaves unexplained which rules apply to men and which to women. More importantly, he suppresses the limitations women would face under Islam.
Ayatollah Khomeini: We want to get rid of this mistaken idea. We want a woman to be a person like other people, a human being like any other human being, to be free as others are free. Do not listen to this propaganda the Shah puts about—on which it is said he spends one hundred million dollars annually. Nobody really pays attention to it any more anyway. He should pack up his things and leave now.	EM64	S7. Does this communication elicit an emotional response?	Terms such as "free," specifically in the context of women in 1978, are highly charged and are invoked here without proper decoding to explain the speaker's conception of the term. Additionally, while the speaker is using charged words such as "propaganda" and "expenditure," he is not providing any proof for his claim.
A French reporter: Some of the Islamic customs, such as the Islamic dress code [hijab], have been given up. Will it become compulsory in the Islamic Republic again? Ayatollah Khomeini: Islamic dress code [hijab] in its general sense which prevails among us and is known as Islamic hijab has no contradiction with freedom. Islam opposes what is opposed to chastity. We will invite them to observe the Islamic dress code. Our courageous women are fed up with the calamities inflicted upon them by the West in the name of civilization and have taken refuge in Islam.	EM65	S8. Is what is said consistent with what is implied?	Inviting women to "observe the Islamic dress code" implies they have a choice, which in reality they do not have.

Evidence seems to support this point of view. Bearing in mind the post-revolutionary laws implemented in Iran, including compulsory hijab, family laws as detailed above, and disqualifying women from certain professions such as Supreme Leadership, judgeship, and studying in certain fields, I think we can safely assume lack of sincerity in those claims. Additionally, the post-revolutionary man at the height of his power insists without that chador, women cannot work in a useful or healthy way. Below is an excerpt from Khomeini's famous interview with Oriana Fallaci in October 1979, well after the revolution had been won and Khomeini had established his authority. In the interview, which was published in the *New York Times*, Fallaci, a fierce reporter and women's rights activist who was forced to wear a chador in order to see the Imam, asks him about compulsory hijab and a woman's freedom to choose.

> Fallaci: Please Imam, there are many things I still want to ask you. For example, this chador that they made me put on, to come to you, and which you insist all women must wear. Tell me, why do you force them to hide themselves, all bundled up under these uncomfortable and absurd garments, making it hard to work and move about? And yet, even here, women have demonstrated that they are equal to men. They fought just like the men, were imprisoned and tortured. They, too, helped to make the revolution.
>
> Khomeini: The women who contributed to the revolution were, and are, women with the Islamic dress, not elegant women all made up like you, who go around all uncovered, dragging behind them a tail of men. The coquettes who put on make up and go to the street showing off their necks, their hair, their shapes, did not fight against the Shah. They never did anything good, not those. They do not know how to be useful, neither socially, nor politically, not professionally. And this is so because by uncovering themselves, they distract men and upset them. Then they distract and upset even other (Fallaci, 1979, 8).

However, as previously detailed, women of all walks of life, with or without hijab, lay and secular, modern and traditional participated in the revolution. Overall, the evidence suggests lack of sincerity in the discourse of Khomeini and points overwhelmingly to communication distortion. Studying Khomeini's discourse points to concealment of his intentions and beliefs deemed unpopular during the revolution, only to be revealed once he was at the helm.

EMPIRICAL ANALYSIS OF LEGITIMACY CLAIMS

What is most striking regarding Khomeini's legitimacy claims regarding women is his sheer comfort and ease in speaking for them. Women are not consulted on any of these matters, and since Shi'ite women are not allowed to practice *fiqh* and to be ordained to the status of a Marja', their voices are completely missing from this discourse. Ayatollah Khomeini is speaking for what Muslim women want even before he is in power. While he asserts in one interview that women have the right to choose their own mode of dress (a distorted concept as we established in the previous section), he also dictates that they don't "have the right to degrade themselves" (EM66). The question to be asked here is who decides what is "degrading" for half the population? Is removing a headscarf, for example, degrading? Concepts such as degradation and "corruption" (EM57, EM68, EM69, EM71) that are brought up frequently in Khomeini's discourse on women's rights are highly problematic in that a male leader ascribes to himself the authority to decide what those concepts entail and what their implications should be for the lives of female citizens. This is in part due to Khomeini's view of his own role in particular and that of the Shi'ite clergy in general as the guardians of the nation. He detailed this view in his book *The Islamic Government* (1970) decades before the revolution and managed to successfully engrave that view in the constitution as the principle of Absolute Guardianship of the Jurisprudent, as discussed in chapter 5.

Ayatollah Khomeini believed, and many other Shi'ite clergy continue to believe, they are the guardians of the public, especially women, who, in their view, cannot make decisions for themselves because their cognitive abilities and knowledge are limited and have thus been placed under male guardianship. This view, which by no coincidence is fully aligned with patriarchal and paternalistic views of women, further pushes women to the margins, scrapping their limited yet hard-earned achievements (such as the 1967 Family Protection Law) over the previous decades. By this logic, the women who by Khomeini's own admission participated widely in the protests (EM68), thus contributing to his ascent to power and exhibiting tremendous courage and more importantly agency over their destiny, need a guardian to prevent them from "indignity" and "corruption." Table 7.3 summarizes those claims.

Additionally, Ayatollah Khomeini persistently ignores Iranian women's diverse religious backgrounds, painting everyone as Shi'ite Muslims. He is well aware that Iran is home to large Christian, Jewish, Assyrian, Zoroastrian, Baha'i, and Sunni minorities, among others. Furthermore, many leftist, nationalist, and liberal women whose contributions were instrumental to the success of the revolution were secular or non-practicing. Yet Khomeini continues to refer to them as Muslims, erasing the diverse population that is Iranian women, distancing those minorities even further from the discourse.

Furthermore, a considerable amount of information is suppressed and details are left out of this discourse that would further reveal women's marginalization and exclusion from Iranian society. Khomeini suppresses the fact, for example, that when it comes to participating in the army, women will only be able to serve in supportive roles (EM69), and he fails to mention what else

Table 7.3. Empirical analysis of legitimacy validity claims of Ayatollah Khomeini regarding women's rights.

Claims regarding Changing Structures	Source	Guiding Questions to Identify Validity Claims of Legitimacy	Evidence of Distortion
A reporter from *Amsterdam Weekly* magazine: What does returning to the laws of the Quran mean as far as women? Ayatollah Khomeini: In an Islamic system, women can actively cooperate with men in building an Islamic society, but they will not be used as objects. Neither do they have the right to degrade themselves, nor do men have the right to hold such a concept of them.	EM66	L1. Who is speaking and who is left silent?	The speaker ascribes to himself the authority to speak for what women can and cannot do, and what is degrading to them and what is not
Ayatollah Khomeini: Who has told you that women will be locked up?! They are free like men.	EM67	L2. What information is suppressed or left silent?	The speaker is suppressing the fact that his views on women places certain limitations on the freedom of women
A Lebanese reporter of the Amal daily, the organ of the youth of Harikat al-Mahrumin [the Movement of the Disinherited]: Women constitute a great multitude of the Muslims. What role or what rights do you consider for women in the Islamic system? Ayatollah Khomeini: Currently the Muslim women of Iran participate in the anti-Shah political struggles and demonstrations. I have been informed that the women in Iran hold political meetings in various cities. In an Islamic	EM68	L3. Is all relevant information communicated without distortion and omission? L4. What group is marginalized or excluded?	3- The speaker omits the severe limits and restrictions of free will for women, and points to "certain cases" being forbidden passing rendering it unimportant 4- Iranian women come from a diverse religious background, not all of which are Islam.

system, the women enjoy the same rights that men do, that is, right to education, right to work, right to property, and right to suffrage. Women enjoy the same rights that men do in all fields. However, there are certain cases that are forbidden for men in order to prevent corruption, likewise there are certain cases that are forbidden for women because they cause corruption. Islam has tried to protect the humane status of men and women. Islam has tried to prevent the women from becoming a plaything in the hands of men. What they have said outside about women, that is, they are treated violently, is incorrect and is false propaganda by those who have prejudice, otherwise, men and women both have their own rights in Islam. If there are differences, it is for both of them that is related to their nature.

(continued)

Table 7.3. *(continued)*

Claims regarding Changing Structures	Source	Guiding Questions to Identify Validity Claims of Legitimacy	Evidence of Distortion
Professor Kirk Croft of Rutgers University: It is said that the former head of Iran's Society of Female Lawyers, Mahvash Safiniya has said that the religious movement in Iran has obliged the Parliament to ratify bills, which limit the women's rights. For example, reducing the marriage age to 15 years, prohibiting women from joining the army and announcing abortion as a crime (Quoted in the *New York Times*, December 17). Do you acknowledge such laws? Ayatollah Khomeini: With regards to marriage, Islam has granted the women the right to choose their husbands. Women can choose their favored husbands, of course in the framework of the Islamic laws. Islam is against abortion and considers it an unlawful act and prohibits it. As I said before, women can join the army. What Islam is against, and prohibits, is corruption, no matter if this corruption is on woman's part or the man's. The people whom you are introducing as lawyers have always misled our women. Today, the prisons are filled with our noble women and these lawyers have always undersigned and confirmed the Shah's crimes. Which one of these two groups is free and noble?	EM69	L5. What information is suppressed or left silent? L6. What groups are marginalized?	5- The speaker leaves out the fact that in reality women often had little choice in who they married and at what age, and that divorce is by default a man's right. Additionally, Ayatollah Khomeini omits the fact that women can only join the army in supportive, none-combat roles 6- What protections are there in the Ayatollah's view for the multitude of girls who are forced to marry someone against their own will? Additionally, allowing girls as young as 15 to be married off marginalizes them for children are not capable of consent at that age

will be "forbidden" to women, which will include judgeship, filing for divorce, and removal of hijab in public. Moreover, he fails to mention that he is against women's suffrage, which was granted to them during the White Revolution. In general, he fails to observe that his views on women will further alienate and exclude them. Thus, it is safe to say Khomeini's validity claims of legitimacy defy the standards of discourse analysis and point to distortion.

Empirical Analysis of Comprehensibility Claims

Reviewing Ayatollah Khomeini's revolutionary discourse for validity claims of comprehensibility reveals his frequent engagement in convoluted language that is difficult for the audience to understand. He often refers to Islamic teachings on women (EM64, EM71, EM72) without clarifying what those teachings are for an audience who, unlike him, are not schooled in *fiqh* and thus are unaware of its inner workings. In other words, at times the level of detail in his responses is considerably burdensome for the audience to fully comprehend what he is saying to them. The lay person could not possibly be expected to have an extensive knowledge of *fiqh*, and not much effort is made on the part of Khomeini to unpack his messages for them. I want to point out as well that Ayatollah Khomeini is not alone in excluding the public from participating in debates on religious matters that impact their lives directly. Historically, the Shi'ite clergy consider interpretation of Shari'a and Qur'an their exclusive purview. A case in point: one of the reasons for the ulama's contentious relationship with Reza Shah was because he secularized public education, which until that point had been the clergy's almost exclusive domain and one of the tools at their exclusive disposal with which to maintain their influence over the public. Comprehensibility claims are detailed in Table 7.4.

Khomeini's answers to pointed questions such as "Will you impose any restriction that currently does not exist in the society on them [women]?" are confusing and difficult to understand.

Georgia Gayer of the L.A. Times: With regard to social issues, how do you envisage the presence of the women in the universities or their working in the society? Will you impose any restriction that currently does not exist in the society, on them? What is your opinion about the family planning and coeducation in the universities?

Ayatollah Khomeini: Women will be free in the Islamic society and there will be no restriction on their admission to the universities, working in the offices and being elected to the houses of the parliament. What will be restricted is moral decadence in whose regard both men and women are treated equally; it is unlawful for both. The family planning will depend on the government's decision (EM61).

Table 7.4. Empirical analysis of comprehensibility validity claims of Ayatollah Khomeini regarding women's rights.

Claims Regarding Changing Structures	Source	Guiding Questions to Identify Validity Claims of Comprehensibility	Evidence of Distortion
A reporter of the Dutch Volt Krant magazine: Specifically, how would women's rights in the Islamic Republic be? What about the coed schools? What would be the case with the issue of birth control and abortion? Ayatollah Khomeini: According to human rights, there is no difference between a man and a woman. Because they are both human, and like men, women have the right to take part in making their own destiny too. Yes, of course there are some differences between men and women that have nothing to do with their humanistic dignity. Anything not against women's dignity and nobility is free. Abortion is prohibited in Islam.	EM70	C1. Is the communication sufficiently clear?	The speaker does not explain his views on the "differences between men and women" and those matters "against women's dignity and nobility" and their implications on restricting women's freedom.
A reporter of the German The Third World magazine: In the opinion of Western countries, Shiism is being considered as a conservative element in progress. We have also heard the Shiah desire to withdraw women from the scene of social life, as well as their wish to return to Shiah laws, which would call for setting religious traditions as the basis of governing laws, as referred to in the constitutional laws, which has become illegally obsolete. We have also heard that Shiism rejects Western life style because it doesn't agree with religious traditions. Will it be possible for you to give your opinion on this matter based on Shiah belief?	EM71	C2. Is the level of detail too burdensome for the audience?	It is left for the audience to decode and understand the details of gender relations in Shi'itism.

Ayatollah Khomeini: Shiism, which is a revolutionary school of thought, and the continuation of the Prophet's (s) true Islam, has always been under the dastardly attacks of the dictators and expansionists. Not only does Shiism not drive away women from the scene of social life, but it places them in their own elevated humane position within the society. We will accept the West's advancements, but not the West's corruptions that they themselves are whimpering about.

A reporter of the Voice of Luxemburg and Radio Luxemburg: How do you foresee social development and progress, particularly the progress of the women, in case your movement attains victory and an Islamic government is established? Will polygamy be allowed, will you permit it?
Ayatollah Khomeini: Women are free, as men are. We will act in accordance to the law of Islam.

EM72	C3. Is the communication clear and without confusion?	Khomeini does not provide a clear answer to the question. Instead he offers an ideological statement.

Asian, European and American reporters: What would be the policy of the Islamic Republic about the freedom of women, illiteracy campaign and cinemas?
Ayatollah Khomeini: The Shah has done nothing positive in Iran. Reconstructing and renovating the Shah's destruction will take a lot of time. Shah has granted freedom neither to the women nor to the men. We will grant freedom to everybody. In the Shah regime, the cinemas were in the service of corruption, while in the future republic they will serve to the nation's benevolence. We will also fight illiteracy in its best way.

EM73	C4. Is the communication clear and without confusion?	Khomeini does not provide a clear answer to the question. Instead, he points to the Shah and draws an unrelated comparison between himself and the Shah in order to elicit an emotional response and distract.

(continued)

Table 7.4. *(continued)*

Claims Regarding Changing Structures	Source	Guiding Questions to Identify Validity Claims of Comprehensibility	Evidence of Distortion
Foreign reporters: What will be the role and position of women in the future government? Ayatollah Khomeini: It will be the condition of a genuine human being and a free personality contrary to the time that we have put behind, when neither our women nor our men were free. A nation whose men and women were not free and were living under repression has been liberated from this situation and henceforth its men and women will be free. But if they decide to commit any act in contravention to the principles of chastity or take measures contrary to the exigencies of the country, they will be of course stopped.	EM74	C5. Is the communication clear and without confusion?	Khomeini does not provide a clear answer to the question. The speaker is vague on the details of his answer.

The difficulty in discerning or comprehending Khomeini's claims is due to his avoiding concise and clear answers to direct questions. EM73 and EM74 further attest to this point, in which Khomeini evades addressing pointed questions about his stance on women. One conclusion we can draw here is that perhaps Khomeini is leaving some of the more controversial questions vague on purpose to avoid further scrutiny and deter the public who would be weary if they knew of the restrictions to be imposed on their freedom and their bodies. Ayatollah Khomeini, as the world came to learn, was not a man of uncertainty. He was clear on his vision for the direction of the revolution: toward creating an Islamic government. Therefore, one is left to speculate why a religiously learned man (a Grand Ayatollah) with a distinct vision would engage in such confusing discourse, making it difficult for his audience to comprehend his message. One argument that can be made here is that he did not want to stir the pot by raising controversial issues that might lose him the popular support he enjoyed until he was in a position of power.

On a separate note, I have to point out the difficulties of working from Khomeini's translated work. *Sahifeh-Ye Imam*, which is twenty-two volumes of his work, has been translated into English by the *Institute for Compilation and Publication of Imam Khomeini's Works*, which is dedicated to promoting the thought and ideology of Khomeini. Comparing the originally transcribed Farsi interviews and the English translation, one can't help but notice the often grammatically and syntactically convoluted and confusing language of Ayatollah Khomeini in the former is cleaned up for the latter. Comparing the Farsi and English texts reveals a clear attempt by the translation team to remedy Khomeini's speaking style, which includes correcting his grammatical and syntactical errors and adding explanatory words and phrases without properly referencing their addition. Therefore, I must point out that the English text doesn't fully represent the truly convoluted language of Khomeini. Like Karoubi and other clerics, Khomeini was especially known for defying the rules of Farsi grammar, using obsolete or difficult to understand Arabic words (Arabic being the language of Islam), or leaving one thought and starting another in the middle of a sentence. The very fact of these corrections in the English version serves as proof that Khomeini's language often hinders understanding, further leading to communication distortions.

CRITICAL DISCOURSE ANALYSIS:
CLAIMS ABOUT DEMOCRACY AND THE CLERGY

In this book, I adopt a basic definition of democracy as a political system "to the extent that its most powerful collective decision makers are selected through fair, honest, and periodic elections in which candidates freely compete for votes and in which virtually all the adult population is eligible to vote" (Huntington, 1991, 7). Schumpeter (1976) emphasizes that virtually all adult members of a population are eligible to vote when arriving at political decisions by "means of a comprehensive struggle for the people's votes" (269). In this context, as asserted by Nobel laureate Amartya Sen (1999), "democracy has complex demands, which certainly include voting and respect for election results, but it also requires the protection of liberties and freedoms, respect for legal entitlements, and the guaranteeing of free discussion and uncensored distribution of news and fair comment" (9). Central to political freedom is respect for human rights and its basic principles as outlined in the United Nation's "Universal Declaration of Human Rights."

CLERICAL LEADERSHIP AND DEMOCRATIC GOVERNANCE

Communication distortions are also present in Khomeini's promises regarding the clergy's role in the new political structure. Toward the end of 1978 when the turmoil in Iran was reaching a climax, the outspoken Ayatollah Khomeini stepped up his attacks on the monarchy. His communiqués (e'lamieh), initially circulating among a small number of his supporters—mainly militant-minded theology students—were now circulated on a much larger scale. His circle now also included many in the Bazaar and the religious intelligentsia. Despite the ideological diversity of the opposition, from Marxist guerillas of Fadayian e Khalgh to moderate liberal nationalists of the National Front, Khomeini's populist style and his charismatic spiritual aura, among a host of other circumstances, helped him emerge as the leader apparent of the movement.

The natural question that emerged in many interviews he gave was Are you going to assume any position of political power should the movement be successful? His firm response to these questions was that he would not assume a position as a leader or any other position of power in the future government (Khomeini, 2008). He pointed out that an Islamic government did not imply rule of the clergy and that "the religious authorities will not rule by themselves; they will rather supervise and direct those executive affairs. The government will rely on the people's vote and will be under public control, evaluation and criticism at all times" (2008, 4:148).

In Paris, Khomeini always maintained that the clergy and the religious authorities, including himself, were not to assume official posts in the government. However, he always remained consistent on their function: to monitor and guide the government (2008). Khomeini remained silent on the extent to which the clergy would exercise control over the government. The citizens of Iran were never informed of the extent of the "monitoring" and "guidance" the clergy was to unleash or the consequences for those who disobeyed their "guidance." The Ayatollah's speeches regarding spirituality and religious guidance resembled those of the pope, being mostly concerned with the spiritual aspects of life and entrusting to politicians matters of the state. Table 7.5 illustrates some of Khomeini's claims regarding this matter before and after the revolution.

A review of Khomeini's speeches and interviews after the revolution (see table 7.5) shows a different stance on the issue of the clergy and governance altogether. He now insisted that no one other than the clergy could run the affairs of the government and declared those who disputed this fact were apostates (*mortad*) who must be executed (2008). He harshly rejected those who believed that he and other Shi'ite clergy should leave politics to politicians and tend to religious matters as they had promised (2008).

Table 7.5. Major claims regarding clerical roles before and after the revolution

Major Claims Regarding Clerical Roles before the Revolution	*Major Claims Regarding Clerical Roles after the Revolution*
Ulama will not rule; they will rather supervise and direct those executive affairs. The government will rely on the people's vote and will be under public control, evaluation and criticism at all times.	They are saying that the clergy should go and attend to their own affairs, and leave the people and politics to them, have not done anything these past fifty years . . . I know you. I do not want to keep mentioning your names. Sit in your place! Mend your ways!
I do not want to head the government. The form of the government will be a republican one, based on people's votes.	All the clerical authorities are now involved in the government activities because they see others cannot direct the country as required by Islam.
I and other clerics will not occupy any position in the government. The duty of the clerics is to guide the governments.	They [the clergy] have their role in the government as well. They clergy should have a significant role . . . The clergy will control the actions of the president.
[Islamic government] does not mean that the religious leaders themselves are to run the government.	I have said this . . . in Najaf and Paris. If Islam emerges victorious, the clerics will go back to their business. However, when we took over, we found out that if we tell all the clerics to go to their mosques, this country would be swallowed by the U.S. or the Soviet Union.

As for the "guidance" and "monitoring" role of the clergy, it was only when Iran's post-revolution constitution was being drafted that the Ayatollah's intended meaning became clear. Ayatollah Khomeini introduced the concept of Guardianship of the Jurisprudent (Velayat-e Faqih) as a pivotal part of the new constitution. Velayat-e Faqih effectively means the leadership of the clergy, and with this declaration, Khomeini became the ultimate power in Iran. As described in chapter 5, based on that clause of the constitution, the Supreme Leader has absolute rule over all elected and non-elected members of the state. Homa Katouzian best puts this into perspective by stating that Velayat-e Faqih "merged religion and government into the formation of an ideological state" (2009, 336). Khomeini also re-introduced the Guardian Council, which was originally introduced by Sheikh Fazlolah Noori during the Constitutional Revolution as discussed in chapter 2 but was harshly rejected by the Constitutionalists. Article 91 of the Iranian constitution describes the Guardian Council as follows.

With a view to safeguard the Islamic ordinances and the Constitution, in order to examine the compatibility of the legislation passed by the Islamic Consultative Assembly with Islam, a council to be known as the Guardian Council is to be constituted with the following composition.

1. Six *adil fuqaha* (just Ulama) conscious of the present needs and the issues of the day, to be selected by the Leader, and
2. Six jurists, specializing in different areas of law, to be elected by the Islamic Consultative Assembly from among the Muslim jurists nominated by the Head of the Judicial Power" (Constitution of Islamic Republic of Iran, Article 91).

For more on the Guardian Council and its function and role in the Islamic Republic of Iran's political apparatus, please refer to chapter 5. Khomeini signed and approved the constitution despite protests by the prime minister, other high-ranking Ayatollahs, and, not surprisingly, Marxists and liberals. He not only went back on his word not to assume political office, but also made the people's vote and political will contingent on the will of God.

In the following sections I will apply CDA to the discourse of Khomeini on democratic governance and the role of the clergy in politics.

Empirical Analysis of Truth Claims

While living in Paris, Khomeini always insisted that a democracy was to replace the existing monarchy and that Islam and by extension its guardians, the clergy, was to serve only as a spiritual guide (EM98). He reassured skeptics who believed in the separation of religion and state that democracy and Islam were not only compatible but that "Islamic government means a government based on justice and democracy" (EM83). Not only that, he went one step further, declaring on many occasions that the government he was fighting for was based solely on the "people's vote" (EM77). In a speech to Iranian students and expatriates he stated that the new government would draw its legitimacy from the people's vote, and further, a state that did not meet this condition was invariably illicit: "And if at any time he acts against the wishes of the nation or against the law, the codified law, then his rule will, as a matter of course, becomes null and void and the government of Iran and the Iranian nation will sweep him aside" (EM89).

Khomeini however, remained silent on the specifics of an Islamic democracy, instead resorting to ideological and populist rhetoric. When asked for details about his vision for the new government, he used broad terms by referring to a government based on "freedom," and "justice" (EM75, EM83, EM84, EM94). At first glance, the Ayatollah's rhetoric sounds highly radical, novel, and authentic for his time, but more careful scrutiny reveals it to be ambiguous and vague on specifics. Khomeini's rhetoric appealed to the revolutionary masses so strongly that they adopted many of those catchphrases as revolutionary slogans. "Neither East nor West but Islamic Republic" was by far the most popular one and remains in use to date. However, the specifics of such a democracy are never discussed, and while the Ayatollah repeatedly reassures the public that the new government will be a democratic one, no evidence is presented to warrant the claim. Consider the following response to a reporter from Austrian Radio and Television.

> By the revolutionary uprising of the people of Iran . . . the state of democracy and Islamic Republic will be established. In this republic, there will be a national parliament consisting of truly nationally elected people, running the country's affairs. The rights of the people, especially the religious minorities, will be valued and observed (EM76).

Table 7.6 Summarizes these claims.

A closer look reveals the half-truths that riddle this statement, including the consequences of the "nationally elected" parliament passing laws deemed religiously unfit. As previously stated, the Guardian Council was established at the request of Ayatollah Khomeini to oversee the laws passed by the parliament for consistency with Shi'ite *fiqh*. A truly democratic parliament is not overseen and overruled by an appointed council of ideologues. Omissions of that nature conceal the speaker's true belief regarding the role of a national parliament and mislead the public. Claims that describe establishing a government based on "divine law" (EM82) or an Islamic government based on

Table 7.6. Empirical analysis of truth validity claims of Ayatollah Khomeini regarding democracy

Claims Regarding Changing Structures	Source	Guiding Questions to Identify Validity Claims of Truth	Evidence of Distortion
A reporter of the French newspaper, Le Figaro: But is the regime (government) you wanted a democratic one? For example, are you in favor of freedom of the press, multi-party system and freedom of parties and syndicates? Ayatollah Khomeini: We want a regime that observes all freedoms. As in every people-based government, Iran's future regime's bounds should embrace the interests of the whole community, and be particular about the dignity of the Iranian society, because offering an unrestricted society would rob men and women of their dignity.	EM75	T1. Is this argument logically consistent?	Observance of "all freedoms" is in conflict with persecuting religious minorities and political opponents such as the Marxists and others. Additionally, the speaker doesn't explain his notion of "unrestricted society," and its connection with the "dignity" of the nation.
A reporter from Austrian Radio-Television: What do you think about Iran's future changes and transformations? Ayatollah Khomeini: By the revolutionary uprising of the people of Iran, the Shah will leave, and the state of democracy and Islamic Republic will be established. In this republic, there will be a national parliament consisting of truly nationally elected people, running the country's affairs. The rights of the people, especially the religious minorities, will be valued and observed. Mutual respect will be considered in relation to foreign countries. We will not oppress anyone nor will we allow ourselves to be oppressed. The country is presently bankrupt and everything has been destroyed. By the establishment of the Islamic Republic, the real construction of the country will begin.	EM76	T2. What evidence has been provided to support these arguments?	This statement omits the consequences of the parliament passing laws deemed to be non-"Islamic." Additionally, the speaker doesn't mention the rights of secular persons and some religious minorities such as the Baha'i, who have been condemned by the Shi'a.

In an address to the Iranian Nation: And the governing system of Iran is an Islamic Republic, which maintains independence and democracy, and it will be announced according to Islamic standards and laws, and soon we will officially resort this suggestion to the people's votes, and anyone, or any group disagreeing with these triple suggestions, will not be with us and the Iranian nation.	EM77	T3. Is this argument logically consistent?	The Islamic ideology is said to be aligned with principals of democratic freedom. Islamic values are presented as the cornerstone of independence and democracy, and clerics who are specialized in Islamic Shari'a are those who will implement these values.
An Egyptian reporter: Why does Your Eminence distance yourself from cooperating with other oppositionist political forces in the struggle toward reaching your goals—for example, the communists who have the very same goal? Ayatollah Khomeini: No, we cannot accept the communists, because their danger to our country is not any less than that of the Shah's. We cannot accept them.	EM78	T4. What evidence has been provided to support these arguments?	Khomeini is simply making an unexamined claim against political opponents with whom he is ideologically at odds. He does not provide any support or evidence for communists being as "dangerous" as the Shah.
In a speech to a group of Iranian students and residents abroad: That which is clear is that all the people are saying this regime and the Shah must go and an Islamic government must be established. This is now on all the people's tongues.	EM79	T5. Is this argument true or false?	In fact, many, including the Left, the Nationalist Front, and others, simply wanted a democracy (i.e., a republic) and not an Islamic Republic.
In an interview with a reporter of Germany's Swiss language Radio-Television: If the Shah leaves and the Islamic Republic, which is the true democratic government, takes its place, these riots will end and stability will return to the country. The regime of Iran would turn into a democracy which will create stability in the region.	EM80	T6. Are the issues and options clearly defined?	Falsehoods are presented as fact. The Islamic Republic of Iran did not contribute to peace and stability in the region.

(continued)

Table 7.6. *(continued)*

Claims Regarding Changing Structures	Source	Guiding Questions to Identify Validity Claims of Truth	Evidence of Distortion
Russell Kerr: What would be the situation of human rights in Iran's future? What is your plan for the State Organization for Information and Security (SAVAK)? Ayatollah Khomeini: SAVAK? No, we won't need it. There will be no pressure. SAVAK has had nothing except oppression, suppression, and encroachment upon the rights of the people; it won't exist in the Islamic government. The Islamic government will be based on the human rights and its observance. No organization or government has cared for the human rights as much as Islam has. The head of the state in an Islamic government is equal with the lowest person.	EM81	T7. Is there an ideological claim here that is unexamined?	The claim "No organization or government has cared for the human rights as much as Islam has" is an ideological and unexamined claim. Khomeini is falsely claiming Islamic ideology is aligned with universal human rights.
In a speech to a group of Iranian students and residents abroad: In this system the government will be just, it will be a national government, a government based on the divine laws and on the consensus of the nation.	EM82	T8. Has the relevant information been communicated without distortion or omission?	The notion of "divine laws" as a guide for political practices led by a government are not defined.
A reporter of the British Time Television: May you kindly refer to some details and elaborate on the Islamic government? Ayatollah Khomeini: The Islamic government means a government based on justice and democracy and a government based on Islamic rules and laws; I do not have time to explain more right now.	EM83	T9. Are there ideological claims here that are unexamined?	There is no guarantee that Islamic ideology as expressed by Khomeini will bring justice and democracy.

"justice and democracy" (EM83) or of aligning Islamic ideology with human rights (EM81) are ideological and value-laden claims for which the speaker provides no evidence yet presents as facts. The truth is, Khomeini's Islamic ideology stands in opposition to many basic tenets of human rights. Yet such bold and broad claims universally declaring Islamic ideology on par with human rights and democratic principles misinforms and hinders further critical examination by the hearer.

While the speaker claims respect for the rights of religious minorities (EM75), he refuses to acknowledge for example Baha'is as a religious minority, thus saying that trampling over their rights is not just acceptable but necessary. The Islamic Republic of Iran's persecution, torture, and execution of those suspected of Baha'ism is well documented.[1]

Furthermore, Khomeini implies that all the people of Iran are of one faith or another, but the question that comes to mind then is what about the rights of secular citizens? How will the new regime handle the rights of its secular, agnostic, or atheist citizens? In reality, the regime Ayatollah Khomeini established treats those citizens as criminals and guilty of crimes that are severely punishable, sometimes even by death. The many thousands of Marxists and Communists who were executed, and continue to be persecuted to this date, were often sentenced to death for the crime of "waging war with God" because of their lack of religious conviction. Yet the above claims, left unexamined by the public, seemed quite innocent and progressive at the time.

Furthermore, while Khomeini remains adamant on the alignment of his version of Islamic ideology with democracy, human rights, and personal freedom (EM81, EM83, EM88) he cleverly leaves out Velayat-e Faqih, which he had proposed in his book *Islamic Government* years earlier in support of theocratic rule. As previously detailed, this is a view far from democracy and free will.

Ayatollah Khomeini's rhetoric goes beyond a democratic movement and into forming an *Ummah*. The "imagined community" (Anderson, 1991) that Khomeini calls upon the Iranians to mobilize in support of is not that of a democratic nation-state in Anderson's context. According to Anderson (1991), an Ummah predates nation-states in that it is a sacred community of the past. Ultimately, it was this that Khomeini was looking to make Iran into, not a democratic republic. This is evident in his book *Islamic Government*—subtitled *Governance of the Jurist*, which was written while he was in exile in Najaf, Iraq, in the early 1970s and in which he argues for the superiority of Islamic government over others and states that the Ummah is in need of a guardian (a jurist) to lead it on the righteous path of Islam.

Moreover, Khomeini strongly opposed the nationalist and democratic parties in Iran and later went as far as banning them from political participation.

This included the secular National Front and even the liberal Islamists of the National Freedom Movement. He said on many documented occasions that nationalism was in utter contradiction with Islamic teachings and was the root cause of all problems in the Muslim world (2008).

Ayatollah Khomeini always maintained that his intention was to unite the Muslim world under one umbrella: an Ummah. Khomeini sought an Islamic government, but in the end he settled for an Islamic Republic.

The evidence clearly point to inconsistencies, falsehoods, biases, ideologically unexamined claims, and half-truths present in the discourse of Ayatollah Khomeini that hinder understanding and lead to distorted communication.

Empirical Analysis of Sincerity Claims

One of the most striking themes that emerges when examining Ayatollah Khomeini's sincerity claims is the Islam-democracy parallel he consistently draws upon (see for example EM76, EM77, EM83, EM84, EM86, EM89). While statements such as "Islamic government is a democratic government in the true sense of the word " (EM84) suggest the newly formed government would be based on the tenets of Islam as well as democratic values, he is deftly silent on which principles would be sovereign should conflict arise. Islam, and specifically Khomeini's interpretation of it in the form of the doctrine of Guardianship of the Jurisprudent, is fundamentally at odds with democratic notions. In its essence, this doctrine renders citizens in need of custodianship and incapable of making informed decisions, thus placing them under the guardianship of a learned group (the jurists) led by the Supreme Leader. Such an understanding of the nature of human beings is in direct contrast to democratic principles that hold adult individuals as rational beings capable of reaching informed decisions in their collective interest. Therefore, while on the surface an Islamic Republic seems like a happy marriage between democracy and theocracy, in practice the leader of the revolution doesn't divulge how those glaringly contradicting philosophies might coexist. Along the same lines, we never clearly know where the speaker stands on citizenship rights. Does being a Muslim trump citizenship? Do Muslim citizens have more rights than non-Muslims? Table 7.7 details validity claims of sincerity.

Failure to further scrutinize the unholy union of democracy and Islamic theocracy was one of the most significant sources of distortion that misled the public, and fatally misdirected revolutionary efforts. Examining the discourse of Ayatollah Khomeini, one can conclude that he successfully managed to conceal his true position on which concept he considered sovereign in a political system: Islam or democracy and human rights. While it is tempting to speculate he might not have hammered out the details at that point, it is almost

Table 7.7. Empirical analysis of sincerity validity claims of Ayatollah Khomeini regarding democracy

Claims Regarding Changing Structures	Source	Guiding Questions to Identify Validity Claims of Sincerity	Evidence of Distortion
In a press conference with Reporters from Brazil, Britain, Thailand, Japan, America, etc.: Your Eminence Ayatullah, is interested in replacing the present regime with an Islamic Republic. Would such a government guarantee democratic freedoms for everyone? And what role would you personally play in such a government? Also, regarding the democratic freedoms, we would like to know whether or not the communists or the Marxists would enjoy freedom of thought and speech. Ayatollah Khomeini: The Islamic government is a democratic government in the true sense of the word, and under which, there are equally complete freedoms for all religious minorities, and everyone will be able to express his or her opinion. And Islam has the responsibility to answer every opinion, and the Islamic government will answer logic with logic. But I am not active within the government and will act the same way as I am right now, and when the Islamic government takes form, I will take a guiding role.	EM84	S1. Is this argument providing false assurances?	In reality, the rights of those citizens who did not believe in Islamic political ideology—such as Marxists, Communists, secular individuals, and many religious minorities—were trampled.
In a speech to a group of Iranian students and residents abroad: We want an Islamic government; an Islamic Republic in which popular votes will be sought and qualifications (for the head of state) will be announced. Islam delineates such qualifications.	EM85	S2. Is what is said consistent with what is implied?	Khomeini implies that the "popular vote" will be a factor but fails to explain which will be sovereign: democracy or Islamic laws.

(continued)

Table 7.7. *(continued)*

Claims Regarding Changing Structures	Source	Guiding Questions to Identify Validity Claims of Sincerity	Evidence of Distortion
A reporter with the Third World Magazine: What kind of rule will you suggest after the fall of the Shah's regime? Do you intend to save the monarchy within the framework of the constitutional law as well as the Pahlavi monarchy? What kind of government do you prefer? Ayatollah Khomeini: The nation of Iran desires an Islamic government, and I have suggested an Islamic Republic that relies on the votes of the nation. And the Pahlavi rule or the monarchial system is something that the Iranian nation has generally been rejecting within last year, and anyone who approves them is a traitor to the nation.	EM86	S3. Is the communication clear and complete?	The communication fails to make clear which set of rules reign will supreme in case of a conflict, Islam or democracy.
A reporter of the British Time Television: May you kindly refer to some details and elaborate on the Islamic government? Ayatollah Khomeini: The Islamic government means a government based on justice and democracy and a government based on Islamic rules and laws; I do not have time to explain more right now.	EM87	S4. Do metaphors and connotative words create false assurances?	What are those "Islamic rules and laws" and who defines them?
Russell Kerr: What would be the situation of human rights in Iran's future? What is your plan for the State Organization for Information and Security (SAVAK)? Ayatollah Khomeini: SAVAK? No, we won't need it. There will be no pressure. SAVAK has had nothing except oppression, suppression, and encroachment upon the rights of the people; it won't exist in the Islamic government. The Islamic government will be based on the human rights and its observance. No organization or government has cared for the human rights as much as Islam has. The head of the state in an Islamic government is equal with the lowest person.	EM88	S5. Is what is said consistent with what is implied? S6. Does the statement provide false assurances?	S5: The speaker is silent about the rights of citizens who may disagree with so-called Islamic values and observance. S6: Additionally, this statement implies the alignment of Islamic rules with those of universal human rights, thus hindering further critical examination by the hearer.

In a speech to a group of Iranian students and residents abroad: A ruler will not be able to bully his way to power and then protect his rule by the same means. No, he will come to power through the nation's vote, and it will be the nation who will protect him. And if at any time he acts against the wishes of the nation or against the law, the codified law, then his rule will, as a matter of course, becomes null and void and the government of Iran and the Iranian nation will sweep him aside.	EM89 S7. Do metaphors and connotative words promote or suppress understanding?	The term "bully" suggests the exercise of oppressive power. Terms such as "acting against the wishes," "law," and "codified law" have juridical meanings, while terms such as "null" and "void" do not.
In a speech to a group of Iranian students and residents abroad: A ruler will not be able to bully his way to power and then protect his rule by the same means. No, he will come to power through the nation's vote, and it will be the nation who will protect him. And if at any time he acts against the wishes of the nation or against the law, the codified law, then his rule will, as a matter of course, becomes null and void and the government of Iran and the Iranian nation will sweep him aside.	EM90 S8. What is missing or suppressed in the discourse?	Khomeini is omitting his theory of *Velayat e Faqih*, which considers the Supreme Leader the nation's guardian and thus above the popular vote.
French reporter of the Le Monde newspaper: You are known as the undeniable leader of the opponents. You have said that you are not going to take the reins of the government. So what would be the form of your Islamic government? Ayatollah Khomeini: We will find a candidate for presidency, who should be elected by the nation. When he is elected, we will back and support him. The laws in the Islamic government would be the Islamic laws. Personally, I will not become the president, and will refuse to accept any governmental responsibility. I will merely guide the nation, just as before.	EM91 S9. Is what is said consistent with what is assumed?	This statement implies that Khomeini will not be taking up a political role, but in actuality, he became the most powerful figure in the new regime, and in fact did take the "reins of the government."

impossible to believe one of the highest-ranking men of religion in Iran didn't already know which doctrine he would hold superior. As I have frequently mentioned in this work, he had even detailed his theory in a book a decade earlier. This creates serious doubts of the sincerity of Ayatollah Khomeini's claims that the new political system would be a seamless union of Islam and democracy in which he and the other clergy would only have a guiding role (EM98). A system based on guardianship of citizens naturally requires a guardian or a "Supreme Leader," and to think the author of this theory was not going to be active in that government (EM84, EM91) is simply naive.

Once he was back in Iran, and as soon as Khomeini realized the power he wielded over the transition process his tone changed completely and he went from supporting democracy to demanding an outright theocracy: "[Those who] are all making a big noise that there should be a democracy in the country . . . these people's ways are different from that of ours . . . Our goal is Islam" (2008, 7:405). The charismatic Ayatollah slowly began to reveal his disdain for democracy and those in favor of it. He denounced democrats, accusing them of contradicting Islam and demanding that they be crushed. He claimed that Iranians rose up not for democracy but to restore the rule of Islam (2008).

In Ayatollah Khomeini's addresses, Islam had now superseded democracy. Rule of the majority no longer mattered if it seemed to contradict Islam. Islam was no longer compatible with democracy but at odds with the very notion. Will of God and rule of Islam had replaced will of the nation. The word *democracy* was now vilified and was deemed to carry a negative stigma, and those who used it were considered anti-revolutionary by Khomeini supporters. The same word that the Ayatollah had used so often and so liberally in Paris to describe the future government was transformed into a label for immorality, corruption, Westernization, and, above all, anti-Islamism.

In the spring of 1979, during a referendum that asked Iranians to vote on whether the new regime was to be a monarchy or a republic, Khomeini prohibited use of the phrase "Islamic Democratic Republic of Iran" and mandated the use of "Islamic Republic of Iran" instead. Oriana Fallaci questioned this move in her October 1979 interview with the Ayatollah, and demanded that he explain why he disliked democracy. In response, Khomeini dismissed democracy as unnecessary.

> To begin with, the word Islam does not need adjectives such as Democratic. Precisely because Islam is everything, it means everything. It is sad for us to add another word near the word Islam which is perfect. Besides, this democracy that you like so much and that you consider so valuable, does not have a precise meaning (Fallaci, 1979, 9).

Many in the political scene, including a number of high-ranking clergy and the prime minister of the interim government, Mehdi Bazargan, did not approve of the two choices afforded by the referendum. They argued that the choices did not offer a fair representation of the people's wishes, but Khomeini insisted on this demand. Bazargan, along with many others on the left and members of the Nationalist intelligentsia, contested the nature of such a "republic" and demanded that the referendum be delayed so as to permit further debate and discussion outlining the contours of the "republic" in more detail. The referendum offered two choices for the future government: the creation of an Islamic Republic or a continuance of the current monarchy. The intelligentsia warned against restricting the choice in this way because the only other alternative to this vague "Islamic Republic" was a monarchy that had been recently ousted so strongly by the people of Iran. The opposition tried in vain to at least incorporate the word "Democratic" into the name of the Islamic Republic, but Khomeini strongly rejected this, saying, "Islamic Republic, not a word more and not a word less" (Fallaci, 1979, 9). As a result, a large faction of the opposition, including the Left, and the Socialist-Islamists who'd fought against the Shah, boycotted the referendum, declaring it theocratic and false.

Hirschheim and Klein (1994) argue that one of the main sources of communication distortions (emanating from the social context) is information-processing biases exerted by authorities and other powerful actors. These distortions hide privileged interests and power through theoretical constructions (verbal pictures) that portray a state of affairs as natural (and therefore unavoidable) or just (and therefore desirable) when in fact, it is neither. By eliminating "Democratic," from the name "Islamic Republic of Iran," Khomeini implies that democracy is unnecessary and redundant in the context of Islam since there are already such provisions in the religion. However, decades later, the Iranian experience reveals the distortion hidden in this claim. As has been made evident by the election of Khatami in 1997, the student uprising in 1999, and the 2009 Green Movement, the Iranian quest for democracy remains unfulfilled as of yet.

Furthermore, to the point above regarding hiding biased power relationships by disguising them as "natural," I will add that by placing Islam and democracy on par with each other and claiming that Islam has all the necessary provisions of democracy, Ayatollah Khomeini naturally places the clergy in a position of power and leadership since they are the learned experts in the field of Islam. On the flip side, however, by continuously assuring the public and inquiring journalists that he and the clergy would not hold political office (EM91, EM98), he is appeasing the fears that were then being stirred by some politicians and revolutionaries warning the public of the dangers of theocratic rule and of giving power to the clerics. Hence, on one hand Khomeini paves the way for theocratic rule, which inherently necessitates clerics in power, and on the other he appeases the public's genuine and growing concern about that very fact until he is in the clear and holds undisputed power.

So far, we have established the incongruence between Khomeini's intentionality and his utterances or his validity claims of sincerity. The question then becomes Why is Khomeini hiding his actual intentions regarding Islamic governance and clerical leadership behind a cloak of ambiguity and misinformation? Perhaps, I would speculate, he was aware that he would lose popular support had his undistorted vision of Supreme Leadership of the jurist as detailed in his book, become public.

Empirical Analysis Of Legitimacy Claims

As we previously discussed, the analysis of validity claims of legitimacy is partly focused on the stakeholders, i.e., who is included in the discourse, who is silenced, who is misrepresented? In his sermons and interviews, Ayatollah Khomeini frequently refers to the people of Iran as Muslims (EM92, EM94, EM95), but in reality, Iran is home to many religious minorities including Sunnis, Baha'is, Zoroastrians, Christians, Jews, and Assyrians, among others. Therefore, right from the beginning, this assumption excludes religious minorities, not to mention seculars, agnostics, and atheists, from the conversation that determines the political faith of their country. Additionally, there are yet again no specifics on how the rights of minorities, religious or otherwise, are to be guaranteed in an Islamic regime that inherently sees Muslims as superior to others. Khomeini, for example, never openly mentions that Baha'is will be punished for practicing their faith or that Marxists will be executed for refuting God. Such a hegemonic view ignores the heterogeneity of Iranian society and collapses the diverse revolutionary forces to their religious affiliation, presenting them as a uniform body of "Muslims" as defined by Ayatollah Khomeini. This is a highly problematic reading of Iranian society because of its assumptions of religious, ideological, and cultural homogeneity in a country that is anything but homogenous. Although Iran is a Shi'ite majority country and the official state religion is Ja'fari Shi'ite, many religious, ethnic, and cultural minorities have resided in the country for centuries. Iran is home to a sizeable number of Zoroastrian, Jewish, and Christian minorities (each with a seat in the parliament), as well as Baha'is, Assyrians, and Mandaiis, among others. The Muslim population is also diverse, being split between minority Sunnis and the majority Shi'ites. Sunnis of different denominations live in parts of Kurdistan, Khuzestan, and Baluchestan but also largely along the coast of the Persian Gulf in the south. Shi'ites are also split between

Twelvers (the majority), Sufis, Ismailis, and other smaller denominations. Iranians are also vastly diverse in terms of ethnicity (Armenian, Azeri, Kurds, Turkman, Baluch, etc.), language (Farsi, Arabic, Turkish, Kurdi, etc.), as well as urban/rural/nomadic (Lur, Bakhtiyari, and Qashqai tribes). Consequently, in addition to religious, ethnic, and cultural affiliations, the Iranian identity is formed against the backdrop of their socioeconomic status, political affiliation or non-affiliation, and level of education. Table 7.8 contains a summary of validity claims of legitimacy.

In this respect, I find that Ayatollah Khomeini in his discourse constructs a static, homogeneous, one-dimensional "Muslim Iranian" whose consciousness or identity is shaped by one factor only—his or her religion. I find this position questionable in that it reduces a diverse population to the universal entity of "Muslim Iranian" based on reductionist claims of religious affiliation (Mojab, 2001). This discourse reduces the socioeconomic, cultural, linguistic, religious, and political diversity of Iranian women to one simplistic unifying factor forming their identity: their supposed religion. Furthermore, Khomeini's rhetoric is based on a brand of *fiqh* interpreted within the confines of Twelvers Shi'itism, as explained above, that marginalizes many who have different religious affiliations, not to mention secular individuals. This critique then, contrary to some claims, is not to deny Muslim Iranians their agency but to question a discourse that claims egalitarian practices but marginalizes secular, Christian, Jewish, Sunni, and non-practicing Iranians, among others, many of whom actively participated in the revolution. Khomeini's construction of Iranians as a unitary "Muslim" denies many, including me, their agency.

The danger of this unitary construction of Iranian identity as "Muslim and God-fearing" (EM94) as produced by Ayatollah Khomeini inevitably materialized once the IRI had been established. In the early 1980s, thousands of political opponents were executed, their primary charge: "waging war on God" or "corruption of the earth." The real horror, however, presented itself in 1988 following the end of war with Iraq when Ayatollah Khomeini personally sanctioned the mass execution of thousands of political prisoners across Iran. The mass murders are considered an unprecedented political purge in the modern history of Iran for their sheer number[2] and the extent of the cover-up. By the direct order of Ayatollah Khomeini, members and supporters of Mojahedin Khalgh, Fadayian, Tudeh Party, and others, many of whom had already served their sentences but had not been released, appeared before a four-member panel, later referred to by the survivors as "death committees," who decided whether the prisoners should live or die. The committees decided whether the prisoner qualified as a *mortad* (apostate) or a *mohareb* (waging war against god), in which case they were sent to the gallows. While

Table 7.8. Empirical analysis of legitimacy validity claims of Ayatollah Khomeini regarding democracy

Claims Regarding Changing Structures	Source	Guiding Questions to Identify Validity Claims of Legitimacy	Evidence of Distortion
In an interview with a reporter from Le Figaro: How do you conceive of the "Islamic government"? Does this mean that the religious leaders will govern? What are the stages of this government? Ayatollah Khomeini: No; it does not mean that the religious leaders themselves are to run the government. They will lead the people in providing for the needs of Islam, and as the vast majority of the people are Muslims, the Islamic government will enjoy their support and will have them to rely on.	EM92	L1. Whose political legitimacy is affirmed? Who is excluded?	There is no guarantee or evidence that religious leaders won't run for government.
And the governing system of Iran is an Islamic Republic, which maintains independence and democracy; and it will be announced according to Islamic standards and laws, and soon we will officially resort this suggestion to the people's votes, and anyone, or any group disagreeing with these triple suggestions, will not be with us and the Iranian nation.	EM93	L2. Who is marginalized or excluded from the discourse?	Alternative points of view and non-Muslims are excluded from the conversation.
In a speech to a group of Iranian students and residents abroad: We want a divine rule that conforms with the desires and choice of the people and God's laws, and a rule that is in accordance with God's will is also concordant with the people's wants. The people are Muslim and God-fearing and when they see that the government wants to implement and execute justice they will support it. God wants justice to prevail among the people.	EM94	L3. Who is speaking and who is left out?	A Shi'ite Muslim clergyman is speaking and representing "the people" as "Muslims," thus he is marginalizing those who are not of that faith.

EM95	An Arab reporter of Al-Bayraq publication: Your Eminence Ayatullah, can the movement that you are introducing, along with the emotional and popular values it holds, come to power by itself in the name of the majority of Iranians, without the involvement of the leftists and the traditional oppositions? And if they hold a referendum today, based on the slogans you raise, what percentage of the votes will you earn? Ayatollah Khomeini: The absolute majority of the Iranian nation is Muslim and will vote for what we call for. The whole nation does not want the Shah. Can't ninety percent of the Iranians who are Muslims, establish an Islamic Republic, as a majority in the society?	L4. Which stakeholders are marginalized? L5. Whose interests are being represented and who is left out?	L4: The speaker ascribes to himself the authority to dismiss as illegitimate opposing voices such as those of "leftists and the traditional opposition," a dismissal he bases on faith. L5: The speaker doesn't mention the rights and the faith of the minorities in an Islamic country. Where do they stand in deciding the faith of their country? Does being a Muslim trump citizenship?
EM96	A reporter of the British Time Television: May you kindly refer to some details and elaborate on the Islamic government? Ayatollah Khomeini: The Islamic government means a government based on justice and democracy and a government based on Islamic rules and laws; I do not have time to explain more right now.	L6. Whose interests are being represented and who is left out? L7. Who is speaking, who is silent, what are their interests?	6- Oppressive for religious minorities (non Islamic Shia) and for those with "modern" interpretations of Islam (e.g., the separation of religion and state) and the secular fraction of society. 7- An Islamic ideologist is speaking with vague definition of democracy and its relation to political Islam, leaving out his self interest in this system.

(continued)

Table 7.8. *(continued)*

Claims Regarding Changing Structures	Source	Guiding Questions to Identify Validity Claims of Legitimacy	Evidence of Distortion
Washington, AFP: Ayatullah Khomeini announced that he will establish a new government to take the position of the Bakhtiyar government and the emergence of an Islamic government in Iran is near. Answering the question, whether he will become—"Iran's powerful man," Ayatullah Khomeini said that he will neither have the same scope of powers of the Shah, nor will become the premier, but that he will maintain his role of guiding people.	EM97	L8. Whose political legitimacy is affirmed? Who is excluded?	It is not clear what happens if decisions and acts of the government or parliament conflict with the counsel of the spiritual leader.
A reporter of the Singapore's Strait Times newspaper: If I have understood correctly, you and your followers want the ouster of the Shah and see the future of Iran only under a complete divine government, which means an Islamic government which is run by a religious leader. Do you say that ideally you should replace the Shah at the apex of the power structure, that Iran be run in a more humanistic manner and directed by the Islamic principles? Ayatollah Khomeini: I and the other clerics will not occupy any position in the government. The duty of the clerics is to guide the governments. But we want the ouster of the Shah and want to replace this corrupt regime with the judicious Islamic government and victory will be ours.	EM98	L9. What are the stakes and interests of those involved or excluded?	The claim that the new government will be Islamic and should act as an Islamic government, as well as Khomeini's claim of not influencing the decision-making process, is not warranted.

the regime continues to deny the killings, Grand Ayatollah Montazeri, who was Khomeini's deputy at the time, sounded the alarm but was dismissed from his post and placed under house arrest until his death a few months after the 2009 uprisings. According to survivors, while the Mojahedin were asked to recant and condemn and expose their comrades, the secular leftists were asked an additional set of questions.

The questions focused on the secular leftists' willingness to practice Islam in the manner decreed by the government. Leftist sympathizers were asked whether they were Muslim, whether they prayed, and whether they accepted the Islamic Republic. Many of the men who refused to pray were executed; others were whipped. The female leftists who refused to pray were whipped five times a day, corresponding with prayer times, until they agreed to pray. Many committed suicide. (Iran Human Rights Document Center, n.d.).

This is simply one example of the death and destruction caused by the singular homogenous construction of what it means to be an Iranian as evident in the revolutionary discourse of Ayatollah Khomeini.

Empirical Analysis of Comprehensibility Claims

As previously discussed, Ayatollah Khomeini and the Iranian clergy in general have a particular style of communication that is not always coherent and clear to a lay audience. A study of the statements of Ayatollah Khomeini regarding democracy and clerical rule reveals that the speaker often leaves the audience to decode significant details in his speech. While Khomeini often engages in ample symbolism and metaphors, he seldom explains them to the audience and makes little effort to provide clarity, thus causing confusion and leaving the audience with a burdensome level of detail to decode: "We believe that noble understanding of Islam will lead us toward advancement of a society which is very talented, has a lot of manpower and social justice" (EM99).

Concepts such as "noble understanding of Islam," a government that is the "shadow of God and is the extension of His hand," and "divine laws" (EM103) are metaphorical and open to various interpretations, and their meaning is missing from the Ayatollah's discourse. Likewise, in an interview with *Le Monde*, when he is asked to elaborate on the nature of the republic he is proposing, he says, "The method of the republic is the same way as elsewhere" (EM104). We the audience, however, are unclear on the notion of "elsewhere," leaving us puzzled as to the meaning of this mysterious place. Is the speaker referring to the French form of republicanism? Or the American form? Or any other form? The fact is we, as his audience, are unclear because this utterance is incomplete, and that is precisely the problem with distorted rhetoric. Table 7.9 Summarizes those claims.

Table 7.9. Empirical analysis of comprehensibility validity claims of Ayatollah Khomeini regarding democracy

Claims Regarding Changing Structures	Source	Guiding Questions to Identify Validity Claims of Comprehensibility	Evidence of Distortion
A reporter of the French newspaper, Le Figaro: In fact, which is the direction of your actions, and what kind of regime do you have in mind to replace the Shah's? Ayatollah Khomeini: Keeping the Shah's regime is indisputably unacceptable. We have always been against it. "Overthrow" is the unchangeable target of our resistance. Besides, it is not the legal form of the regime that counts, but rather its content. An Islamic Republic can naturally come into consideration, because we believe that noble understanding of Islam will lead us toward that advancement of a society which is very talented, has a lot of manpower and social justice. Before anything, we have set our hopes on the social contents of the future political regime.	EM99	C1. Is the communication clear and without confusion?	The meaning of "noble understanding of Islam" is unclear. Also, we don't know who provides that understanding. The audience is also unclear on how that understanding leads to the development of a political system and society.
A delegate with Amnesty International: Would the Marxists have freedom of speech and thought under the Islamic Republic? Would they have freedom of choosing a career? Ayatollah Khomeini: a) In the Islamic Republic, everybody would be free to hold any kind of belief, but they won't be free to cause sabotage. b) In Islam, the right of anyone to choose a career is protected in accordance with the legal regulations.	EM100	C2. Is this utterance complete and intelligible?	The speaker leaves the audience to decode what he means by such terms as "free," "sabotage," and political protection "in accordance with legal regulations."

A reporter of the Lebanese An-Nihar newspaper: What is the nature of your desired Islamic Republic? And what are its features? Ayatollah Khomeini: The nature of the Islamic Republic is such that it will be established under the conditions set forth by Islam for government, relying on the public votes of the nation and enforcing the Islamic laws.	EM101	C3. Is the level of detail too burdensome for the reader or hearer?	Too many messages are left for the audience to decode such as "set forth by Islam for government," and the nature of that relationship with the public's vote. Which "Islamic laws" will be enforced, to what extent, and how?
An Egyptian reporter: In Your Eminence Ayatullah's opinion, what is the quality and nature of the Islamic Republic which you propose? And what is the difference between that and the Islam observed in the constitution? In the plans for an Islamic state, is more attention paid to social or political affairs of Islam? Does the precise execution of Islam's commands mean, for example, the amputation of the hand of a thief from now on? What is your perception? Ayatollah Khomeini: What is intended is that when a system is against the system of Islam in every aspect, such as its culture, its army as well as its economy and politics, that system must be overturned and the Islamic system established. Once the Islamic system becomes established, there would be a parliament, the votes of the members of the parliament. . . . We intend to enforce all Islamic commands and we would practically prove that Islamic laws are progressive and more than arresting and releasing a thief.	EM102	C4. Is the communication clear and without confusion?	Khomeini does not provide a clear answer to the questions.

(continued)

Table 7.9. *(continued)*

Claims Regarding Changing Structures	Source	Guiding Questions to Identify Validity Claims of Comprehensibility	Evidence of Distortion
In a speech to a group of Iranian students and residents abroad: The Islamic government we are talking about, that is, the government we want is one which the people desire and one to which God, the Blessed and Exalted, could say that these people who pledged their allegiance to you had pledged their allegiance to God. It should be a governing body allegiance to which is allegiance to Allah. In wars, when an arrow is shot, God will say: "When thou threwest (a handful of dust), it was not thy act, but Allah's," meaning that the hand that threw the dust was God's hand. The government that we want is one which is the shadow of God and is the extension of His hand; a government that is divine. The government that we want is such a government. Our wish is for a governing body to come to power that will not transgress against divine laws.	EM103	C5. Is the communication sufficiently clear?	Despite the metaphors and the symbolism, the details of the Khomeini's intended Islamic Government are still unclear. Concepts such as a government that is the "shadow of God" and an "extension of His hand," as well as "divine laws," are confusing, unclear, and too burdensome for an audience to decode.

A reporter of the French Le Monde newspaper: Your Eminence declares that an Islamic Republic must be established in Iran, and this doesn't make much sense for us French because a republic can be established without religious grounds. What do you think? Is your republic based on socialism, constitutionalism, elections, democracy, or what? Ayatollah Khomeini: As to the republic, it means as it is elsewhere although, this republic is based on a constitutional law, which is the law of Islam. We say Islamic Republic because the terms of the elected, as well as the commands enforced in Iran, would all based on Islam. However, the choice is the nation's, and the method of the republic is the same way as elsewhere.	EM104	C6. Is the communication complete?	"Elsewhere" is not defined. The reader or hearer is left to decode what "elsewhere" means and how an Islamic democracy will compare to a democracy of "elsewhere."
A reporter of the British Time Television: May you kindly refer to some details and elaborate on the Islamic government? Ayatollah Khomeini: The Islamic government means a government based on justice and democracy and a government based on Islamic rules and laws; I do not have time to explain more right now.	EM105	C7. Is the communication sufficiently intelligible? C8. Is the level of detail too burdensome for the reader or hearer?	C7: The claim equates democracy with Islamic rules and laws without explaining how these laws and rules map onto democracy. C8: Level of detail is burdensome for religious minorities (e.g., non-Islamic Shia) and for those with a modern interpretation of Islam (e.g., separation of religion and state) as well as for secular hearers of readers.

Furthermore, even when asked pointed and direct questions to provide detail regarding his notion of Islamic government, Khomeini avoids providing sufficiently intelligible answers.

> A reporter of the British Time Television: May you kindly refer to some details and elaborate on the Islamic government?
>   Ayatollah Khomeini: The Islamic government means a government based on justice and democracy and a government based on Islamic rules and laws; I do not have time to explain more right now (EM83).

Such claims hazily associate democratic principles with laws of Islam, especially Khomeini's political interpretation of those laws, without describing how they map onto a democratic state. Despite Khomeini's repeatedly being asked to explain the enigma of an Islamic republic or an Islamic democracy (EM76, EM77, EM84–86, EM93, EM102, EM104, among others), we never once receive a coherent, well-detailed answer, leaving us to conclude these validity claims are primarily made to justify power dominance in the future.

In summary, evidence of communication distortion is widely present when testing for validity claims of comprehensibility in the discourse of Ayatollah Khomeini. His language is often vague and his communication is incomplete, leaving the audience with a considerably unintelligible amount of detail to decode.

STRUCTURES OF SIGNIFICATION AND LEGITIMATION

Similar to the discourse of the Green leaders, the discourse of Ayatollah Khomeini largely points to structures of domination such as the political system, governing bodies, and the constitution. Moreover, Ayatollah Khomeini's rhetoric also touches on religion as a structure of domination. He is the father of the Islamic revolution for legitimizing Islam as the guiding authority and ideology of the Iranian government. However, there is very little evidence to suggest any attempt by the Ayatollah to alter structures of signification.

THE IMPACT AND IMPLICATIONS OF THE DISCOURSE OF AYATOLLAH KHOMEINI

There is ample evidence presented in this chapter to suggest the discourse of Ayatollah Khomeini was directed toward systematically distorted communication and not communicative action aimed at mutual understanding. The validity claims are often proven false, the evidence points to communication distortion, and overall the conditions of constructive rational discourse oriented toward the mutual goal of building a democratic nation are broken. Violations of validity claims that then lead to a verdict of systematically distorted communication are explained in more detail in the next chapter.

The question, remains however, what was the impact of the Ayatollah's rhetoric? In other words, how did Khomeini's distorted communication impact the 1979 revolution and by extension the Green Movement? One conclusion to be drawn here is that the impact of this type of goal-oriented communication in practice translated into the oppressive political, social, and religious structures established by the new regime. A constitution that not only concentrates political and economic power in the hands of the clergy and pro-regime, Islamist forces but also justifies inequality, prejudice, and marginalization of minorities, renders women second-class citizens, and severely suppresses freedom of expression is without dispute Ayatollah Khomeini's legacy. Khomeini's distorted revolutionary discourse paved the way for him to consolidate his political power and establish his vision in the many oppressive structures that continue to exist to date—the very same structures against which the Green Movement protests occurred, and within which the Green Movement leaders operated.

NOTES

1. For more on Iran's treatment of Baha'is, read Human Right's Watch's latest report here www.hrw.org/world-report/2016/country-chapters/iran.

2. While Amnesty International recorded over two thousand cases of execution during that wave, Ayatollah Montazeri claims the numbers exceeds thirty thousand.

8

The Impact and Implications of Speech: An Overview of the Findings

The empirical analysis discussed in the previous chapter illustrates the use of systematically distorted communication by both Ayatollah Khomeini and the leaders of the Green Movement. In this chapter, I will offer a theoretical explanation of the impact and implications of distorted communication for the Green Movement as based on the structuration-communicative action framework developed in chapter 4. While my primary focus is on the impact and implications of speech in the Green Movement, applying the framework allows us to draw further inferences regarding the Reform Movement and the state of civil society as well as the public sphere in Iran. Thus, this chapter elaborates on the findings of this project and discusses their impact on the survival of the 2009 uprising.

IMPACTS AND IMPLICATIONS OF DISTORTED DISCOURSE

My analysis of the communications of Mousavi and Karoubi regarding changing the two structures of the economy and patriarchy uncovered frequent violation of validity claims of truth, sincerity, legitimacy, and comprehensibility, thus revealing an orientation to success rather than mutual understanding. Furthermore, it is my contention that the Green leaders engage in systematically distorted communication since the evidence suggests they are participating in self-deception. As the evidence in chapters 3 and 6 reveal, the interests and aspirations of the three main categories of actors in the movement often stand in contrast to each other, and very little is done to bridge that gap (RQ4 and RQ5). The evidence indicates that those contrary aspirations are never reconcilable, especially as far as the Reformers and civil society groups are concerned. In other words, the leaders of the movement had no plans to achieve mutual understanding when it came to matters so important to civil society groups as women's rights. Thus, they engaged in systematically distorted communication to conceal their true intentions and generate popular support to get elected to office.

As described in chapter 4, unconscious deception or systematically distorted communication requires that at least one party engage in self-deception. The two leaders along with their wives have been under house arrest since February 2011 and under strict supervision. Prior to that, once the protests erupted, they were publicly discredited and attacked by the ruling party and excluded from politics for refuting the official recount results. Considering all they had to lose—their freedom and their social and political status—along with the humiliation, character assassination, and threat of execution they continue to face, leads me to conclude that at some level they believed in what they communicated to the people, however distorted it may have been. Consequently, although we can never be absolutely certain of what goes on in other actors' minds, based on critical hermeneutics, we can interpret the congruency between an actor's utterances and his or her actions, and the actions of the two leaders of the Green Movement speak to self-deception rather than manipulation. Thus, it is my contention that based on the evidence above, the language of Mousavi and Karoubi is largely systematically distorted communication.

Similar arguments can be made for the discourse of Ayatollah Khomeini during the 1979 revolution because the evidence suggests he too is engaging in systematically distorted communication. This demonstrates a long legacy of communication distortions from the beginning of the Islamic Republic and particularly at such pivotal moments as mass uprisings. Khomeini's rhetoric and misleading communication managed to channel the revolutionary zeal and democratic aspirations of the Iranian people into creating a theocratic regime. Similar tactics were employed by the leaders of the Green Movement in order to contain the movement and direct its energy toward achieving their own goals: securing the presidency. In other words, while a certain degree of goal orientation goes into political campaigns, systematically distorted communication, which is a particularly destructive form of strategic action, seems to be the thriving and preferred mode of political communication during social movements in Iran.

As outlined in chapter 4, totalitarian regimes such as the IRI rely on ideology, e.g., the Shi'ite doctrine of Velayat-e Faqih, to dominate the population. The IRI's hegemonic tendencies thus limit freedom of speech, critical debate, and rational argumentation where the only force is the power of the better argument aimed at mutual understanding and not furthering the Islamic ideology of the regime. To put this in Habermasian terms, Islamic ideology has colonized the public sphere in Iran with systematically distorted communication. Perhaps if freedom of speech were not so limited, journalists and other social actors would have been able to publicly scrutinize the validity claims of the Green leaders and point to the distortions present in their communication. And had those leaders not been concerned with crossing the multitude of red lines protected by the regime, they might have put forth arguments that would present their message in a better light. For example, it would have been easier to question and receive an answer from Ms. Rahnavard regarding her attire (that is to say, forced hijab) and its contradictory nature with reference to women's rights when she brought up the subject of furthering that cause.

In other words, the evidence suggests the two leaders of the Green Movement are expressing a somewhat altered version of the official regime narrative through systematically distorted communication. Additionally, the real and structural violence of the Iranian regime, including the harsh consequences hindering free critical debate, make it difficult for the citizenry, scholars, and other stakeholders to investigate the validity of the Green leaders' claims, uncovering communication distortions and unexamined convictions (ideologies) present in their message.[1]

However, while investigating the claims of the Green politicians proves to be challenging in the Iranian public space, social actors may still examine political communications directed at them with respect to the four validity claims. Critical Theory posits that

1. Intelligent social actors are not mere receptacles of meaning directed at them but actively process, interpret, and enact meaning from what they hear or read.
2. Social actors are not restricted to merely interpreting the messages they receive for consistency with mutual understanding, i.e., how well one actor comes to understand what the other means. They can also be critical of the messages they receive.
3. Social actors accomplish this by engaging in cycles of critical reflection (Giddens, 1984; Habermas, 1984; Ngwenyama and Lee, 1997); that is, they continually assess one or more validity claims present in the speaker's discourse against the social context of their action.
4. Therefore, the inference of the social actor's reflection is not always mutual understanding and could lead to a more critical outcome in which he or she can emancipate themselves from distorted communicative acts (Ngwenyama, 1991).

In the context of the Green Movement, this means protesters in their role as engaged readers or listeners (social actors) participating in the uprising possessed the capability to not merely achieve mutual understanding with the leaders of the movement and to comprehend the political communications directed at them but to assess the truthfulness, clarity, sincerity, and legitimacy of those communications over a period of time. The framework suggests knowledgeable social actors critically examine the messages directed at them within their sociopolitical context. We know the supporters of the movement were engaged in the discourse and knowledgeable of their sociopolitical context because they would not otherwise be participating in the uprising. Ngwenyama and Lee (1997) state that the social context "serves as a reference schema that enables actors to act and to interpret the actions of others" (152). Through a mutual stock of knowledge (shared norms, laws, rules, customs, and traditions) as well as material and non-material resources,[2] the social context affords the actors the potential and possibilities of social action.

The concept of reflexive monitoring of action (chapter 4) defined by Giddens (1984) reminds us that social actors continually monitor and critically reflect on their own actions, their consequences, the actions of others, and the domain of action within which they operate. It is due to this subconscious and continuous monitoring, and during critical reflection on all that is happening, from receiving the messages of their leaders to facing the consequences of protesting on the streets and enduring the violence directed at them, that doubt arises and there is a breakdown in communication. Doubt arises when actors fail to establish congruency between the messages they receive and their mutual stock of knowledge and decide, although not always consciously, to test the validity claims. In the case of the Green Movement, through critical reflection and in a process similar to that detailed in chapter 6, the protesters tested the communications of their leaders and detected evidence of distortion such as half-truths, unclear language, and insincerity. At some point in the life of the movement, they too, as intelligent social actors, were able to critically analyze Zahra Rahnavard's brand of women's rights and Karoubi's promises of economic prosperity and detect evidence of systematic distortion in those messages.

According to the theory of communicative action (Habermas, 1984), breakdown in communication occurs when doubts about the validity claims implied in a social action are raised and an actor fails to observe orientation to mutual understanding. For example, at some point in the Green Movement, the protesters realized their aspirations were not aligned with those of their leaders and that what was promised was not going to be delivered.

A FOCAL POINT OF THE MOVEMENT

Research shows that one such pivotal moment, during which a breakdown in communication gave rise to doubts about the movement, was the shooting death of Neda Agha Soltan on June 20, eight days after the elections.[3]

In a study of the causes of demobilization in the Iranian Green Movement, Kevan Harris demonstrates that the largest protest day of the movement was June 15, three days after the elections, in which an estimated 1–3 million participated (2012).[4]

More significantly, Harris notes that "the post-election uprising quickly spread beyond initial protest participants, peaked only a few days after the election, and then narrowed to a generally consistent size that continued to sporadically punctuate the post-election order" (2012, 436). June 20, the day Neda Agha Soltan was shot, acted as a focal point in the movement after which participation sharply declined and demobilization of the masses set in. A focal point is a temporal context that instigates action within a crowd in the absence of direct communication because it appears to be the logical choice (Schelling, 1960, 57). Collins (Goodwin, Jasper, and Polletta, 2001, 41) adds that at this point in social movements individuals "decide" which route to take and which coalition to support, that of the insurgents or of the status quo. The logical choice for the Green Movement protestors here seemed to be dispersion and, consequently, demobilization, essentially returning to the status quo. Thus, the evidence suggests Neda's death acted as a focal point of the movement at which point protesters were forced to weigh their convictions about the movement against the consequences of continued participation, and large numbers decided against further street action.

In short, the supporters of the Green Movement became aware of distortions in the discourse of the movement as knowledgeable actors essentially do. Critical monitoring and reflection thus empowered the protesters to emancipate themselves from distorted communicative acts. Some of the practical manifestations of emancipation from the distorted communication stemming from the movement's ideological discourse was for protesters to withdraw their support from the uprising, to stop participating in the protests, and, essentially, to become disillusioned with the cause. According to the above data, Neda's shooting provided an occasion for protesters to begin weighing the consequences of their participation in the protests against what they were promised, and they deemed the cost of participation too high. This is evident in the downward shift in public presence that took place after June 20. Therefore, when evidence of communication distortion surfaced and disillusionment with the direction of the movement gradually set in, the protesters were no longer willing to endure the harsh consequences of further participation (being beaten, arrested, jailed, or killed) in a cause that was not aligned with their goals. Reflexive monitoring is critical in the sense that it enables the actor to "free himself not only from false or unwarranted beliefs and assumptions about the other person or her action, but also from constraints to enacting coherent meaning of the situation and taking appropriate counteraction" (Ngwenyama and Lee, 1997).

In other words, because the protesters were engaged audiences, the distortions in the communication of the leaders of the movement became evident to the protesters and indicated that the movement no longer embodied their aspirations. While they originally believed they were fighting for values such as democracy, women's rights, transparent and fair elections, economic development, etc., at some point they realized these values were not going to be achieved by what was being promised by Mousavi and Karoubi. The government was cracking down on the participants harshly by beating, arresting, and even shooting them down. Many were jailed, raped, and tortured while under arrest. Some were barred from going to school (particularly university students) or continuing in their profession (lawyers, doctors, etc.). Naturally, disillusionment with the movement meant they were no longer willing to face the violence and severe consequences they had previously endured, and thus protesters gradually abandoned the movement and stopped participating. If the protestors had still believed in the cause of the movement and trusted it would help them in their struggle for democracy, they would have continued to fight and the Green uprising would not have faltered.

While I don't intend to imply that the movement faltered solely because of demobilization, I suggest that the systematic communication distortions of the leaders of the movement contributed to its demise considerably. Additionally, not all actors follow the same path to emancipation. Some fail to detect communicative distortions altogether, while others engage in self-deception despite questioning the truth of what is being communicated, and yet others become disillusioned and withdraw their support. To this date, there are those who continue to view the path offered by Mousavi and Karoubi and the Reform Front in general as the only viable roadmap to democracy and to achieving a more open and free state in Iran. This is despite both leaders' numerous assertions that they were fighting to save the regime and uphold its values. Nevertheless, in my view the movement lost a significant share of its support once it was increasingly seen to be "more of the same old regime." Building on the above discussion, I am led to draw two conclusions: (1) the Reform strategy currently doesn't seem like a plausible alternative, and (2) the absence of a strong civil society further feeds into the confusion created by the communication distortions of both sides. I will discuss both as follows.

THE REFORM PHILOSOPHY AS AN ALTERNATIVE

The Reform philosophy as an alternative to the dominant regime narrative that has been put forth for two decades doesn't seem to have the ability to serve the purpose of providing a plausible alternative to that narrative. Reformers have been trying to use the presidential elections platform since 1997 to legally present and implement their ideas within the red-lined boundaries of the regime to claiming that would ultimately steer the nation toward democracy. However, presidential elections in Iran are not a true exercise of democracy where critical debate takes place in the public sphere and subsequently the citizenry speak their choice by popular vote. As discussed previously, the Guardian Council (Shoraye Negahban) and the Assembly of Experts (Majlis e Khobregan)—two unelected bodies, among others— already limit the people's choice and override democracy by vetting and hand selecting presidential candidates to ensure their adherence and loyalty to the regime and its ideologies. Therefore, this practice proves to be nothing more than an exercise in pseudo-democracy where elections are held every four years but the citizens don't truly have a vote. Perhaps more importantly, the distortions gripping the communications of Mousavi and Karoubi make it difficult to discern their agenda, to put it in Western terms. My analysis shows that once put to the test, most of their promises are vague at best, leading the audience into interpretations that may not be true, and do not offer solid blueprints and plans. For example, although women's rights were a major election issue, there was very little in solid plans and programs offered to the electorate to elaborate on how the two candidates would set about fulfilling that promise. As the Green leaders represent the hopes and aspirations of the Reform Movement, their communications can be extended to those of the movement's, which is how I am able to draw my conclusions. Furthermore, reviewing the constitutional framework of the country and past events tells us that the office of the president is not the most powerful institution in the Iranian political hierarchy. The Supreme Leader holds the ultimate power and thus dictates policy and ensures its adherence to the official regime lines.

Therefore, the systematically distorted communication of Mousavi and Karoubi, the two figureheads embodying the Reform Front's ideals, obstruct our perception and hinder the process of reaching mutual understanding. It is difficult for us, the audience, to determine where they stand on many controversial issues. In other words, what reforms do they plan to implement to the system? For example, is removing mandatory hijab on their agenda? Second, the structural limitations of the Islamic Republic, at least at this point in time, don't leave much room for reform as that would mean some of the political powerhouses would lose their tight grip on the nation. Thus, while I am making this observation independent of presenting an alternative, the evidence overwhelmingly suggests that the Reform Front is not a viable political alternative for the emancipation of the Iranian public. I, however, concede that the Reformers are the embodiment of the hopes and aspirations of a large segment of Iranian society that is craving for change, for more freedom, and for a more open and transparent society. Nevertheless, the absence of a free and open public sphere where ideas can be freely debated has helped, over the years, to reinforce the illusion of reform in the Iranian social and political arena.

ABSENCE OF A STRONG CIVIL SOCIETY

On another note, the absence of a strong civil society that could advocate and lead critical debate in the public sphere helps reinforce the illusion of reform in the Iranian social and political arena. Strong civic engagement helps consolidate democracy by advocating for open and free debate that uncovers communication distortions, contradictions, and incongruences between speech and action on one hand and mediate between the state and people on the other hand to reduce real and structural violence. But since the Iranian political apparatus systematically restricts the activities of nongovernmental organizations and discourages civic engagement beyond what is allowed within the confines of the regime ideology, Iranian civil society has never had a chance to flourish. Ideally, with the help of civil society members such as the One Million Signatures Campaign, citizens could uncover discrepancies in the speech and actions of the political elite such as those under study here. However, in the absence of any public opportunity to analyze the communications and promises of political leaders, concepts such as gender equity and women's rights are largely devoid of their intended meaning and merely utilized as tools for furthering an ideology—in this case that of the IRI and by extension the Reformist doctrine.

Moreover, both Green leaders engage in a rhetorical strategy of repetition of positive opinions and campaign promises (e.g., change, women's rights, economic growth) to establish them in the taken-for-granted lifeworlds of the masses as established facts. There is, however, very little in the data to support many of these opinions and promises. Yet by repeating them over and over again in the course of a few months, Mousavi and Karoubi and their respective campaigns managed to establish these goals as attainable within the current regime framework. The absence of a strong civil society and free press has heightened this situation since those largely unsubstantiated promises remain unexamined, and because they are powerful statements made in a systematically distorted discourse, they manage to colonize the lifeworlds of Iranian individuals.

It is clear the data overwhelmingly support an argument that the structures of domination are largely targeted, which speaks volumes for the dominating nature of a totalitarian regime such as that of the IRI. This argument is further evident in the fact that while economic structures dominated the election campaign discourse, with social justice and class differences being discussed and candidates paying lip service to women's causes, women are largely excluded from the economic debate. Social justice and gender equality are practically meaningless if half the population is excluded from a conversation that essentially determines women's economic power. Thus, colonizing the public consciousness with half-truths and suppressing understanding by means of distorted communication merely hinders emancipation from an oppressive government rather than brings about the change so often promised by Mousavi and Karoubi and other Reformists. In other words, based on the evidence, the two leaders are essentially another tool to broadcast the ideology of a hegemonic regime. The public sphere tends to be colonized by those with privileged access, i.e., politicians. Similarly, the Reformers colonize the Iranian political arena by systematically distorting its political communications and thus obstructing the consciousness of the general public on their path to democracy. The next section will discuss the public sphere and its implications in Iran in more detail.

THE PUBLIC SPHERE IN THE IRANIAN CONTEXT

Iran's campaign for democracy is a lengthy one dating back to the Constitutional Revolution at the turn of the twentieth century (Katouzian, 1998; Kamrava, 2008; Jahanbegloo, 2013) when the intellectual elite drafted the country's first constitution in an attempt to limit the state's absolute and arbitrary exercise of power, subjecting its practices to a legal framework and paving the way for a more representative government. The 1979 Islamic Revolution and the 2009 Green Movement were a continuation of the same quest to establish a democratic government dominated by the rule of law and prevalence of justice. The public sphere is the cornerstone of a democratic society for it stands up to state authority through open debate that forms public opinion, thus critically steering the political establishment in a democratic direction. In the absence of a critical public sphere, democracy suffers as the political elite, special interest groups, and capitalist interests colonize that space, strategically influencing social and political decisions making without being subject to the deliberation of the citizens and the scrutiny of critically developed public opinion.

As described in chapter 4, freedom of expression and political participation without fear or threat of reprisal are fundamental to the concept of a free and flourishing public sphere. Furthermore, an independent judiciary to mediate between the state and citizens at times when conflict about those rights arises is imperative to the survival of the public sphere, protecting individuals and their freedoms from state encroachment. However, it is my contention that these conditions are not satisfied in the Iranian context as is evident by the large number of journalists, civil society activists, and political figures held in Iranian prisons essentially for overstepping state-sanctioned lines of discussion. Considering that these fundamental conditions are broken, it is my belief that a public sphere, based on the definition expressed by Habermas, does not exist in the Iranian context despite the multitude of references alluding to the concept in the literature in the field of Iran Studies.

Broken Conditions and Principles of the Public Sphere in Iran

State authority in Iran, despite limited provisions in the constitution, increasingly infringes on the citizens' right to freedom of expression (including freedom of speech and press) and continues to restrict expression via legal avenues as well as classified ones. Journalists, bloggers, civil rights activists, lawyers, trade unionists, artists, women's rights activists, minorities (ethnic and religious), LGBTQ members, and human rights advocates are frequently arrested, prosecuted, punished, and even put to death for crossing government sanctioned red lines. The UN's special rapporteur's report on the situation of human rights in Iran states,

> As of 14 January 2014, at least 895 "prisoners of conscience" and "political prisoners" were reportedly imprisoned. This number includes 379 political activists, 292 religious practitioners, 92 human rights defenders (including 50 ethnic rights activists), 71 civic activists, 37 journalists and netizens, and 24 student activists (United Nations, 2014).

Moreover, freedom of expression assumes a secular backdrop, and the Islamic Republic of Iran, as evident in its very name, is a religious state whose laws and regulations must all be aligned with a specific reading of Islamic teachings. Although republicanism implies some degree of representative government, that aspect of the Islamic Republic of Iran's constitution is crippled by Shi'ite philosophies. According to Article 99 of the Iranian constitution, the Guardian Council, an appointed body consisting of six clerics (faqihs) appointed by the Supreme Leader and six jurists appointed by the Majlis is empowered by the principle of approbation supervision, as discussed in chapter 3. Among other things, this principle means that legislation passed by the Majlis has no legal status without the approval of the Guardian Council, which scrutinizes each bill based on its adherence to Islamic law. Additionally, approbation supervision empowers the Guardian Council to veto legislation passed by the elected representatives of the people if that legislation is deemed to be in conflict with a strict reading of Shi'ite Islam. Moreover, the religious oversight embedded in the Iranian constitution constrains the Majlis, which is among the main institutions of the public sphere, essentially stripping it of its role in providing a platform for open debate of matters of public interest. Consequently, in an environment where any and all aspects of an Iranian citizen's life are bound by religious boundaries, freedom of speech and public use of reasoned argumentation are significantly restricted.

The Habermasian public sphere is founded on the principles of communicative rationality, detailed in chapter 3, that demand public use of reasoned argumentation, but when we juxtapose that with a regime that has legislated faith and demands undisputed belief in religious principles, the logical conclusion is that the public sphere cannot survive under these conditions.

Next, I'd argue that freedom of assembly and political participation is equally constrained. Presidential, parliamentary, and city council candidates, to name a few, are subject to approval by the Guardian Council and other monitoring bodies for adherence to Islam. However, in reality this process is an arbitrary process that gauges alignment with the dominant ideology of the regime, including allegiance to the concept of Supreme Leadership and the person of Ayatollah Khomeini. Over the years, the candidacies for various elected positions (sometimes the very same positions they have held before) of many once-influential regime insiders have been rejected by the Guardian Council because of the candidates' criticism or policies or diversions from the official line defined by the institute of Supreme Leadership. Grand Ayatollah Montazeri, Ayatollah Bayat Shirazi, Ayatollah Zanjani, Ayatollah Hashemi Rafsanjani, and lately Hojatol Islam Karoubi and Mir Hossein Mousavi are some of those who were once instrumental in the regime apparatus but have now fallen out of grace with the leadership.

Peaceful assemblies and rallies in Iran are frequently and violently broken up and the participants arrested. Women, religious minorities, and anyone with a record of political activism against the regime (albeit none proven in court) are barred from seeking certain high office. Despite Iranian authorities' official stance that there are no political prisoners in Iranian jails, political activists, and often their families, pay a heavy price for their advocacy. They are routinely imprisoned without counsel, raped, tortured, forced to make false confessions, and executed in secret. The violent crackdowns on peaceful protesters in 2009 and in 1999 are symbolic of how restricted political participation and freedom of assembly are in the Islamic Republic of Iran.

The Habermasian public sphere assumes freedom of expression and the right to political participation and assembly:

The principles of the public sphere involved an open discussion of all issues of general concern in which discursive argumentation was employed to ascertain general interests and the public good. The public sphere thus presupposed freedoms of speech and assembly, a free press, and the right to freely participate in political debate and decision-making (Kellner, 2000, 262).

However, in Iran these principles are routinely violated, a breach that serves as an impediment to the formation of a public sphere in its true sense. Continuous persecution of opinions, restriction of political participation, and aggressive suppression of citizens along with an imposed religious ideology interfere with the backdrop necessary for the public sphere to materialize. Perhaps the Reform philosophy would have had no support at all had it been presented in a country with a flourishing public sphere, which in turn had given rise to a strong civil tradition, both of which are impediments to the spread of ideologies and their linguistic manifestation in the form of politically distorted communication. It is precisely because Iranians' access to an open public sphere where ideas can be critically debated is blocked that the illusion of reform has had a chance to flourish over the past two decades, presenting itself as the alternative.

THE STRUGGLE FOR ESTABLISHMENT OF
DEMOCRACY AND FREE PUBLIC DISCOURSE IN IRAN

While I maintain that a public sphere in the Habermasian sense does not exist in Iran, my research reveals there is a strong political undercurrent in Iran attempting to create a public sphere in the democratic sense. Post-presidential election events in 2009 speak of a strong tendency, specifically among women and youth, toward a realm of rational debate in which the public can openly discuss their collective concerns. The protests of June 2009 ostensibly began with a peaceful march of silence and the slogan "Where is my vote?" I believe that this is the single most powerful slogan that has emerged from the Iranian public psyche since the revolution—one that captures the soul of the Green Movement. On one hand, it points to the broken conditions of democratic governance (which republicanism implies for after all, the country is called the "Islamic Republic of Iran") where there should be respect for the popular vote of the citizens, and on the other hand, it recognizes the individual's right to questioning political authority and enter into rational and critical debate with it when those conditions are violated, which is the essence of the public sphere. The above example, although not unique, suggests that while a true public sphere has yet to form in Iran, a strong collective will among the youth, women, activists, and the intelligentsia is working toward it.

Studying the emergence of the public sphere within Iran from another angle reveals that while a physical manifestation of the concept has failed to form, the virtual space of the internet has been more welcoming to the idea. Social media particularly has afforded an effective platform for those actively trying to develop the Iranian public sphere. Social media and the internet also provide an opportunity for the Iranian public sphere to form online when its manifestation in the physical world is faced with great resistance. While the Iranian authorities crush any attempt at creating an open space for critical debate and severely restrict freedom of expression and political participation in the physical world, they have far less authority over the virtual space of which social media is a big part. The internet and particularly social media contribute greatly to the development of a free and inclusive virtual public sphere that gives a voice to many who would be otherwise silenced. A multitude of blogs, Twitter and Facebook accounts, YouTube videos, podcasts, etc., provide a wealth of information that was previously inaccessible and scattered. They essentially provide a platform for debate and the exchange of ideas by Iranians within Iran and those in the Diaspora, bridging a gap that had been widening between those groups since the revolution, a welcome phenomenon that was not possible before.

While this is not to say that online activism is risk-free in Iran, the anonymity, ease, and global reach that the internet affords makes for a more democratic and tolerant atmosphere for political activists. As previously discussed, Iranian authorities continue to suppress internet activism by limiting access to the internet by controlling available bandwidth, censoring content, and prosecuting known bloggers. But monitoring every blog entry, every Facebook post, and every video shared requires unlimited resources. Thus, Iranian activism thrives online, and while the authorities might be successful at crushing attempts to form a public sphere in the physical world, that public sphere has a better chance of emerging online.

YouTube videos developed by the protesters (both within and outside the country) within the Green Movement and without have been of particular importance in the struggle to form a public sphere. A large number of videos were made and posted online during the Green Movement both prior to and after the disputed elections. While the majority of the videos are of an informative nature, capturing the events of the movement such as demonstrations, discussions, and confrontations with the security forces, a considerable number also engage in a form of dialogue with the authorities. On June 14, 2009, two days after the disputed elections, footage of President Ahmadi Nejad calling those protesting the results "dust and dirt" (in Farsi, خس و خاشاک) caused an uproar. Within a few days a video featuring a song by a young Iranian artist Hamed Nikpay lashed back at the president's speech, lamenting his calling the dissidents "dust and dirt." Essentially, this video and many more like it are an attempt to engage in a dialogue with Iranian authorities, which goes to the heart of a free public sphere and demonstrates the Iranian struggle to create one.

NOTES

1. This book will not investigate the context and circumstances that left unexamined distortions in Ayatollah Khomeini's discourse or silenced dissenting voices.

2. As outlined in chapter 4, Giddens (1984) describes those resources as interpretive scheme, facility, and norm.

3. Neda Agha Soltan was a twenty-seven-year-old philosophy student who, according to Human Rights Watch (2009), was a bystander to the protests when she was shot in the chest and died at the scene. She quickly became a symbol of the movement in the face of the regime's violent crackdown on the protesters since she was widely believed to have been shot by the Basij militia. Her shooting and consequent death were captured on video and aired internationally on CNN, FOX, the BBC, etc.

4. For a more detailed discussion of the data see Harris (2012).

Epilogue

What About Us? The Political Protests of Working Workers, Unemployed Workers, Peasants, and the Poor of Iran (2017–2018) and What This Means for the Future of Modern Iran

As this manuscript was about to be forwarded to its publisher, a round of protests by Iran's workers, unemployed peasants, and the poor erupted in late December 2017/January 2018. Security forces attempted to disperse the protesters and were unevenly successful as across the country strikes broke out, the grievances of the protesters common to many of Iran's subjects: the high prices of everyday necessities of life like rice, butter, bread, cooking oil, petroleum, and eggs.

This book has focused on engaging the reader in an examination of the rhetorical acts of deception knowingly or unknowingly engaged in by the political leaders of the Green Movement of 2009, a movement partly encouraged by the language of Western political liberalism promoting its cause for political transformation in Iran. The Green Movement was an urban middle-class movement genuinely concerned with regaining its loss of political rights and central place in the creation, ownership, and distribution of the economic surplus of Iran. Women's rights, which have regressed significantly since the 1979 revolution, and fading economic prosperity—two of the major themes examined in this book—point to this claim. However, analysis of the street protests by the country's poor, unemployed, and low-paid workers (for the purpose of this epilogue, Iran's dispossessed) is a significant factor in the evolution of modern Iran since previous protests against the Islamic government were led by the country's urban middle and upper classes. This protest was the first independent protest by the dispossessed against the government, a government that has promoted itself as existing to materially better their collective lot since they were its source of political legitimacy.

In protesting their material grievances against the Islamic government, the dispossessed were adding their voice to the voices of resistance against the very Islamic government studied in this book. Needless to say, this is a cause of concern for the government for without the support of their claimed base, they are absent the appearance of legitimacy necessary for their globally unique form of government to survive domestically.

Moreover, the Green Movement assumed its interests were identical to those of the working class and that the latter's task was to identify with the former's vision of a nationally unified and secular Iran. They promoted this vision though Iran is home to many ethnic minorities for whom nationalism has meant erasure of their heritage and identity (i.e. the Kurds, Turkmans, Baloochis, etc.). Throughout the life of the Islamic government, the middle classes have often assumed their political grievances (e.g. women's rights, social liberty, freedom of expression) were those of the entire nation, and they have been repeatedly and bitterly bewildered by the lack of support among working-class Iranians for their oppositional initiatives. This recent eruption by the working class is an exercise of their agency in finding their own voice and speaking their own truth to power. In essence, this struggle against the Islamic regime is no longer a universal narrative but rather a constellation of a plurality of forces and diversity of interests in negotiation and contention with the government: the middle class with their political grievances, the dispossessed in their struggle to ease material pressures, and women and minorities standing up for equal rights, to name a few.

Such is the measure of identification between the Islamic government and Iran's dispossessed. It makes these recent protests a threat to the political authority of the Islamic government and promises the government a very unstable future. These independent protest actions of the dispossessed against the government's authority have the potential to persuade the dispossessed to seek alternative sources of political leadership to meet their material interests since the government, in their eyes, under these circumstances, has failed to do so? These alternatives might not include the Islamic government as presently constituted. It is this possibility of a rupture in the relationship between ruler (the Islamic government) and ruled (Iran's dispossessed) that so haunts my analysis of the Green Movement in its political contest vis-à-vis the same government of Iran: Are the dispossessed an ally of the Green Movement because they have grievances against the government even though the grievances of the two are not identical in nature? Are the dispossessed capable of acting politically, and in their own self-interest, without support from the crowds of the Green Movement? What would be the political purpose of another uprising led by the middle class when and if the dispossessed act independently of both it and the Islamic government? What would be the shape of future Green Movements if the Islamic government recognizes the political movement of the dispossessed to the disadvantage of the Green Movement and its allies in an effort to co-opt the former and politically alienate or neutralize the Green Movement? Are these street protests early signs of the beginning of the end of the Islamic government, or is their cessation evidence of the solidity of the government's authority? Are the protests early evolutionary steps in the transformation of the governing structure of the Iranian nation from its present Islamic form to another more inclusive, more tolerant, and less repressive Islamic government? Or is it early evidence of a post-Islamic, secular form of government? These are questions the recent street protests of the dispossessed pose for my analysis of the Green Movement.

THE 2017–2018 REVOLT: A MOVEMENT FROM BELOW

This more recent vintage of popular revolt is coming from classes and regions distant from Tehran in geographic terms that hope they will get some attention paid to their agendas for jobs and lower costs for basic necessities. Recent media analysis has reduced the 2017–2018 unrest primarily to economic grievances; social movement scholars, however, have long established there is no direct correlation between economic deterioration and political insurgence. Harris and Kalb (2018) accurately observe that "Iran's 1979 revolution, the 2011 Arab uprisings and the 2013 Gezi Park protests in Turkey all followed booms in economic growth." Similarly, while Iran's non-oil GDP actually grew around 6 percent between 2016 to 2017, it is the uneven distribution of that growth that further fueled the conflict. The growth that followed the lifted sanctions after the Iran nuclear deal in 2015 largely benefited the upper and middle classes, whereas the working classes and the poor failed to see a tangible, material improvement in their lot. These grievances were manifest in one of the protesters' most striking and prevalent slogans, "Bread, Work, Freedom!" From the above, it is somewhat logical the upper classes ignored the 2017–2018 protests because they felt little kinship with the cause of the working class who had in turn showed little support for the Green Movement's protesters of 2009.

Harris and Kalb (2018) report that of the seventy-five cities and towns where the 2017–2018 protests erupted, all had experienced some degree of labor unrest since 2013. At the same time, preliminary observations and research indicate that the protests are shifting away from Tehran and other large urban centers where the affluent and the professional middle classes are concentrated. In other words, the emergent social unrest is spreading to and out of small towns and peripheral cities in overlooked provinces such as Kurdistan, Lorestan, Khouzestan, and Baluchestan. This phenomenon further manifests in the movements' identification on Twitter with the hashtag "Eterazat_Sarasari" or "Tazahorat_Sarasari" which translates to "protests everywhere."

Reformers within the Islamic government who provided the agenda and organized the logistics of the 2009 uprisings entirely abandoned working-class protesters in 2018. Some high-profile Reformers, including former president Khatami, the proverbial father of reform, called the 2018 protesters "anarchists." President Rouhani on the other hand, went as far as downplaying the magnitude of their grievances while maintaining their voices needed to be heard even if some of them were infiltrators fomented by foreign powers. Once the street protests waned, Rouhani proudly announced that they were finally "wrapped up" (Euronews, 2018), and since then no plans to address the grievances of the protesting crowd have been declared. Additionally, while the president maintained the seemingly moderate stance of letting the protesters be heard, security forces and local police across the country were tasked with repressing the demonstrations. Interestingly, unlike the IRGC and the Basij militia that are under the Supreme Leader's command, the police and the security forces fall under the purview of the president!

In 2018 the protesters quickly recognized the political roots of their grievances, realizing the rulers, Hardliners or Reformers, were unsuited to be such and implied that their political authority should be superseded by an alternative political administration. This evolution in the collective consciousness of the rioting public, who were already on a path to disillusionment with the Reformers, is also captured in the popular slogan "Hardliners! Reformers! The game is over!" In other words, while the 2009 Green Movement displayed the public delegitimization of the governing Hardliners, in 2018, protesters went full circle by refusing to further consider the Reformers as a democratic alternative. Perhaps, as we established above, the Reformers were never representative of the interests of the dispossessed to begin with. It is perhaps no surprise then that protesters received no support and only condemnation from the Reformist administration.

On another note, while many have pointed out the unorganized and leaderless quality of the recent wave of protests and have painted the protests as insignificant, I would argue for their power to disrupt accepted political norms in Iran. Despite having no leader and no collectively agreed upon mandate, the protesters managed to shift the political frame from Hardliner or Reformer and to move on to a third alternative: neither. In the short time the 2017–2018 unrest lasted, it managed to encourage the collective political consciousness of the nation to move beyond the regime in its entirety. Furthermore, as I have argued throughout this book, the protests were leaderless because of continuous repression of civil society throughout the life of the Islamic Republic of Iran (Harris and Kalb, 2018).

The protests further suggest the political reality of modern Iran is by no means a fixed one but rather a fluid, open, evolutionary political reality capable of giving birth to realities present stakeholders cannot forecast since they are attached to the nation's past. My study of the Green Movement, given the eruption from below of the dispossessed, is but one contribution to a body of scholarship and commentary about modern Iran—a moment in Iran's history—that is trying to capture the present moment while being aware of and open to the possibility that with modern Iran, any outcome is possible. Here, time and struggle will bring the unforeseen, the silent, the taken for granted of political struggle in modern Iran into clear and resolved relief.

Appendix A:
Video Transcriptions of the Green Movement

Empirical Observations: Women's Rights	File Name	Time Stamp
The footage begins with the meeting of Zahra Rahnavard, Fatemeh Mo'tamed Arya and an unidentified woman: **Rahnavard:** A government that is run without women executives will definitely be a harsh one. Women's presence in executive positions makes society healthier, more equal, more balanced. It creates a more passionate and loving society. **Unidentified woman:** One of the most important topics in social justice is the issue of gender equality. Discussing that first and foremost our girls and boys must feel safe. **Rahnavard:** All forms of discrimination must be eliminated in society. We are against all forms of discrimination. Discrimination disrupts human growth. Now gender discrimination is one of its forms . . . there has to be a new reading of the role of women. Women are saying we are present, we have expectations, and we still want to take part in deciding our destiny. **Mo'tamed Arya:** If I want to travel to a different city I can't check into a hotel. Either my father, husband, or brother has to accompany me. **Rahnavard:** Worse than that, if you need surgery you are not considered to be in charge of your body. A man has to authorize the surgery, as if saying, Are you dying, no, wait until a man allows you to solve your problem. **Unidentified woman:** Sadly there is no security for a woman who has lost her male protector.	Mir Hossein Mousavi Second Campaign Video—2	0:37

(continued)

Empirical Observations: Women's Rights	*File Name*	*Time Stamp*
Rahnavard: Why shouldn't our women be safe in our society? Why are so many women killed? Why are so many women killed under the pretense of honor. Although, honoring the codes of chastity is not harmful if they are bound by law.		
In a speech to university students, Mousavi: "I am against the polygamy bill." He says this to the loud uproar of the crowd. While we hear the above words, the footage that is shown in the background is him holding a piece of paper on which is listed gender-based admission policies (*sahmieh bandi e jensiaty*), and women's rights—among other things.	Mir Hossein Mousavi Campaign Video— Mehrjouyi	2:00
Young girls and boys chanting together: "Rahnavard, Rahnavard, stands for equality of men and women."	Mir Hossein Mousavi Campaign Video— Mehrjouyi	4:30
The video starts by Mousavi praising his wife's scholarly achievements and then he moves on to talk about women: Mousavi: The issue of women in our country is both extensive and multidimensional. There are certain discriminations and disenchantments, both from a legal perspective and from the execution perspective. Also from an employment perspective. We have a large number of female university students who seem to face enormous problems once they want to enter the labor market. They feel discriminated against in this respect. We similarly have huge problems when it comes to domestic women. Part of the solution is women should be present in high-ranking decision-making.	Mousavi on Women	0:33
Mousavi: In my opinion, women must be present in the cabinet.	Mousavi on Women	2:06
Rahnavard and Mousavi meet with women's rights activists on the prophet's daughter Fatimah's birthday. The voice-over quotes Mousavi as follows. Mousavi: There are no differences between men and women when it comes to freedom and working toward achieving democracy, and everyone must march together on this path. Mousavi: I believe women play a critical role in the Green Movement. The women's movement is a part of the Green Movement. The future of the Green Movement is intertwined with all democratic and justice-seeking movements, including the women's movement.	Mousavi on Women on Hazrat e Fatimah's Birthday	1:55

Empirical Observations: Women's Rights	*File Name*	*Time Stamp*
Mousavi: Women's issues in our country won't be solved unless they become a national problem, and there should be no segregation between men and women. Gender segregation is the root of discrimination, which renders the problem unsolvable. We cannot have a free and just society unless we solve women's problems.		
Mousavi: Considering the turn of events in the past year, women and youth have a new understanding of themselves and have a renewed sense of identity. Their worldviews and thoughts have changed. Therefore a certain pain is felt that is related to this renewal of identity because our governing, legal, and traditional structures are incompatible with this newly born identity. We have to study this issue.	Mousavi on Women on Hazrat e Fatimah's Birthday	2:55
Mousavi: There are many things that under the name of Islam and securing family values, but in reality influenced by discriminatory gender views and legal issues, have created serious hurdles for women in society.	Mousavi on Women on Hazrat e Fatimah's Birthday	3:15
Mousavi: The concerns of Iranian women are the concerns of both men and women . . . Men's and women's happiness is intertwined and we can only solve this by seeing them as one.	Mousavi on Women on Hazrat e Fatimah's Birthday	
Mousavi: The faith of the Green Movement is tied to the women's movement in the future, and I don't think the Green Movement can achieve its goals without being accompanied by women every step of the way. The opposite is true too, meaning if we fail to promote political change, women's conditions won't change either.	Mousavi on Women on Hazrat e Fatimah's Birthday	4:27
In response to a question about the Green Movement's strategy regarding some Friday Prayers' clerics about women's cover and recent earthquakes and also the resurgence of Islamic Guidance crews: Mousavi: Certain events are happening in society and certain decisions are being made that instead of solving problems are creating conflict. For example, our country is prone to earthquakes and parts of Tehran are on a fault line, which certainly is very dangerous, and we have to stop it, and the government is better off taking care of this instead of confusing it with a dream or a deed like women's cover . . . This is diversion from truth that wants to keep people busy with such discussions and create division. Even the purpose of Islamic Guidance crews is not really for rectifying scantily covered women, they are largely meant to create diversion in minds.	Mousavi on Women on Hazrat e Fatimah's Birthday	4:45

(continued)

Empirical Observations: Women's Rights	File Name	Time Stamp
Mousavi: The Green Movement is after justice and freedom and the execution of the law, and if we achieve those, other issues stemming from those will be solved too. The reason we are facing actions that are causing us pain is because our conditions are not aligned with the constitution and human dignity and honor.	Mousavi on Women on Hazrat e Fatimah's Birthday	5:35
Mousavi: They want to keep our minds busy.	Mousavi about Women on Hazrat e Fatimah's Birthday	5:40
In response to a question about the One Million Signatures Campaign, and noting the Green human chain formed last year from Tajrish Square to Railroad Square as a symbol of reconciliation and national unity: **Mousavi:** I consider that day a great representation of the Green Movement. In previous years we have put forth "reconciliation" as our motto, which was a good motto for our national unity that will solve and even bring forward our problems. Some benefit from not reconciling. Currently, in different formats, including the families of political prisoners, different groups and movements have been created that didn't have the possibility to organize prior to the Green Movement. The women's movement is of those movements too. Some women used to participate in certain activities under the umbrella of the One Million Signatures Campaign Against Discrimination who were even criminalized maybe because they were conducting those activities apart from each other. But due to the colorful and diverse nature of the [Green] Movement, today they are joined with the extensive Green mass movement without the presence of suspicion against this group.	Mousavi on Women on Hazrat e Fatimah's Birthday	5:45
Karoubi: I will say this bluntly here, Imam [Khomeini] was very sensitive to moves that would demotivate people from participating in the elections and would readily oppose them. At a point in time, it hasn't been forgotten, that it was said that women shouldn't participate and don't get elected into the *Majlis*. Emam readily said that women must participate in the elections and be able to get elected to the *Majlis*	Mehdi Karoubi's First Televised Speech—Part 1—May 25, 2009	4:58

Empirical Observations: Women's Rights	File Name	Time Stamp
Karoubi: We published our third campaign promise during the month of Farvardin which was about civil rights. Civil rights bound by the constitutional framework. Regarding women, regarding ethnicities, regarding the various religions that exist in Iran, regarding universities, regarding prisoners that people get into, the pointless restrictions they place on people's lives and the bitter incidents [they have caused], pointless nuances, interfering with the private lives of families that Islam has so advised [against], civil rights in general bound by the constitutional framework or those principles of the constitution that are left vague.	Mehdi Karoubi's First Televised Speech—Part 2—May 25, 2009	7:20
All questions are directed at Karoubi. **Jamileh Kadivar:** Do you think forced hijab is a wise idea? Has it worked? You are a cleric after all, do you think, based on Islamic principles and religious teachings, it is right to force hijab? **Karoubi:** I think we have to do two things. One thing is to remove the aggressive way because that hasn't worked and in many cases they were counterproductive. **Jamileh Kadivar:** What about polygamy? **Karoubi:** Polygamy will destroy lives in our society for certain.	Mehdi Karoubi Campaign Video—1	5:16
Female Voice-Over: If he [Karoubi] is victorious in the presidential elections, he intends to create an organization for the defense of human rights and civil rights and intends to study and correct the behavior of governmental and national security institutions on a regular basis.	Mehdi Karoubi Campaign Video—1	2:16
Female Voice-Over: Karoubi considers solving women's problems an important and critical goal of his government and will try to execute the 6th *Majlis'* bill to join Iran to the [UN's] Convention on the Elimination of All Forms of Discrimination Against Women. He has certain plans to encourage and support non-governmental women's organizations and groups, and he plans to have at least one female minister in his cabinet.	Mehdi Karoubi Campaign Video—1	4:45

Empirical Observations: Economy	File Name	Time Stamp
Unidentified woman in chador: We are looking to return to an era where I can at least say class separation was minimal.	Mir Hossein Mousavi Campaign Video—1	0:55
The clip shows a man on a bike with his child. He comes up to a bus that carries Mousavi to complain of his employment and economic problems.	Mir Hossein Mousavi Campaign Video—1	5:00
Mousavi: When people's incomes shrink, when they don't have employment prospects, you can be sure these youth that see no light at the end of the tunnel turn to drugs and foul behavior (*bad akhlaghi*), and these types of crimes will spread. But when in a society, clear [economic] goals are stated, and there is hope for the future—which was the case during the war era despite all the hardship—I think all these foul behaviors could be drastically reduced.	Mir Hossein Mousavi Campaign Video—1	6:25
A woman talking about how no job prospects and economic hardship have turned her son to drugs.	Mir Hossein Mousavi Campaign Video—1	7:35
Mousavi: I have described these [economic conditions] as turning a society based on higher values into a commercial society. In a commercial society everything becomes utility-based and monetary-based. Cultural values turn into market values and economic values where everything has a monetary price—even human values are set a monetary value. There comes a point, for example, when a person bribes a member of parliament with $5 million Tomans to buy their vote. This is a consumerist society. The current situation with this way of looking at a society and with false promises, and superstitions and such are far from the [value-based] era we went through [at the beginning of revolution].	Mir Hossein Mousavi Campaign Video—1	8:15
Unidentified woman: Excuse me, Mr. Mousavi, but for years we have been asking [the government] to solve the problem of unemployment. Employment should be for our own city first and then other cities. Not only did this did not happen, they brought in the Chinese. They fired thousands from domestic companies and brought in Chinese [workers instead].	Mir Hossein Mousavi Campaign Video—2	2:15
Mousavi: On one hand, we export crude oil, and on the other hand, imported consumer goods are flooding our market at the cost of destroying our domestic production.	Mir Hossein Mousavi Campaign Video—2	5:31

Empirical Observations: Economy	File Name	Time Stamp
A scene in the northern provinces and a discussion of how the tea industry is being destroyed because of excessive imports.		6:40
Mousavi: Wealth distribution is both in our religious beliefs, and [my] economic policy does not mean, obviously, that we would take money from one person's pocket by force and put it in another's. Our argument is that our collective economic policies should be designed in such a way that they don't cause wide economic class gaps, and the middle class prospers so we can help the poor. But when over 50 percent of the society collapses into the lower classes, it is impossible for the government to help the poor. Which is what is happening now.	Mir Hossein Mousavi Campaign Video—2	7:08
Unidentified young man no. 1: We have so many resources in this country, oil, gas, mining industry, what happened to those incomes? What happened to the $260 million that was mostly Khatami's and Rafsanajani's governments' oil income? **Unidentified young man number 2:** We have so many charity donation boxes (*sandgh sadaghat*), why does the government gives people handouts (*sadagheh*)? We don't want a handout, we want jobs. **Unidentified young woman:** The country's projects have been left incomplete because Iran has been sanctioned against. My father works on oil, gas, and mixed cycle projects, and because of four mere screws, because Mr. Ahmadi Nejad doesn't want to build relations with others [countries], all the projects are sanctioned against. Why?	Mir Hossein Mousavi Campaign Video— Mehrjouyi	4:08
Mousavi: I have come to advocate for the poor (*mostaz'afan*). Those whose backs are breaking under the pressures of inflation, and flawed economic policies have targeted their dignity.	Mir Hossein Mousavi **Second** Campaign Video—1	1:40
Image reading: Where is the $270 billion in oil income?	Mir Hossein Mousavi Second Campaign Video—1	4:49
Mousavi to a roaring crow while he wears a green scarf: Iran's destiny is not poverty.	Mir Hossein Mousavi Second Campaign Video—1	5:04

(continued)

Empirical Observations: Economy	File Name	Time Stamp
Mousavi (same speech as above): Weakness in the national economy means humiliation in the world.	Mir Hossein Mousavi Second Campaign Video—1	5:30
Mousavi: We are occupying our thoughts with disputes outside [the country], mostly for domestic consumption, and have overlooked our vital interests in the region.	Mir Hossein Mousavi Second Campaign Video—1	5:34
Mousavi: We ask, during these past years, what great mission have you accomplished considering you spent $300 billion. Twenty-five percent inflation means the downfall of social security. Twenty-five percent inflation means addiction, foul behavior. Twenty-five percent inflation is like a tax the rich charge the poor. This is what the handout economy (*eghtesad sadagheyi*) has inflicted on us.	Mir Hossein Mousavi Second Campaign Video—1	5:42
Mousavi: If old-age pensions must rightly increase, why on election night? If teachers' back pay must be paid, why on election night?	Mir Hossein Mousavi Second Campaign Video—1	6:19
Mousavi: What employment outlook do our 3 million university students have? It is easy to kickstart a project, it is easy to kickstart a project, [repetition is intentional] securing the outcome is difficult.	Mir Hossein Mousavi Second Campaign Video—1	7:25
Mousavi: Any policy that diminishes our national identity and our Iranian dignity and eminence is in the wrong.	Mir Hossein Mousavi Second Campaign Video—1	7:54
Mousavi: Our people gave birth to many martyrs because they believed in their future, they believed in the system's righteous directions.	Mir Hossein Mousavi Second Campaign Video—1	8:33
Mousavi: We have come to investigate the lost billions.	Mir Hossein Mousavi Second Campaign Video—2	4:50

Empirical Observations: Economy	*File Name*	*Time Stamp*
Mousavi: Even if one rial is given to the people by the government, that is the people's right not a present to them.	Mir Hossein Mousavi Second Campaign Video—2	4:53
Mousavi: When I was in the North, the discussion was that while the rice produced by Iranian farmers is left in the warehouses, Pakistan and India's basmati rice is being sold at a lower price in the Rasht markets. On top of that they were also discussing oranges, saying our oranges are left unpicked on the trees and imported oranges such as Egyptian and so on are in the market and this is causing our fruit farmers to go bankrupt. They were talking about tea fields. I went to a tea farm where there were both tea farmers and tea specialists, and I was in those green gardens, and they showed me there how the fields are shrinking and talked about the problems they were facing. They were saying while over 180,000 metric tons of Iranian tea are left in the warehouses . . . our own markets are flooded with imported tea, and this has eliminated the possibility of healthy competition and growth. The same problem appeared when I went to Kerman. Fruit farmers there were also telling me that their oranges are left [in the warehouse] while the importing of oranges is increasing. Then I went to the silk industry. There I said the silk industry at some point was critical to the Safavid's economy. Shah Abbas was one of the major silk merchants in the country who would both use silk imports to Europe for political purposes and also use it to find a way to preserve Iran's interests in the face of the Ottoman's threat.	Mir Hossein Mousavi Second Campaign Video—2	7:25
Karoubi: Our second manifesto . . . was about oil shares . . . as we can see the large and unprecedented revenues that were at the disposal of the current honorable government in the past few years—hopefully they can explain what changes they have produced for our society with this unprecedented revenue where we sold oil at $100 and $120 [a barrel]. It's obvious how much the revenue levels were. Inflation, unemployment, the high cost of living, and recession are things that people are fully familiar with. They don't need opinion polls and central bank benchmarks, which are their rights, they see their lives and how much it has changed. Therefore the oil shares as we detailed, which we are not going to get into how we're going to deal with them.	Mehdi Karoubi's First Televised Speech—Part 2—May 25, 2009	5:50

(continued)

Empirical Observations: Economy	File Name	Time Stamp
Karoubi: And another more important issue that is very very important to me, us, the government should oversee, the government shouldn't take over, the government should not interfere in the private sector and create limitations for them so much. The government should accommodate them, the government should create security for them so they can bring their capital in with confidence and don't continue to take them outside [the country] and don't run away. This is the first point. Second we have many Iranians . . . We truly have many interested many Iranians all around the world who are willing to come and invest here and develop our economy. The government takes in more in taxes, takes in more revenue, [the government] won't be reliant on oil so much, won't use up, and sell and spend its capital so much. Next, partnership with foreign economies, and foreign investment—again we attract them and bring them in. First off, professionals will come in, technology will come in, management will come in, we transfer our management to them, they transform their management to us, in all of this we will fully hold our national interests, our principles.	Mehdi Karoubi's First Televised Speech—Part 3—May 25, 2009	0:03
Karoubi: And if I spend time, my own shortcomings, create crises and dump it on this or that person, please note, what hurdles are the private banks facing in our country? They have even gone to the verge of getting arrested. In a country like this where certain high-ranking individuals or legitimate powerhouses have to intervene and prevent a certain bank CEO's arrest. Can investment be done in something like this? Is there security? If we want economic development, if we want high inflation to not exist, if we want sometimes we have to increase inflation we have to make it up, we have to couple it with extra revenues so we can make up for the inflation.	Mehdi Karoubi's First Televised Speech—Part 3—May 25, 2009	4:45
Karoubi: If we want everyone to be employed, we have no other way than to reinforce the private sector and enter them into the job market. Naturally, we will oversee and we will take care, we have to do it so misuse doesn't happen, and that in itself doesn't create a new problem for us. And this is a very simple thing to do and it is regularly and frequently practiced.	Mehdi Karoubi's First Televised Speech—Part 3—May 25, 2009	5:40

Empirical Observations: Economy	File Name	Time Stamp
Mohammad Najafi (questioning the candidate's stance on the following issue): One of the most important issues regarding higher education of the youth is the expense of that education. Both those who study in state universities and some of them have to go far away from home to other cities, and covering their expenses is difficult, or those in private universities whose primary concern is covering their tuition and expenses. **Karoubi:** *I* see how education affects people and families, and how difficult this burden is for them	Mehdi Karoubi Campaign Video—1	5:54
Morteza Alviri: If you become president, what do you think is the first thing to do to set this train in motion to get to the higher goal so in any case we can have an economically developed country, is going to be? **Karoubi:** My first thing to do, my first manifesto, the manifesto that I published in [the month of] Bahman, my first manifesto was to revive the [center] for planning and management, which unfortunately got dissolved.	Mehdi Karoubi Campaign Video—1	6:35
Gholamhossein Karbaschi: And I pointed out that you know the poverty line better than us because you frequently deal with the veterans and martyrs (God's heaven be upon them). In any case when this election and the political discussions are over, at least 12 million of our population will be poor. What are you going to do for them as a cleric president? **(he says this while getting tears in his eyes).** **Karoubi:** When Mr. Karbaschi remembers things, he unwillingly gets affected and becomes upset. The other day too in a meeting when they came to my office and had a meeting, he got upset again. **(He says all this while the camera zooms on Karbaschi's face and his tears).** The answer is the same, you are sure I alone can't say, I have to think about it and sit on it first, the solution is with all the factions who want to work with me, and even those who may not work with us but they still feel for these issues. Let's sit down and think, I am ready to spend all my energy for things like this. **Karbaschi (jumping in):** I'm sure you are like that, all I want to say is, in the position of the president let's set all considerations aside. Talking about the poor and justice is easy. But feeding off of their share and not doing anything for them in the name of "we will be a world hero," saying things that end up putting more pressure on people and not doing anything for them is not the decent thing to do.	Mehdi Karoubi Campaign Video—1	7:50

(continued)

Empirical Observations: Economy	*File Name*	*Time Stamp*
Karbaschi (video continues from previous section showing Karbaschi's tears): In the position of president, are you determined to use any tool at your disposal, even your reputation, for this purpose? **Karoubi:** I will definitely do this. First of all, I'm not a hero, first of all. Second, we have, as you know, a certain record and that I'm not dependent on fake heroism. And I will truly go into my own purview which is working as the country's president and solving problems, and I am willing, as your honor has seen, I, to free a prisoner, when I was the *Majlis* speaker, I'd make a phone call to a colleague and he'd tell me you don't have to do this yourself, tell your office to call, you don't have to tell me, people's problems, people's lives, people's dignity and authority are really important to us	Mehdi Karoubi Campaign Video—2	0:01
Karbaschi: In any case our main problem is the United States. If we can't enter the international political club and if we can't solve our problems, these issues, these problems' consequences will put more pressure on the people, Mr. Karoubi. When you mention "our people's dignity," our people's dignity is their stomachs should be full. Poverty is befitting our leaders, but they have to strive, at any price, so people are not poor.	Mehdi Karoubi Campaign Video—2	3:50
Female voice-over: Are you still asking yourself why Mehdi Karoubi is running for president? Maybe you remember in the last election, Mehdi Karoubi promised that if he gets elected president, he will set a salary of 50,000 Tomans a month for all Iranians eighteen and older. **Esma'il Gerami Moghadam**: Is this the continuation of your last plan, when you stated 50,000 Tomans a month will be given to all Iranians eighteen and older, and . . . it is also a solution for many unemployment challenges, is this a continuation of that plan and a more complete version of it? If this is the case please explain a little. **Karoubi:** This time around I think it is more comprehensive, it's better, meaning we have made it more detailed and more clear. **Female voice-over:** This plan, of course, was mocked by the other incumbents and was considered impossible. But after the elections many economists agreed with it and experts reviewed and completed it. Today this plan is completed under "assigning oil revenue shares to people," and is ready for execution.	Mehdi Karoubi Campaign Video—2	5:22

Empirical Observations: Economy	*File Name*	*Time Stamp*
Female voice-over: Karoubi has other economic plans too, including exempting small businesses from taxes and reinforcing the private sector in the fields of production, commerce, and services through tax exemption and through partnership with private and public banks	Mehdi Karoubi Campaign Video—2	7:01

Appendix B:
A Summary of Ayatollah Khomeini's Claims

Empirical Observations: Khomeini—Women's Rights	Source[1]
Elizabeth Targood, a reporter with The Guardian: Will the Islamic laws be put into effect? And what difference will they make in daily life, compared to the current laws? May Ayatullah precisely explain whether women could choose between Islamic and Western dress freely, under the banner of Islam? **Ayatollah Khomeini:** Women are free to choose their own activities and destiny as well as their mode of dress within Islamic standards.	4:231 November 1, 1978
A reporter of the Dutch Volt Krant magazine: Specifically, how would women's rights in the Islamic Republic be? What about the coed schools? What would be the case with the issue of birth control and abortion? **Ayatollah Khomeini:** According to human rights, there is no difference between a man and a woman. Because they are both human, and like men, women have the right to take part in making their own destiny too. Yes, of course there are some differences between men and women that have nothing to do with their humanistic dignity. Anything not against women's dignity and nobility is free. Abortion is prohibited in Islam.	4:349 November 7, 1978
A reporter from Amsterdam Weekly magazine: What does returning to the laws of the Quran mean as far as women? **Ayatollah Khomeini:** In an Islamic system, women can actively cooperate with men in building an Islamic society, but they will not be used as objects. Neither do they have the right to degrade themselves, nor do men have the right to hold such a concept of them.	4:392–93 November 9, 1978

(continued)

211

Empirical Observations: Khomeini—Women's Rights	Source[1]
Who has told you that women will be locked up? They are free like men.	4:404 November 9, 1978
A delegate with *Amnesty International*: From an Islamic point of view, to what extent would women be allowed to participate in the construction of an Islamic government? **Ayatollah Khomeini:** Women play a significant role in building an Islamic society; Islam promotes women to where they can realize their humanistic values in the society, and more beyond the boundaries of being simply an object, and along with such growth, they can assume responsibilities in constructing an Islamic government.	4:412 November 10, 1978
An interview with a German reporter: How the freedom of women in the future government will be? Will they have to leave schools and stay at home or will they have the chance to continue their educations? **Ayatollah Khomeini:** What you have heard about women and other issues are all propaganda spread by the Shah and the biased people. Women are free; they are also free in regard to education and they are free in other things as men are. It is now that neither women nor men are free.	4:450 November 13, 1978
A reporter of the German *The Third World* magazine: In the opinion of Western countries, Shiism is being considered as a conservative element in progress. We have also heard the Shiah desire to withdraw women from the scene of social life, as well as their wish to return to Shiah laws, which would call for setting religious traditions as the basis of governing laws, as referred to in the constitutional laws, which has become illegally obsolete. We have also heard that Shiism rejects Western lifestyle because it doesn't agree with religious traditions. Will it be possible for you to give your opinion on this matter based on Shiah belief? **Ayatollah Khomeini:** Shiism, which is a revolutionary school of thought, and the continuation of the Prophet's (s) true Islam, has always been under the dastardly attacks of the dictators and expansionists. Not only does Shiism not drive away women from the scene of social life, but it places them in their own elevated humane position within the society. We will accept the West's advancements, but not the West's corruptions that they themselves are whimpering about.	4:472 November 15, 1978

Empirical Observations: Khomeini—Women's Rights	*Source[1]*
In An Interview with Russell Kerr, a member of the British House of Commons and member of the Labor Party. Shah's Critic for human rights violations **Russell Kerr:** Your enemies claim that the rights of the women in the Islamic government will be violated, the present rights that the women have gained during the Shah's rule will be revoked. Of course, I do not personally believe in it. What is your opinion? **Ayatollah Khomeini:** The women are free in the Islamic government; their rights will be identical with those of men. Islam emancipated the women from the captivation of men and put them on an equal footing with men . . . The propaganda carried out against us aims to misguide the people. Islam has guaranteed all human rights and issues.	5:68 November 1978
Georgia Gayer of L.A. Times: With regard to social issues, how do you envisage the presence of the women in the universities or their working in the society? Will you impose any restriction that currently does not exist in the society, on them? What is your opinion about the family planning and coeducation in the universities? **Ayatollah Khomeini:** Women will be free in the Islamic society and there will be no restriction on their admission to the universities, working in the offices, and being elected to the houses of the parliament. What will be restricted is moral decadence in whose regard both men and women are treated equally; it is unlawful for both. The family planning will depend on the government's decision.	5:179 December 7, 1978
A Lebanese reporter of the Amal daily, the organ of the youth of *Harikat al-Mahrumin* [the Movement of the Disinherited]: Women constitute a great multitude of the Muslims. What role or what rights do you consider for women in the Islamic system? **Ayatollah Khomeini:** Currently the Muslim women of Iran participate in the anti-Shah political struggles and demonstrations. I have been informed that the women in Iran hold political meetings in various cities. In an Islamic system, the women enjoy the same rights that men do, that is, right to education, right to work, right to property, and right to suffrage. Women enjoy the same rights that men do in all fields. However, there are certain cases that are forbidden for men in order to prevent corruption, likewise there are certain cases that are forbidden for women because they cause corruption. Islam has tried to protect the humane status of men and women. Islam has tried to prevent the women from becoming a plaything in the	5:185–86 December 7, 1978

(continued)

Empirical Observations: Khomeini—Women's Rights	*Source[1]*

hands of men. What they have said outside about women, that is, they are treated violently, is incorrect and is false propaganda by those who have prejudice, otherwise, men and women both have their own rights in Islam. If there are differences, it is for both of them that is related to their nature.

Ayatollah Khomeini: This regime has disseminated propaganda to the effect that were Islam to come to power, women, for example would have to remain at home with the doors locked to prevent them from getting out! Such falsehoods they spread about Islam . . . of course there are certain rules which apply only to men and others which apply only to women, but this does not mean that Islam discriminates against women. Both women and men are free to attend university, both are free to vote and stand as parliamentary representatives.

5:213–14
December 11, 78

Ayatollah Khomeini: Islam does not oppose any of the manifestations of civilisation and is not against any one particular group of you. When it first appeared, Islam took women by the hand and made them equal with men. Even though women were regarded as nothing at the time the Prophet of Islam began his teachings. Islam gave women strength. Islam put women on a par with men and made them equal with men. Of course, there are certain rules which apply only to men and others which apply only to women, but this does not mean that Islam discriminates against women.

5:213–14
December 11, 1978

Ayatollah Khomeini: We want to get rid of this mistaken idea. We want a woman to be a person like other people, a human being like any other human being, to be free as others are free. Do not listen to this propaganda the Shah puts about—on which it is said he spends one hundred million dollars annually. Nobody really pays attention to it any more anyway. He should pack up his things and leave now.

5: 214
December 11, 1978

A reporter of the Voice of Luxemburg and Radio Luxemburg: How do you foresee social development and progress, particularly the progress of the women, in case your movement attains victory and an Islamic government is established? Will polygamy be allowed, will you permit it? **Ayatollah Khomeini:** Women are free, as men are. We will act in accordance to the law of Islam.

5:220
December 12, 1978

Empirical Observations: Khomeini—Women's Rights	*Source*[1]
Professor Kirk Croft of Rutgers University: Which changes, in your opinion, are necessary to be made in the current status of women in the Iranian society? How do you think the Islamic government will change the status and situation of women? For example, the employment of women in governmental jobs or in different occupations such as medical practices, engineering, etc. and also some occasions including divorce, abortion, the right to travel and the compulsory observance of veil (chador).	5:287 December 28, 1978

Ayatollah Khomeini: The disinformation campaign of the Shah and those who are employed by him have distorted the issue of freedom of women in a way that people think that Islam has come to merely confine the women to the four walls of their houses. Why should we be against women's education? Why should we be against women's employment? Why shouldn't women hold governmental positions? Why should we be against women's traveling? Women are free in all these affairs as men are. There is no difference between men and women . . .That is right, women should have hijab [Islamic dress code], but their hijab should not necessarily be a veil [chador]. They can choose any kind of clothes that covers them. We cannot and Islam does not want us to make dolls of women. Islam intends to preserve the dignity of the women and make them efficient and serious human beings. We will never let the men to use women as a doll for their caprices and whims. Islam prohibits abortion and women can procure the right to take divorce in their marriage contract. No law or school has given as much freedom and respect to women as Islam has.

| **Professor Kirk Croft of Rutgers University:** It is said that the former head of Iran's Society of Female Lawyers, Mahvash Safiniya has said that the religious movement in Iran has obliged the Parliament to ratify bills, which limit the women's rights. For example, reducing the marriage age to 15 years, prohibiting women from joining the army and announcing abortion as a crime (Quoted in the New York Times, December 17). Do you acknowledge such laws? | 5:287 December 28, 1978 |

Ayatollah Khomeini: With regards to marriage, Islam has granted the women the right to choose their husbands. Women can choose their favored husbands, of course in the framework of the Islamic laws. Islam is against abortion and considers it an unlawful act and prohibits it. As I said before, women can join the army. What Islam is against, and prohibits, is corruption, no matter if this corruption is

(continued)

Empirical Observations: Khomeini—Women's Rights	*Source[1]*
on woman's part or the man's. The people whom you are introducing as lawyers have always misled our women. Today, the prisons are filled with our noble women and these lawyers have always undersigned and confirmed the Shah's crimes. Which one of these two groups is free and noble?	
Asian, European and American reporters: What would be the policy of the Islamic Republic about the freedom of women, illiteracy campaign and cinemas?	5:411 January 11, 1979
Ayatollah Khomeini: The Shah has done nothing positive in Iran. Reconstructing and renovating the Shah's destruction will take a lot of time. Shah has granted freedom neither to the women nor to the men. We will grant freedom to everybody. In the Shah regime, the cinemas were in the service of corruption, while in the future republic they will serve to the nation's benevolence. We will also fight illiteracy in its best way.	
Foreign Reporters: What will be the role and position of women in the future government?	5:472 January 16, 1979
Ayatollah Khomeini: It will be the condition of a genuine human being and a free personality contrary to the time that we have put behind, when neither our women nor our men were free. A nation whose men and women were not free and were living under repression has been liberated from this situation and henceforth its men and women will be free. But if they decide to commit any act in contravention to the principles of chastity or take measures contrary to the exigencies of the country, they will be of course stopped.	
In an interview with the reporters of Iranian Keyhan and Etela'at Dailies:	5:505 January 23, 1979
Q: What will be the role of the women in the Islamic government? Will they, for instance, participate in the state affairs? For example, will they become minister or members of the parliament, if they demonstrate their competence?	
A: The Islamic government will decide about these issues. It is not an appropriate time to express ideas about these issues now. Like men, women too will play a role in the construction of the Islamic society of tomorrow. They will enjoy the right to elect and the right to be elected. In current the struggles in Iran, women's contribution is similar to that of the men. We will grant all sorts of freedoms to the women. Of course, we will stop corruption and in this regard there will be no differences between men and women.	

Empirical Observations: Khomeini—Women's Rights	*Source*[1]
A French Reporter: Some of the Islamic customs, such as the Islamic dress code [hijab], have been given up. Will it become compulsory in the Islamic Republic again? **Ayatollah Khomeini:** Islamic dress code [hijab] in its general sense which prevails among us and is known as Islamic hijab has no contradiction with freedom. Islam opposes what is opposed to chastity. We will invite them to observe the Islamic dress code. Our courageous women are fed up with the calamities inflicted upon them by the West in the name of civilization and have taken refuge in Islam.	5:524 January 27, 1979

Empirical Observations: Khomeini — Democracy	*Source*
In an interview with a reporter from Le Figaro: How do you conceive of the "Islamic government"? Does this mean that the religious leaders will govern? What are the stages of this government? **Ayatollah Khomeini:** No; it does not mean that the religious leaders themselves are to run the government. They will lead the people in providing for the needs of Islam, and as the vast majority of the people are Muslims, the Islamic government will enjoy their support and will have them to rely on.	3:485 September 14, 1978
A reporter of the French newspaper, Le Figaro: But is the regime (government) you wanted a democratic one? For example, are you in favor of freedom of the press, multi-party system and freedom of parties and syndicates? **Ayatollah Khomeini:** We want a regime that observes all freedoms. As in every people-based government, Iran's future regime's bounds should embrace the interests of the whole community, and be particular about the dignity of the Iranian society, because offering an unrestricted society would rob men and women of their dignity.	4:2 October 14, 1978
A reporter of the French newspaper, Le Figaro: In fact, which is the direction of your actions, and what kind of regime do you have in mind to replace the Shah's? **Ayatollah Khomeini:** Keeping the Shah's regime is indisputably unacceptable. We have always been against it. "Overthrow" is the unchangeable target of our resistance. Besides, it is not the legal form of the regime that counts, but rather its content. An Islamic Republic can naturally come into consideration, because we believe that noble understanding of Islam will lead us toward advancement of a society which is very talented, has a lot of manpower and social justice. Before anything, we have set our hopes on the social contents of the future political regime.	4:2 October 14, 1978
A reporter from Austrian Radio-Television: What do you think about Iran's future changes and transformations? **Ayatollah Khomeini:** By the revolutionary uprising of the people of Iran, the Shah will leave, and the state of democracy and Islamic Republic will be established. In this republic, there will be a national parliament consisting of truly nationally elected people, running the country's affairs. The rights of the people, especially the religious minorities, will be valued and observed. Mutual respect will be considered in relation to foreign countries. We will not oppress anyone nor will we allow ourselves to be oppressed. The country is presently bankrupt and everything has been destroyed. By the establishment of the Islamic Republic, the real construction of the country will begin.	4:228 November 1, 1978

Empirical Observations: Khomeini—Democracy	*Source*
In an address to the Iranian Nation: And the governing system of Iran is an Islamic Republic, which maintains independence and democracy, and it will be announced according to Islamic standards and laws, and soon we will officially resort this suggestion to the people's votes, and anyone, or any group disagreeing with these triple suggestions, will not be with us and the Iranian nation.	4:299 November 5, 1978
In a press conference with Reporters from Brazil, Britain, Thailand, Japan, America, etc.: Your Eminence Ayatullah, is interested in replacing the present regime with an Islamic Republic. Would such a government guarantee democratic freedoms for everyone? And what role would you personally play in such a government? Also, regarding the democratic freedoms, we would like to know whether or not the communists or the Marxists would enjoy freedom of thought and speech. **Ayatollah Khomeini:** The Islamic government is a democratic government in the true sense of the word, and under which, there are equally complete freedoms for all religious minorities, and everyone will be able to express his or her opinion. And Islam has the responsibility to answer every opinion, and the Islamic government will answer logic with logic. But I am not active within the government and will act the same way as I am right now, and when the Islamic government takes form, I will take a guiding role.	4:389–90 November 9, 1978
A delegate with Amnesty International: Would the Marxists have freedom of speech and thought under the Islamic Republic? b) Would they have freedom of choosing a career? **Ayatollah Khomeini:** a) In the Islamic Republic, everybody would be free to hold any kind of belief, but they won't be free to cause sabotage. b) In Islam, the right of anyone to choose a career is protected in accordance with the legal regulations	4: 412 November 10, 1978
A reporter of the Lebanese An-Nihar newspaper: What is the nature of your desired Islamic Republic? And what are its features? **Ayatollah Khomeini:** The nature of the Islamic Republic is such that it will be established under the conditions set forth by Islam for government, relying on the public votes of the nation and enforcing the Islamic laws.	4:421 November 11, 1979

(continued)

Empirical Observations: Khomeini—Democracy	*Source*
An Egyptian reporter: In Your Eminence Ayatullah's opinion, what is the quality and nature of the Islamic Republic which you propose? And what is the difference between that and the Islam observed in the constitution? In the plans for an Islamic state, is more attention paid to social or political affairs of Islam? Does the precise execution of Islam's commands mean, for example, the amputation of the hand of a thief from now on? What is your perception? **Ayatollah Khomeini:** What is intended is that when a system is against the system of Islam in every aspect, such as its culture, its army as well as its economy and politics, that system must be overturned and the Islamic system established. Once the Islamic system becomes established, there would be a parliament, the votes of the members of the parliament . . . We intend to enforce all Islamic commands and we would practically prove that Islamic laws are progressive and more than arresting and releasing a thief.	4:431 November 12, 1979
An Egyptian reporter: Why does Your Eminence distance yourself from cooperating with other oppositionist political forces in the struggle toward reaching your goals—for example, the communists who have the very same goal? **Ayatollah Khomeini:** No, we cannot accept the communists because their danger to our country is not any less than that of the Shah's. We cannot accept them.	4:431 November 12, 1979
In a speech to a group of Iranian students and residents abroad: That which is clear is that all the people are saying this regime and the Shah must go and an Islamic government must be established. This is now on all the people's tongues.	4:432 November 12, 1978
In a speech to a group of Iranian students and residents abroad: The Islamic government we are talking about, that is, the government we want is one which the people desire and one to which God, the Blessed and Exalted, could say that these people who pledged their allegiance to you had pledged their allegiance to God. It should be a governing body allegiance to which is allegiance to Allah. In wars, when an arrow is shot, God will say: "When thou threwest (a handful of dust), it was not thy act, but Allah's," meaning that the hand that threw the dust was God's hand. The government that we want is one which is the shadow of God and is the extension of His hand; a government that is divine. The government that we want is such a government. Our wish is for a governing body to come to power that will not transgress against divine laws.	4:433 November 12, 1978

Empirical Observations: Khomeini—Democracy	Source
In a speech to a group of Iranian students and residents abroad: We want an Islamic government; an Islamic Republic in which popular votes will be sought and qualifications (for the head of state) will be announced. Islam delineates such qualifications.	4:433 November 12, 1978
In a speech to a group of Iranian students and residents abroad: We want a divine rule that conforms with the desires and choice of the people and God's laws, and a rule that is in accordance with God's will is also concordant with the people's wants. The people are Muslim and God-fearing and when they see that the government wants to implement and execute justice they will support it. God wants justice to prevail among the people.	4:434 November 12, 1978
A reporter of the French Le Monde newspaper: Your Eminence declares that an Islamic Republic must be established in Iran, and this doesn't make much sense for us French because a republic can be established without religious grounds. What do you think? Is your republic based on socialism, constitutionalism, elections, democracy, or what? **Ayatollah Khomeini:** As to the republic, it means as it is elsewhere although, this republic is based on a constitutional law, which is the law of Islam. We say "Islamic Republic" because the terms of the elected, as well as the commands enforced in Iran, would all based on Islam. However, the choice is the nation's, and the method of the republic is the same way as elsewhere.	4:449 November 13, 1979
An Arab reporter of Al-Bayraq publication: Your Eminence Ayatullah, can the movement that you are introducing, along with the emotional and popular values it holds, come to power by itself in the name of the majority of Iranians, without the involvement of the leftists and the traditional oppositions? And if they hold a referendum today, based on the slogans you raise, what percentage of the votes will you earn? **Ayatollah Khomeini:** The absolute majority of the Iranian nation is Muslims and will vote for what we call for. The whole nation does not want the Shah. Can't ninety percent of the Iranians who are Muslims, establish an Islamic Republic, as a majority in the society?	4:451 November 13 1978
In an interview with a reporter of Germany's Swiss language Radio-Television: If the Shah leaves and the Islamic Republic, which is the true democratic government, takes its place, these riots will end and stability will return to the country. The regime of Iran would turn into a democracy which will create stability in the region.	4:470 November 15, 1978

(continued)

Empirical Observations: Khomeini—Democracy	*Source*
A reporter with the *Third World* Magazine: What kind of rule will you suggest after the fall of the Shah's regime? Do you intend to save the monarchy within the framework of the constitutional law as well as the Pahlavi monarchy? What kind of government do you prefer? **Ayatollah Khomeini:** The nation of Iran desires an Islamic government, and I have suggested an Islamic Republic that relies on the votes of the nation. And the Pahlavi rule or the monarchial system is something that the Iranian nation has generally been rejecting within last year, and anyone who approves them is a traitor to the nation.	4:471 November 15, 1978
In An Interview with Russell Kerr, a member of the British House of Commons and member of the Labor Party. Shah's Critict for human rights violations **Russell Kerr:** What would be the situation of human rights in Iran's future? What is your plan for the State Organization for Information and Security (SAVAK)? **Ayatollah Khomeini:** SAVAK? No, we won't need it. There will be no pressure. SAVAK has had nothing except oppression, suppression, and encroachment upon the rights of the people; it won't exist in the Islamic government. The Islamic government will be based on the human rights and its observance. No organization or government has cared for the human rights as much as Islam has. The head of the state in an Islamic government is equal with the lowest person.	5:68 November 1978
A reporter of the British *Time* Television: May you kindly refer to some details and elaborate on the Islamic government? **Ayatollah Khomeini:** The Islamic government means a government based on justice and democracy and a government based on Islamic rules and laws; I do not have time to explain more right now.	5:131 November 27, 1978
In a speech to a group of Iranian students and residents abroad: In this system the government will be just, it will be a national government, a government based on the divine laws and on the consensus of the nation.	5:211 December 11, 1978
In a speech to a group of Iranian students and residents abroad: A ruler will not be able to bully his way to power and then protect his rule by the same means. No, he will come to power through the nation's vote, and it will be the nation who will protect him. And if at any time he acts against the wishes of the nation or against the law, the codified law, then his rule will, as a matter of course, become null and void and the government of Iran and the Iranian nation will sweep him aside.	5:211 December 11, 1978

Empirical Observations: Khomeini—Democracy	Source
French reporter of the Le Monde newspaper: You are known as the undeniable leader of the opponents. You have said that you are not going to take the reins of the government. So what would be the form of your Islamic government? **Ayatollah Khomeini:** We will find a candidate for presidency, who should be elected by the nation. When he is elected, we will back and support him. The laws in the Islamic government would be the Islamic laws. Personally, I will not become the president, and will refuse to accept any governmental responsibility. I will merely guide the nation, just as before.	5:401 January 9, 1979
Washington, AFP: Ayatullah Khomeini announced that he will establish a new government to take the position of the Bakhtiyar government and the emergence of an Islamic government in Iran is near. Answering the question, whether he will become—"Iran's powerful man," Ayatullah Khomeini said that he will neither have the same scope of powers of the Shah, nor will become the premier, but that he will maintain his role of guiding people.	5:433 January 14, 1979
A reporter of the Singapore's Strait Times newspaper: If I have understood correctly, you and your followers want the ouster of the Shah and see the future of Iran only under a complete divine government, which means an Islamic government which is run by a religious leader. Do you say that ideally you should replace the Shah at the apex of the power structure, that Iran be run in a more humanistic manner and directed by the Islamic principles? **Ayatollah Khomeini:** I and the other clerics will not occupy any position in the government. The duty of the clerics is to guide the governments. But we want the ouster of the Shah and want to replace this corrupt regime with the judicious Islamic government and victory will be ours.	5:458–59 January 15, 1979

1. All references are to Khomeini, *Sahifeh-Ye Imam: An Ontology of Imam Khomeini's Speeches, Messages, Interviews, Decrees, Religious Permissions, and Letters*, vols. 1–22 (Tehran: Institute for Compilation and Publication of Imām Khomeinī's Works, 2008).

References

Abrahamian, E. (1982a). "Ali Shariati: Ideology of Iranian Revolution." *Middle East Research and Information Project*, 102, 24–28.

———. (1982b). *Iran between two revolutions*. Princeton, NJ: Princeton University Press.

Abrahamson, M. (1983). *Social research methods*. Englewood Cliffs, NJ: Prentice-Hall.

Adib-Moghaddam, A. (2006). The pluralistic momentum in Iran and the future of the reform movement. *Third World Quarterly, 27*(4), 665–74. doi:10.1080/01436590600720868.

Ahmadian, A. (2013). Ahmadinejad and Khamenei: End of a love story? http://foreignpolicyblogs.com/2013/05/30/ahmadinejad-and-khamenei-end-of-a-love-story/.

Anderson, B. R. (1991). *Imagined communities reflections on the origin and spread of nationalism*. London: Verso.

Arif, R. (2014). Social movements, YouTube and political activism in authoritarian countries: A comparative analysis of political change in Pakistan, Tunisia and Egypt. University of Iowa.

Babbie, E. R. (2015). *The practice of social research*. 14th ed. Belmont, CA: Wadsworth Cengage Learning.

Baqi, E. (2003). *The clergy and power: Sociology of religious institutions*. Tehran: Saraee.

Bennett, W. L., and Segerberg, A. (2011). "The logic of connective action the logic of connective action: Digital media and the personalization of contentious politics." *6th General Conference of the European Consortium for Political Research*, 19–54. doi:10.1017/cbo9781139198752.002.

Berelson, B. (1952). *Content analysis in communication research*. Glencoe, IL: Free Press.

Blaikie, N. W. (2010). *Designing Social Research: The Logic of Anticipation* (2nd ed.). Cambridge, UK: Polity Press.

Buchta, W. (2000). *Who rules Iran? The structure of power in the Islamic Republic.* Washington, DC: Washington Institute for Near East Policy.

Burrell, G., and Morgan, G. (1979). *Sociological paradigms and organisational analysis elements of the sociology of corporate life.* London: Heinemann.

Carney, T. F. (1971). Content analysis: A review essay. *Historical Methods Newsletter, 4*(2), 52–61. doi:10.1080/00182494.1971.10593939.

Civil Code of the Islamic Republic of Iran. (n.d.). www.alaviandassociates.com/documents/civilcode.pdf.

Constitution of the Islamic Republic of Iran. (n.d.). www.iranchamber.com/government/laws/constitution.php.

Convergence of Women's Movement to Convey Demands during Elections. (2009). www.feministschool.com/spip.php?article2461.

Cordesman, A. H. (2007). Iran, oil, and the Strait of Hormuz. https://csis-prod.s3.amazonaws.com/s3fs-public/legacy_files/files/media/csis/pubs/070326_iranoil_hormuz.pdf.

Cross, K. (2010). Why Iran's Green Movement faltered: The limits of information technology in a rentier state. *SAIS Review of International Affairs, 3*(2), 169–87.

Ctrl+Alt+Delete: Iran's response to the internet. (n.d.). www.iranhrdc.org/english/english/publications/reports/3157-ctrl-alt-delete-iran-039-s-response-to-the-internet.html?p=10%29%28I+have+the+PDF+of+this+saved+in+the+methods+folder%29.

Cukier, W., Ngwenyama, O., Bauer, R., and Middleton, C. (2009). A critical analysis of media discourse on information technology: Preliminary results of a proposed method for critical discourse analysis. *Information Systems Journal, 19*(2), 175–96. doi:10.1111/j.1365-2575.2008.00296.x.

Dahlberg, L. (2005). The Habermasian public sphere: Taking difference seriously? *Theory and Society, 34*(2), 111–36. doi:10.1007/s11186-005-0155-z.

Dahlgren, P. (2005). The internet, public spheres, and political communication: Dispersion and deliberation. *Political Communication, 22*(2), 147–62. doi:10.1080/10584600590933160.

Demands of the Coalition of the Iranian Civil Society Groups. (2009). http://payamekarfarmayan.com/spip.php?article338&lang=fa.

Derayeh, M. (2006). *Gender equality in Iranian history: From pre-Islamic times to the present.* Lewiston, NY: Edwin Mellen Press.

Duriau, V. J., Reger, R. K., and Pfarrer, M. D. (2007). A content analysis of the content analysis literature in organization studies: Research themes, data sources, and methodological refinements. *Organizational Research Methods, 10*(1), 5–34. doi:10.1177/1094428106289252.

Iran's Twitter revolution. (2009). www.washingtontimes.com/news/2009/jun/16/irans-twitter-revolution/.

Esposito, J. L., and J. O. Voll, eds. (2001). *Makers of contemporary Islam.* New York: Oxford University Press.

Euronews. (2018). «اعتراضات ایران به نفع روحانی تمام شد». http://fa.euronews.com/
2018/01/17/iranians-protest-benefits-president-rohani.

Fallaci, O. (1979). An Interview with Khomeini. *New York Times*, October 7, 8–10.

Fateh, M. (1956). *Panjah sal-e naft-e Iran*.

Fraser, N. (1990). Rethinking the public sphere: A contribution to the critique of actually existing democracy. *Social Text* (25/26), 56. doi:10.2307/466240.

Ghobadzadeh, N. (2013). Religious secularity: A vision for revisionist political Islam. *Philosophy and Social Criticism, 39*(10), 1005–27. doi:10.1177/0191453713507014.

Giddens, A. (1979). *Central problems in social theory: Action, structure, and contradiction in social analysis*. Berkeley: University of California Press.

———. (1984). *The constitution of society: Outline of the theory of structuration*. Berkeley: University of California Press.

Goodwin, J., Jasper, J. M., and Polletta, F., eds. (2001). *Passionate politics: Emotions and social movements*. Chicago: University of Chicago Press.

Gross, A. G. (2010). Systematically distorted communication: An impediment to social and political change. *Informal Logic, 30*(4), 335–60.

Habermas, J. (1979). *Communication and the evolution of society*. Boston: Beacon Press.

———. (1984). *The theory of communicative action.* 2 vols. Boston: Beacon Press.

———. (1991). *The structural transformation of the public sphere: An inquiry into a category of bourgeois society*. Cambridge, MA: MIT Press.

———. (1996). *Between facts and norms: Contributions to a discourse theory of law and democracy*. Cambridge, MA: Polity.

———. (2000). *On the pragmatics of communication*. Edited by M. Cooke. Cambridge, MA: MIT Press.

Harris, K. (2012). The brokered exuberance of the middle class: An ethnographic analysis of Iran's 2009 Green Movement [abstract]. *Mobilization: An International Quarterly, 17*(4), 435–55.

Harris, K., and Kalb, Z. (2018). How years of increasing labor unrest signaled Iran's latest protest wave. www.washingtonpost.com/news/monkey-cage/wp/2018/01/19/how-years-of-increasing-labor-unrest-signaled-irans-latest-protest-wave/?utm_term=.9475cab34ec0.

Hazra, U. T. (2014). *Understanding Acceptance Decisions and Identity Associated with Smartphones: A Qualitative Enquiry*. University of Cape Town.

Hirschheim, R., and Klein, H. K. (1994). Realizing emancipatory principles in information systems development: The case for ETHICS. *MIS Quarterly, 18*(1), 83–109.

Hirschl, R. (2011). *Constitutional theocracy*. Cambridge, MA: Harvard University Press.

Holsti, O. R. (1969). *Content analysis for the social sciences and humanities*. Reading, MA: Addison-Wesley.

Holtan, C. (2005). *Iran—From an Islamic state to an Islamic democracy? A study of the thoughts of Abdolkarim Soroush on religion and state* (master's thesis), University of Oslo.

Human Rights Watch. (2009) Iran: Violent crackdown on protesters widens. www
.hrw.org/news/2009/06/23/iran-violent-crackdown-protesters-widens.

Huntington, S. P. (1991). *The third wave: Democratization in the late twentieth century*. Norman: University of Oklahoma Press.

———. (2006). *Political order in changing societies*. New York: Yale University Press.

Ilias, S. (2009). *Iran's economic conditions: U.S. policy issues*. Washington, DC: Congressional Research Service, Library of Congress.

Internet Live Stats. (n.d.). www.internetlivestats.com/internet-users/.

Internet Society. (2014). Internet Society global internet report 2014: Open and sustainable access for all. www.internetsociety.org/wp-content/uploads/2017/08/IS_ExSummary_30may.pdf.

Iran Human Rights Document Center. (n.d.). Deadly fatwa: Iran's 1988 prison massacre. www.iranhrdc.org/english/publications/reports/3158-deadly-fatwa-iran-s-1988-prison-massacre.html.

Iran's Mousavi Says He Will Continue Fight For Reform. (2010). http://news.bbc.co.uk/2/hi/middle_east/8492941.stm.

Jahanbegloo, R. (2002). *The fourth wave*. Translated by M. Goodarzi. Tehran: Nashr-e Ney.

———. (2012). Iranian intellectuals: From revolution to dissent. http://jahanbegloo.com/content/iranian-intellectuals-revolution-dissent.

———. (2013). *Democracy in Iran*. New York: Palgrave Macmillan.

Jones, P. (2011). Succession and the Supreme Leader in Iran. *Survival, 53*(6), 105–26. doi:10.1080/00396338.2011.636514.

Kadivar, M. (n.d.). http://en.kadivar.com/.

Kamali Dehghan, S., and Borger, J. (2011). Ahmadinejad's enemies scent blood in Iran power struggle. http%3A%2F%2Fwww.theguardian.com%2Fworld%2F2011%2Fmay%2F19%2Fahmadinejad-iran-power-struggle.

Kamrava, M. (2008). *Iran's intellectual revolution*. Cambridge: Cambridge University Press.

Katouzian, H. (1998). Problems of democracy and the public sphere in modern Iran. *Comparative Studies of South Asia, Africa and the Middle East, 18*(2), 31–37. doi:10.1215/1089201X-18-2-31.

———. (2009). *The Persians: Ancient, mediaeval and modern Iran*. Princeton, NJ: Yale University Press.

Keddie, N. R., and Richard, Y. (2006). *Modern Iran: Roots and results of revolution*. Princeton, NJ: Yale University Press.

Keller, J. (2010). Evaluating Iran's Twitter Revolution. www.theatlantic.com/technology/archive/2010/06/evaluating-irans-twitter-revolution/58337/.

Kellner, D. (2000). Habermas, the public sphere, and democracy: A critical intervention. https://pages.gseis.ucla.edu/faculty/kellner/papers/habermas.htm.

Keyhan. (2009). www.shafaf.ir/fa/news/3472/%D8%A7%D8%AE%D8%A8%D8%A7%D8%B1-%D9%88%DB%8C%DA%98%D9%87-%DA%A9%DB%8C%D9%87%D8%A7%D9%86.

Khatami Drops His Presidential Candidacy in Support of Mousavi. (2009). www
.iranianuk.com/article.php5?id=35856

Khatami: Many Mistakes Are Made in the Name of the Regime. (2010). www
.asriran.com/fa/news/107346/%D8%B3%DB%8C%D8%AF-%D9%85%D8
%AD%D9%85%D8%AF-%D8%AE%D8%A7%D8%AA%D9%85%DB%8C
-%D8%A8%D9%87-%D9%86%D8%A7%D9%85-%D9%86%D8%B8%D8
%A7%D9%85-%DA%A9%D8%A7%D8%B1%D9%87%D8%A7%DB
%8C-%D8%A7%D8%B4%D8%AA%D8%A8%D8%A7%D9%87%DB
%8C-%D8%B5%D9%88%D8%B1%D8%AA-%D9%85%DB%8C-%DA
%AF%DB%8C%D8%B1%D8%AF.

Khomeini, R. M. (1967). *Tahrir al-wasilah*. Vols. 1–2. Najaf: Matba'at al-Adab.

———. (1970). *Islamic government: Governance of the jurist*. Translated by H. Al-
gar. Tehran: Institute for Compilation and Publication of Imām Khomeinī's Works.

———. (2008). *Sahifeh-Ye Imam: An ontology of Imam Khomeini's speeches, messages, interviews, decrees, religious permissions, and letters*. Vols. 1–22. Tehran:
Institute for Compilation and Publication of Imām Khomeinī's Works.

———. (2015). *Islam and revolution: Writings and declarations of Imam Khomeini
(1941–1980)*. Mizan Press.

Kian-Thiébaut, K. (1996). Iranian women take on the mullahs. http://mondediplo
.com/1996/11/women.

Krippendorff, K. (2004). *Content analysis: An introduction to its methodology*. 2nd
ed. Thousand Oaks, CA: Sage Publications.

Krippendorff, K., and Bock, M. A. (2009). *The content analysis reader*. Thousand
Oaks, CA: Sage Publications.

Kurzman, C. (1996). "Structural Opportunity and Perceived Opportunity in Social-
Movement Theory: The Iranian Revolution of 1979." *American Sociological
Review*, 153–170.

———. (1999). Liberal Islam: Prospects and challenges. *Middle East Review of International Affairs, 3*(3), 11–19.

———. (2009). *The unthinkable revolution in Iran*. Cambridge, MA: Harvard University Press.

Long, D. E., and Reich, B., eds. (1995). *The government and politics of the Middle
East and North Africa*. Boulder, CO: Westview Press.

Lyytinen, K. J., and Ngwenyama, O. K. (1992). What does computer support for
cooperative work mean? A structurational analysis of computer supported cooperative work. *Accounting, Management and Information Technologies, 2*(1), 19–37.
doi:10.1016/0959-8022(92)90007-f.

Markel, N. N. (1998). *Semiotic psychology: Speech as an index of emotions and attitudes*. New York: Peter Lang.

Milani, A. (2000). *The Persian sphinx: Amir Abbas Hoveyda and the riddle of the
Iranian Revolution, A biography*. London: IB Tauris.

Moaveni, A. (2002). Why Iran's president has forced a showdown. http://content
.time.com/time/world/article/0,8599,345297,00.html.

Mojab, Shahrzad. "Theorizing the politics of 'Islamic feminism.'" *Feminist Review* *69*, no. 1 (2001): 124–146.

Mojtahed Shabestari, M. (1998). *Faith and freedom*. Tehran: Tarh-e No.

Momen, M. (1985). *An introduction to Shiʻi Islam: The history and doctrines of Twelver Shiʻism*. Oxford: G. Ronald.

Moosavi, N. (2007). Secularism in Iran: A hidden agenda? In B. A. Kosmin and A. Keysar, eds. *Secularism and secularity: Contemporary international perspectives*. Hartford, CT: Institute for the Study of Secularism in Society and Culture.

Mousavi: I Don't Dare Ask Khatami for His Help. (2009). www.asriran.com/fa/pages/?cid=71438.

Mousavi: I Have Come Independently. (2009). http%3A%2F%2Fwww1.jamejamon line.ir%2Fnewstext2.aspx%3Fnewsnum%3D100906303528.

Navai, R. (2014). Breaking bad in Tehran: How Iran got a taste for crystal meth. http%3A%2F%2Fwww.theguardian.com%2Fworld%2F2014%2Fmay%2F13%2F breaking-bad-tehran-iran-crystal-meth-methamphetamine.

Neuendorf, K. A. (2002). *The content analysis guidebook*. Thousand Oaks, CA: Sage Publications.

New York Times. (1999). Iran's ex-president backs a jailed aide. www.nytimes.com/1999/05/09/world/iran-s-ex-president-backs-a-jailed-aide.html.

Ngwenyama, O. (1991). The critical social theory approach to information systems: Problems and challenges. *Information Systems Research: Contemporary Approaches and Emergent Traditions*, 267–80.

Ngwenyama, O. K., and Lee, A. S. (1997). Communication richness in electronic mail: Critical social theory and the contextuality of meaning. *MIS Quarterly, 21*(2), 145. doi:10.2307/249417

Ngwenyama, O., and Nielsen, P. A. (2003). Competing values in software process improvement: An assumption analysis of CMM from an organizational culture perspective. *IEEE Transactions on Engineering Management, 50*(1), 100–112. doi:10.1109/tem.2002.808267.

Nikfar, M. (1999). The essence of a thought. In *Abdolkarim Soroush: Exploring the prophetic experience* (29–82). Tehran: Serat.

OPEC. (2015). *Petroleum: An engine for global development*. 6th OPEC International Seminar. Austria, Vienna. www.opec.org/opec_web/static_files_project/media/downloads/publications/ASB2014.pdf.

Paidar, P. (1997). *Women and the political process in twentieth-century Iran*. Vol. 1. Cambridge: Cambridge University Press.

Patton, M. Q. (2002). *Qualitative research and evaluation methods*. Thousand Oaks, CA: Sage Publications.

Penal Code of the Islamic Republic of Iran. (n.d.). Retrieved August 14, 2017, from https://www.unodc.org/tldb/pdf/Islamic_Penal_Code_in_Farsi.pdf.

Pike, J. (2009). Grand Ayatollah Ali Khamenei. www.globalsecurity.org/military/world/iran/khamenei.htm.

Pope, C., Ziebland, S., and Mays, N. (2006). Analysing qualitative data. *Qualitative Research in Health Care, 63*–81. doi:10.1002/9780470750841.ch7.

Profile: Zahra Rahnavard. (2009). http://news.bbc.co.uk/2/hi/middle_east/8101384
.stm.

Rahnavard, Z. (1987). *Beauty of concealment and concealment of beauty*. Translated
by S. Naqvi. Islamabad: Cultural Consulate, Islamic Republic of Iran.

Razzaghi, S. (2010). State of civil society in Iran. www.docstoc.com/docs/150594437/
state-of-civil-society-in-iran-Arseh-Sevom.

Rutledge, R. (2009). Iraqi insurgents' use of YouTube as a strategic communication
tool: An exploratory content analysis. Florida State University.

Safeguarding and Strengthening the Islamic Republic Is a Duty for All of Us.
(2014). www.irna.ir/fa/News/81190477/%D8%B3%D8%A7%DB%8C%D8%B1
/%D8%B3%DB%8C%D8%AF%D9%85%D8%AD%D9%85%D8%AF%D8%A
E%D8%A7%D8%AA%D9%85%DB%8C__%D9%88%D8%B8%DB%8C%D9
%81%D9%87_%D9%87%D9%85%D9%87_%D9%85%D8%A7_%D8%AD%D9
%81%D8%B8_%D9%88_%D8%AA%D9%82%D9%88%DB%8C%D8%AA
_%D8%AC%D9%85%D9%87%D9%88%D8%B1%DB%8C_%D8%A7%D8
%B3%D9%84%D8%A7%D9%85%DB%8C_%D8%A7%D8%B3%D8%AA
__%D8%A2%DB%8C%D8%AA_%D8%A7%D9%84%D9%84%D9%87_%D
9%85%D9%87%D8%AF%D9%88%DB%8C_%DA%A9%D9%86%DB%8C
_%D8%A7%D8%B2_%DA%86%D9%87%D8%B1%D9%87_%D9%87%D8
%A7%DB%8C_%D8%A7%D8%B1%D8%B2%D9%86%D8%AF%D9%87_%D
8%A7%D9%86%D9%82%D9%84%D8%A7%D8%A8_%D8%A7%D8%B3%D
8%AA.

Sahraei, F. (2012). Iranian university bans on women causes consternation. www.bbc
.com/news/world-middle-east-19665615.

Schelling, T. C. (1960). *The strategy of conflict*. Cambridge, MA: Harvard University
Press.

Schumpeter, J. A. (1962). Capitalism, socialism, and democracy. New York: Harper
Perennial.

Sen, A. (1999). Democracy as universal value. *Journal of Democracy, 10*(3), 3–17.

Sethi, A. (2013). Banistan: Why is YouTube still blocked in Pakistan? www.newyorker
.com/tech/elements/banistan-why-is-youtube-still-blocked-in-pakistan.

Soroush, A. (1996). A conversation with Abolkarim Soroush. *Q–News International*,
220–21.

———. (1999). Bast-i tajrubih-i nabavi (Expansion of Prophetic experience). *Tehran: Sirat publication*.

———. (2003). Democracy and rationality: An interview with Abdolkarim Soroush
by *Shargh*. www.drsoroush.com/English/Interviews/E-INT-20031200-1.htm.

Sreberny, A., and Mohammadi, A. (1994). *Small media, big revolution: Communication, culture, and the Iranian revolution*. Minneapolis: University of Minnesota Press.

Stahl, B. C. (2007). Privacy and security as ideology. *IEEE Technology and Society
Magazine*.

Subani, H. (2013). *The secret history of Iran*. Cabal Times.

Tabari, A. (1980). The enigma of veiled Iranian women. *Feminist Review, 5*, 19–31.

Toulmin, S., Rieke, R. D., and Janik, A. (1979). *An introduction to reasoning*. New
York: Macmillan.

Tusa, F. (2013). How social media can shape a protest movement: The cases of Egypt in 2011 and Iran in 2009. *Arab Media and Society, 17.*

United Nations. (n.d.). OSAGI gender mainstreaming—Concepts and definitions. www.un.org/womenwatch/osagi/conceptsandefinitions.htm.

———. (2014) Special rapporteur's March 2014 report on the situation of human rights in the Islamic Republic of Iran. www.iranhrdc.org/english/human-rights -documents/united-nations-reports/un-reports/1000000443-special-rapporteurs -march-2014-report-on-the-situation-of-human-rights-in-the-islamic-republic-of -iran.html.

Vakili, V. (2001). Abdolkarim Soroush and critical discourse in Iran. In J. L. Esposito and J. O. Voll, eds. *Makers of contemporary Islam,* 150–76. New York: Oxford University Press.

Van Dijk, T. A. (1991). The interdisciplinary study of news as discourse. In K. B. Jensen and N. Jankowski, eds. *A handbook of qualitative methodologies for mass communication research.* London: Routledge.

———. (2006). Discourse and manipulation. *Discourse and Society, 17*(3), 359–83. doi:10.1177/0957926506060250

Van Engeland, Anicée. "Transcending the Human Rights Debate: Iranian Intellectuals' Contemporary Discourses and the New Hermeneutics of the Sharia." *Middle East Journal of Culture and Communication 4,* no. 1 (2011): 72–89.

Wehrey, F. M., Green, J. D., Nichiporuk, B., Nader, A., Hansell, L., Nafisi, R., and Bohandy, S. R. (2009). *The rise of the Pasdaran: Assessing the domestic roles of Iran's Islamic Revolutionary Guards Corps.* Santa Monica, CA: RAND National Defense Research Institute.

The World Factbook: IRAN. (2018, May 01). Retrieved from https://www.cia.gov/ library/publications/the-world-factbook/geos/ir.html.

Wright, R. B. (2000). *The last great revolution: Turmoil and transformation in Iran.* New York: A.A. Knopf.

———. (2008). *Dreams and shadows: The future of the Middle East.* New York: Penguin Press.

Index

233

About the Author

Maral Karimi was born in Iran during the transition period between the 1979 revolution and the war with Iraq. The violence, volatility, and vengeance that she witnessed and that touched her life made her acutely aware at an early age of the political conditions of the world surrounding her. Those conditions gave rise to questions that she then carried into her adult life and sent her on an academic quest in search of answers, a journey that ultimately led to this critical inquiry. Maral is pursuing a PhD in social justice education at the University of Toronto. She specializes in media and communication studies with a special focus on Iranian and Middle Eastern politics, where she is interested in examining the role of media in general and political communications in particular in social movements. Her research interests extend beyond media to the intersection of critical cultural studies with feminist pedagogies and social media analysis. This book is based on her dissertation for her MA at York University. Maral lives in Toronto, Canada, where she has spent most of her adult life.